Donald M. Matthews   The Kassite Glyptic of Nippur

ORBIS BIBLICUS ET ORIENTALIS

Published by the Biblical Institute of the University
of Fribourg Switzerland
the Seminar für Biblische Zeitgeschichte
of the University of Münster i.W. Federal Republic of Germany
and the Schweizerische Gesellschaft
für orientalische Altertumswissenschaft
Editor: Othmar Keel
Coeditors: Erich Zenger and Albert de Pury

The author

Donald Matthews was born in Edinburgh in 1962 and educated in Scotland. He has excavated in Britain and in Jordan, Syria and Iraq, especially at Tell Mohammed Arab (1983–84), Tell Abu Salabikh (1988) and Tell Brak (1984, 1990). He obtained a B.A. at Cambridge University in Archaeology and Anthropology (1983) and a PhD on Mesopotamian cylinder seals at Cambridge in 1988. The materials for the present volume were collected in Philadelphia and Chicago in 1989. Since 1990 he has been studying third millennium B.C. glyptic from Tell Brak at Oxford University. He is the author of «Principles of Composition in Near Eastern Glyptic of the Later Second Millennium B.C.»
(Orbis Biblicus et Orientalis. Series Archeologica 8), Freiburg / Schweiz – Göttingen 1990, and of various scholary articles.

Orbis Biblicus et Orientalis   116

Donald M. Matthews

The Kassite Glyptic of Nippur

Inscriptions by W. G. Lambert

Universitätsverlag Freiburg Schweiz
Vandenhoeck & Ruprecht Göttingen

Die Deutsche Bibliothek – CIP-Einheitsaufnahme

Matthews, Donald M.:
The Kassite glyptic of Nippur/Donald M. Matthews. – Freiburg, Schweiz: Univ.-
Verl.; Göttingen: Vandenhoeck und Ruprecht, 1992
  (Orbis biblicus et orientalis; 116)
  ISBN 3-525-53750-6 (Vandenhoeck und Ruprecht)
  ISBN 3-7278-0807-1 (Univ.-Verl.)
NE: GT

Publication subsidized by The British Academy, London
and the Swiss Academy of Humanities, Berne

© 1992 by Universitätsverlag Freiburg Schweiz
  Vandenhoeck & Ruprecht Göttingen
  Paulusdruckerei Freiburg Schweiz

ISBN 3-7278-0807-1 (Universitätsverlag)
ISBN 3-525-53750-6 (Vandenhoeck & Ruprecht)

Contents

PREFACE

This research was funded by a British Academy Personal Research Grant and a Fulbright Travel Grant with further support from the Society of Antiquaries of London. I am most grateful to the Society for holding their grant over while the other applications were pending.

In Philadelphia everyone at the University Museum did their utmost to be helpful. Professor Åke Sjöberg and Professor Erle Leichty gave me free access to the Tablet Room, a privilege not obtainable in most museums, which was essential in enabling me to search a very large number of tablets for impressions. They were always ready to answer queries and allowed me to use the excellent library in their offices. Hermann Behrens welcomed me when I arrived and was very generous with his time in helping me at a moment when he was beset by a publication deadline. I owe to him, and to Atsuko Hattori, much help with the collection during my stay. Richard Zettler and Maude de Schauensee gave me access to the archaeological collections and allowed me to look at seals and impressions in the basement. Professor Zettler also gave me a draft of his forthcoming paper on the Nippur glyptic and very generously showed me casts and photographs of his material.

Professor J.A. Brinkman invited me to visit Chicago and facilitated my stay there. He showed me the Philadelphia tablets in his possession and cleared up a number of difficulties in matters Kassite. He proposed that we send a joint Note on no. **61** to *N.A.B.U.* He had the best impressions of the Amil-Marduk seal, no. **149**, and was able to disentangle its attestations in Istanbul from those of the Rimutu seal, no. **148**. Professor Gibson showed me unexpected kindness when I met him in Chicago, giving me free access to the casts and impressions of the glyptic he has discovered at Nippur and allowing me to publish those that are not committed elsewhere. John Nolan and Ray Tindel assisted me with the collection of the Oriental Institute. I am particularly grateful to them for allowing me access to the splendid seal A29349, which I saw in the public gallery.

Professor Edith Porada returned some sealings to Philadelphia so that I could study them. It was my very good fortune that she spent a long time in the Tablet Room with me on two occasions, so that I was able to profit from her experience with the original material before us. Her minute observation suggested a number of significant corrections to my drawings. Later, she invited me to visit New York and did everything possible to make my stay there pleasant.

I have also to thank Dr. J.V. Canby, Dr. P. Harper, Dr. M.V. Harris, Dr. Ran Zadok, Fritz Knobloch, Branwen Denton, Bonnie Magness-Gardiner, Irene Winter, Richard and Maria Ellis, Eva Braun-Holzinger,

Michelle Marcus, Darlene Loding, Judy Montgomery-Moore and Eileen Matshiqi for their help, hospitality and conversation while I was in America.

In Britain, I am indebted to Dominique Collon, Nicholas Postgate, Roger Moorey, Joan Oates and Alison Wilson for their help at various points in the project. Stephanie Dalley and Dr. J. Oelsner assisted me with some textual problems. The Assyriologists I have consulted are not responsible for any philological errors.

Professor W.G. Lambert kindly undertook the editing of the inscriptions at the last moment. The text, translations and immediately associated words (in the Catalogue, after 'Inscription:' in each case) are his sole responsibility. My greatest debt is, as ever, to my parents, and to Frances.

For the abbreviations used in the text, see p. 141. For the other conventions used in the Catalogue and the picture captions, see pp. 63-68.

I. COMMENTARY

1. Introduction

1.1 The material

The Kassite seals have long been recognised as a distinct phase in the history of Mesopotamian glyptic, on account of their characteristic royal inscriptions,[1] though some basic aspects of their development remained unrecognised until after the last war (cf. Frankfort 1939, 188). The division by Beran (1957-8) into three groups is the foundation of the present work, with the addition of a fourth group, pseudo-Kassite, whose importance only became clear with the publication of the seals from Choga Zanbil (Porada 1970).

In my former study (Matthews 1990, henceforth *PC*) I collected most of the known Kassite seals and studied their classification, their phylogeny and their principles of composition. I have preferred here with minor sources of seals to give a reference to the illustrations in *PC* rather than to the original publication, as the detailed arguments here are in any case often dependent on it, and I think that consulting one volume should be less troublesome to the reader. Many of the seals from major sources cited here are also illustrated in *PC*.

It proved difficult to place the development of the Kassite seals on a sound foundation because of the shortage of dated designs and the restricted period of time to which the known dates belonged (*PC* pp. 58, 70). At the same time the work of Brinkman (1976) in collecting the extant dated tablets made it clear that even if only a small proportion of them bore impressions this would still represent a major increase in the evidence available. There are only a few hundred surviving Kassite designs (*PC* p. 55) while Brinkman lists thousands of tablets.

These tablets, however, are still somewhat restricted in chronological scope. The Kassite period, according to ancient tradition and modern convention, lasted for something in the order of half a millennium; but nearly all of the economic texts date from between the reigns of Burnaburiaš II and Kaštiliaš IV, a span of less than one and a half centuries. The great bulk of the archives was found by the American expedition to Nippur at the turn of the century, and through the kindness of Professor Sjöberg and Professor Leichty I was allowed to search through the Tablet Room in Philadelphia where a large part of the material is kept. The Catalogue presented here, containing some two

---

[1]   E.g. Ménant 1883, 193-197.

hundred seals, almost all from Nippur, includes about one third of all the Middle Babylonian designs now extant, and a much higher proportion of those with some geographical or chronological context.[2] Although actual seals of the Third Kassite style have been found at Nippur and elsewhere in Babylonia (*PC* p. 64 n.92) none of the Philadelphia impressions is of this type, no doubt because the style originated after the end of the thirteenth century;[3] so I shall not refer to it again.

In my former work I proposed a distinction between the *Babylonian tradition*, derived from Old Babylonian (*PC* pp. 51-54), and the new styles originating in the fourteenth century which ultimately, after the end of the Kassite period, centred on an *Assyrian standard* (*PC* pp. 115-117). First Kassite and pseudo-Kassite belonged to the older Babylonian tradition, while Second Kassite was one of the main pillars of the new order.

1.2 Description

The convention used for the depiction of human forms in First Kassite and pseudo-Kassite (and also in some Mitannian styles) was quite rigid. In this work I shall use the same code as formerly (*PC* pp. 18-24), but as I require less fluidity of expression here I shall use words rather than numbers, with one exception. These words are simply labels for regular forms, and are used irrespective of their meaning.[4] The rules described here are true for Nippur though there are some exceptions elsewhere (see *PC* pp. 71-72). For clarity, I am giving here a summary of the scheme worked out in *PC*, but it does not seem necessary to provide a complete discussion of it. Humans are described by three primary attributes, posture, dress and arms, though other aspects such as headgear may sometimes be important.

Posture appears to be an indicator of status (*PC* p. 84) and there are three Kassite types, kneeling, standing and sitting. There are again three Kassite *Dress* types. The long or bordered dress is a plain dress covering both legs, with a line or a ladder-patterned strip down the middle. It is worn by all classes of person. The open dress is similar to this but is drawn up in front, either to the knee, often exposing tassels between the legs (**89**), or to the waist to show an under-tunic. The flounced dress appears on the face of it to be divine, especially when combined with a pointed hat (**1, 10, 15, 16, 81, 88, 96**), but it is frequently interchangeable

---

[2] See *PC* for sketches of 276 Babylonian seals, including 23 of those given here.

[3] Porada 1970, 128; *PC* p. 66.

[4] So for example the 'martial' posture is a particular arm attitude and is used irrespective of whether this posture actually had a martial meaning.

with figures in ordinary dresses.[5] Naked figures in Kassite, the kneeling man and the nude female, are always shown at a smaller scale.

The *arm positions* are strictly governed by orientation and provide the basic definitions of figure types. The upper arms always hang down. The forward forearm can either be raised to place the hand at shoulder height, or held in at the waist; and the rear forearm can occupy these two positions (the former now held across the chest to lie over the opposite shoulder), or hang downwards. This gives a total of six arm positions, of which one (forward arm up, rear arm down) was not preserved in Kassite. As for the others, the *interceding* position (both hands raised)[6] defines the Intercessor who stands in a plain or flounced dress and may face either way. She only occurs in First Kassite (**1**, **10-17**) with very rare exceptions such as **78** and possibly **84**.

In the *devotional* posture[7] the forward arm is held in and the rear arm is raised. This man always wears a plain robe and faces right, either kneeling (**57-60**) or standing.[8] The *martial* posture[9] has the forward arm in and the rear arm lowered: the forward hand may hold a mace (**3**, **6**, **87-89**) and the rear arm usually, though not always[10] grasps a curved sword. This man always stands facing right and may wear any dress. He is rare in the First Kassite of Nippur (**2-4**, **6-10**) but is the most common person in pseudo-Kassite (**81-84**, **87-119**, **127**, **128**). The posture where both arms are held in at the waist[11] is only regularly used in Kassite for the nude female (**11**, **12**) but occasionally occurs elsewhere, such as **18**.

The fifth posture, with the forward arm raised and the rear held in, is so common that it needs a short label: but I cannot think of a better term than *arm type 11*.[12] All seated persons have these arms, face left, and are[13] dressed in a plain robe - **65** is the only flounced case at Nippur. The position also occurs in standing persons in a plain robe, almost always facing left.[14]

It should be stressed that the terms used here, interceding, devotional and martial, are purely descriptive and are used entirely without reference

---

5   **81**, **88**, **96**, **98** and compare **65** with **61-64**.

6   Type 2 in *PC*.

7   Type 3 in *PC*.

8   **11?**, **61-68**; in pseudo-Kassite **78-82**.

9   Type 7 in *PC*.

10 Certainly absent in **87**, **89**, **128**.

11 Type 10 in *PC*.

12 I have preferred to maintain conformity with *PC* than to adopt a label like Type A or Type X which might look better.

13 **16-18**, **29-42**, **60-65**, **69-78**.

14 **6-9**, **53-58**, **85-88**; **5** faces right.

to their significance. It would, admittedly, be less misleading to use code numbers; but I have no doubt that most readers would prefer to use words. I have discussed elsewhere the further use that may be made of such terms, on a grammatical analogy (*PC* p. 28-29). Briefly, I understand the Babylonian designs as simple sentences, essentially consisting of two Persons facing each other. The Persons may be affected ("inflected") with reference to each other. The primary Kassite Persons are the King and the God, the King facing right and the God, with arms 11, facing left.[15] The God varies only in posture (seated or standing) while the King varies both in posture (standing or kneeling) and in aspect, devotional or martial. There is also the Intercessor, who may face in either direction, and some lesser persons, the female attendant in **69-73** and the male attendant with a fan in **74-76**. As a general rule, a scene should always represent the interaction of two Persons of different kinds, but the King is often shown repeated, either to combine the force of different aspects (**81, 82**) or more often in repetition of the martial aspect (**88-90, 93-108**).

2. The Babylonian Tradition

2.1 First Kassite

The First Kassite style is only known in quantity at two sites, Nuzi and Nippur. There are certain structural and formal differences between the designs found at these places which led me to define the Northern and Central groups of seals (*PC* pp. 70-87). The most distinctive scenes (though not the most typical) are those where two Persons face each other. In common with most of the other styles in the Babylonian tradition, the arm types of the Persons are subject to strict rules of orientation, which are shared by the two groups, and of combination, which differ. The fundamental difference occurs in the *King-God* scene. In Central seals the King (the figure on the left in the two-figure scene) is always in an inferior posture to that of the God (the figure on the right), while in Northern both figures are always standing (cf. Porada 1970, 10). A kneeling figure is inferior to a standing one, so if the God in Central is standing then the King is kneeling.[16] The arms and posture are thus essential to the structure of the scene, while the dress is variable. The *King-Intercessor* scene does occur in Central,[17] but rarely, and not at

---

[15] As before, the validity of the structural concepts to which these terms refer is unaffected by the appropriateness or otherwise of the actual terms chosen.

[16] For a discussion of this type of analysis, see *PC* p. 28; and for this interpretation of First Kassite, *PC* p. 84.

[17] *PC* p. 86, C1.

Nippur. It is more common in Northern.[18] The Intercessor also combines with the seated God in Central (16, 17), though not in Northern. The seated God in Central also combines with a female figure[19] and this scene also occurs in pseudo-Kassite (71-73) where she may be replaced by a standing man with a fan (74-76). Most Central scenes show only a single figure, normally a seated or standing God but occasionally a King in devotional aspect. A martial King sometimes occurs alone in Northern, but is more often duplicated (*PC* pp. 76-8).

The distinction between the Northern and Central groups, which was derived from differences in the figure combinations and the geographical provenances, is confirmed by a corresponding difference between the repertories of filling symbols used in each. The Central group uses the symbols which are conventionally thought of as 'Kassite': dog, cross, rhomb, corn ear, insect, rosette and locust; while in Northern these are rare or absent, being replaced by a small animal or bird, an isolated vessel, or a nude female at a smaller scale than the main figures. The fly occurs in some Northern scenes but is also a common Elamite symbol and may have impinged slightly on Central from there (*PC* p. 76).

2.2 Pseudo-Kassite

The pseudo-Kassite style (*PC* pp. 66-70) is a close relative of First Kassite. The Intercessor is rare but the other three Kassite Persons are common, normally a *King-God* scene of Northern type (both figures standing) or the component figures of this scene on their own. As in Northern, the King is often duplicated, and is normally in martial form. Unlike in Northern, a seated person occurs and this, together with the isolated standing God and many of the symbols, creates a superficial similarity to the Central group.[20] However the standing God, though not present alone in Northern, is a typical figure there in the *King-God* scene, so a derivation by simplification of Northern makes sense. As for the seated figure, he occurs in pseudo-Kassite in the scene with the attending person who seems to have Elamite connections (*PC* p. 84). As pseudo-Kassite is well known in Elam, at Susa and Choga Zanbil, it is possible that the scene impinged on pseudo-Kassite from the east.[21]

Apart from its structural peculiarities, which thus seem to derive most naturally from Northern, pseudo-Kassite has distinctive features both in

---

[18] 10, doubtless 11.

[19] 69, 70, cf. 18.

[20] *PC* p. 69 nn. 163, 166.

[21] *PC* p. 53. The Central First Kassite examples of this scene, cited in *PC* nos. 30 and 32, are reassigned here to pseudo-Kassite (76 and 75) while no. 31 was misunderstood (here 70); so the problem of this scene in First Kassite no longer exists.

cutting style and subject. The style is strongly linear with much use of hatching and no subtly modelled planes as in the best First Kassite. Most pseudo-Kassite seals are quite crude though a few are finely and precisely cut. In most pseudo-Kassite seals there are items such as hatched bands, a frieze over the inscription, a monster or a volute tree which do not occur in First Kassite. Such seals are almost invariably made of a soft material, often glass, whereas First Kassite is almost always in hard stone. This difference in material is the most convenient distinguishing criterion between the styles, but there are some actual glass seals which do not have any of the specific pseudo-Kassite features[22] and a number of impressions which are thus rather difficult to assign.[23] This raises the question of whether pseudo-Kassite is really a separate style or merely what happens when First Kassite is engraved into a soft material, which would automatically alter the appearance of the engraving.[24] It is true that almost every First Kassite figure and symbol type occurs, at least occasionally, in pseudo-Kassite, and that there are seals in both groups whose style of engraving is not distinctive. However, nearly every known actual seal in a soft material has clear pseudo-Kassite features, and nearly every hard stone seal does not. The choice of subject is as much a stylistic matter as the manner of the engraving. The material of the seal does not constrain the choice of subject in any way, so we have to acknowledge that the choice of material and of subject are both governed by a stylistic difference, which in many seals in both groups extends also to the cutting style. The undistinctive pieces may then be understood in one of two ways. Either they are transitional between the styles, like "franglais"; or they are independently constructed by the productive conventions of their respective styles, which happen in those instances to coincide. The latter case is not surprising, since both styles have the same Babylonian inheritance;[25] and the former is also possible since pseudo-Kassite presumably originated by adapting some variety of First Kassite, most probably the Northern group.

2.3 Chronology and development

The phylogeny of these three closely related versions of the Babylonian standard is not easily understood without knowledge of their chronology: but this remains obscure. The extreme limits can be judged from seals with inscriptions naming kings, but the names in question occurred more

---

22 E.g. Choga Zanbil 2, 6.

23 *PC* p. 67 n. 144: most of the Philadelphia ones are now demonstrably pseudo-Kassite.

24 I am indebted to Dr. Joan Oates for asking me this question.

25 Cf. parallel usage of Greek and Latin roots in modern French and English technical terms.

than once and we do not know which one is correct.[26] The earliest certain date for a seal of clear Central First Kassite character is Burnaburiaš II, c. 1340 B.C.,[27] though seals with inscriptions referring to Kurigalzu and Kadašman-Enlil could be earlier if they refer to the first monarchs of those names. Paradoxically, the latest certain date for a typically Central seal[28] is Kadašman-Enlil I,[29] that is, in the previous reign; but again seals of Kurigalzu and Burnaburiaš could be later if the second kings of those names are described. These limits are, of course, mutually inconsistent, and there are several possible solutions. Given that there are dated impressions in the reigns of Kurigalzu II and Nazi-Maruttaš, the most convenient estimate of the span of the Central seals with royal names is between Kadašman-Enlil I and Nazi-Maruttaš, c. 1370-1300 B.C. They are not likely to continue much later because of their rarity among the thirteenth century impressions presented here; but there is no firm evidence on their beginning.

The difference in the type of evidence is significant, as an inscribed name refers to the *date of engraving*, which is the date we want in terms of artistic history; while an impression only gives the *date of use*, which might be much later. Nonetheless, the fact that styles can often be shown to change over time from impressions demonstrates that the overall picture they give is useful. We need only remember that there is probably a small time-lag between the general pictures obtained from the two sources (a lag possibly insignificant compared to the length of reigns which I am using as a chronological framework); and that individual impressions may be very misleading. The stratigraphy of actual seals found in excavations, on the other hand, is in my opinion virtually useless.[30]

The seals with royal names belong to the Central group; but for the Northern designs we have the impressions from the Nuzi archive. This archive is not, unfortunately, fixed with respect to Babylonian chronology, but we may place its end, following Stein (1989) between 1350 and 1330 B.C., and therefore not necessarily overlapping with Central for more than a generation or so. The Northern group is attested in the second generation at Nuzi (Nuzi 689) which may be placed 75-100 years before the end of the archive, thus c. 1450-1400 B.C. (cf. *PC* p. 57). Before the

---

[26] See p. 66 for a king list.

[27] VR 554 and CANES 577: *PC* pp. 57-8.

[28] I am not counting atypical seals such as PBS XIV 530 (Kara-indaš), where the inscription is not in a separate panel, and there is no royal title.

[29] Walters Art Gallery 42.619 (Brinkman 1976, 136). Dr. J.V. Canby kindly showed me a photograph of this seal which has a seated figure in a flounced robe holding a rod and ring, on a panelled throne, with a cross in the field; seven line inscription.

[30] For the chronological significance of high regnal years, see below p. 45.

examples in this book were known, there was no good evidence for the date of the pseudo-Kassite seals, though some indications pointed towards the thirteenth century (*PC* p. 69).

On this basis I suggested that the Northern and Central groups existed concurrently in different places throughout the fourteenth century, though there was a possibility that the distinction was chronological. In the thirteenth century First Kassite was replaced by pseudo-Kassite (*PC* p. 69-70). But this remained little more than a guess, and a main aim of my research in Philadelphia was to find further evidence bearing on the question. Since the Philadelphia material derives from Nippur, there was little prospect of obtaining much information on Northern; but there was every reason to expect some good evidence for pseudo-Kassite.

The dated *Central* designs here all belong to the reigns of Kurigalzu (**16, 56, 60**) and Nazi-Maruttaš (**19, 20, 48, 55, 57, 61**). Since none of the some thirteen designs dated later than the latter reign were First Kassite (with the possible exception of **14**, a very obscure design), this seems to be reasonable evidence that I was correct in placing the end of First Kassite at the close of the fourteenth century. As there were only five designs dated before Kurigalzu, one of which could belong to the Central group,[31] it is still not possible to assign a beginning to the style. The two earliest impressions, however, though they do not prove anything, may be indicative. **1** is dated by J.A. Brinkman probably to Kadašman-Enlil I or Kadašman-Ḫarbe I in the early fourteenth century,[32] thus perhaps a generation earlier than the earliest existing Central designs. It has a marked Old Babylonian character.[33] **6**, on the other hand, again dated possibly to Kadašman-Enlil I, belongs to the Northern group with its two standing figures facing each other.[34] These impressions leave open the possibility that the Babylonian glyptic of the fifteenth century was essentially Old Babylonian in style, and that the Northern tradition was a general Babylonian phase of the early fourteenth century, divided from Central more by time than by space.

The difficulty with this theory previously was that there was no reason to believe that pseudo-Kassite, which can hardly be kept entirely unconnected to Northern, existed before c. 1300 B.C., and indeed no proof that it existed within the following fifty years. The most startling chronological discovery in Philadelphia was that pseudo-Kassite existed already in a developed form in the reign of Burnaburiaš II (**116**),

---

[31]   **15**: we know already (see above) that Central seals existed in the time of Burnaburiaš.

[32]   See catalogue entry.

[33]   Cf. BM III 578, 608, 609, 613, 616, VR 487, CANES 567.

[34]   Cf. Nuzi 689, 700.

continuing at least until the time of Kadašman-Turgu (**115, 117, 133**).[35] This means that there is no evidence placing Central First Kassite earlier than pseudo-Kassite. Whether they are both derived from Northern, or it is presumed that Central coexisted with Northern in the earlier fourteenth century, it is now certain that Central First Kassite and pseudo-Kassite were both in use in parallel at Nippur throughout the second half of the fourteenth century. When we recall that Second Kassite is also known to have existed throughout the same fifty years (*PC* p. 63) then it is clear that we need an explanation for the concurrence of three different styles in the same place for at least two generations. This problem will be discussed later (pp. 55-57).

2.4 Survey of the designs.

2.4.1 Old Babylonian and Northern First Kassite.

As was explained above, the very earliest impressions (**1** and **6**) are not of classic Central First Kassite character, and it remains possible, though not proven, that the seals in use at Nippur before the middle of the fourteenth century were Old Babylonian and Northern First Kassite in style. There are only thirteen designs of this general type, which may be due either to the overall shortage of dated tablets before the time of Burnaburiaš II, or to these styles being native at Nippur at no time in the Kassite period. **6, 7** and **8** all show a man in martial posture facing a standing God. Such a scene with both figures standing is quite foreign to the Central seals, but is typical of Northern (*PC* nos. 96-107). The crudity of **7** is striking: although fine engraving is not unknown in Northern seals they more commonly include coarse pieces than the Central group does (*PC* p. 73, n. 206). **9** is another example, but should not now be assigned to Nippur (see catalogue entry).

2 and **3** are examples of the martial figure on his own, again a standard Northern subject (*PC* nos. 73-79). The small spare precise engraving of **2**, however, reminds me more of Old Babylonian cutting, as also do **5** and **13**.[36] The figure in **5** faces right,[37] where we would expect the opposite in Central (**54-58**). If I am right in seeing a Common Mitannian impression in **5** as well, this would not be significant as this style often occurs in Babylonia;[38] but it may constitute another link with the north. In **4** the martial figure faces two indeterminate persons, perhaps

---

[35]   For textual corroboration, see Amiet (1990) *Marlik et Tchoga Zanbil* (*RA* 84), 44-47.

[36]   Cf. BM III 620-632, VR 494.

[37]   Cf. in Old Babylonian, BM III 580, 614, 623, 630.

[38]   See below, pp. 52-54.

9

COMMENTARY

Intercessors, in a manner reminiscent of some pseudo-Kassite designs;[39] but the impression shows no pseudo-Kassite traits and seems to have a firmer and harder manner of engraving than is normal in that style, so it may be better to compare it to the Northern three-figure scenes.[40]

10 is a very unusual scene with a flounced martial person facing, no doubt, an Interceding Goddess. The Intercessor in Northern normally has a plain robe,[41] but the martial King in a flounced robe is a standard Northern form.[42] The Central version has a dress open in front.[43] **11-13** are more typically Northern, especially the first two which show the nude female, a typical Northern figure.[44] We may note the almost complete absence of the classic Central symbols, with the very doubtful possible exception of a cross in **8**.[45] I have included **14** here because it may possibly show an Intercessor: but its date in the late thirteenth century is so much beyond the end of First Kassite that it may be better to give it some quite different interpretation.

2.4.2 Central First Kassite

This group is overwhelmingly dominated by the figure of the seated God, to the extent that he is even faced by the Intercessor (**15?-17**), contrary to the usage normal in most of the other styles related to the Old Babylonian convention (*PC* p. 38 nn. 50, 55). Unlike most Kassite figure types, where the headdress seems to be immaterial or stylistic, the Intercessor almost always has a pointed hat with a flounced dress, and a round hat with a plain dress, as in **1**, **10-12**, **15**, **16**.[46] The Central tradition seems to have been more interested in devotional religion than the Northern (*PC* p. 84) so it is appropriate that the more divine version of the Intercessor was preferred. We notice now the typical Kassite symbols, locust (**16**) and cross (**17**).

18 is an extremely unusual design. The figure on the left has the long hair that may be a mark of females,[47] though **58** seems to show it on a

[39] Cf. **87**, **88**, Subeidi 6.

[40] E.g. *PC* nos. 93, 100, 108.

[41] E.g. Nuzi 686, 687, 694.

[42] Nuzi 688, Ash 561.

[43] PBS XIV 530, FI 236, BM 102420.

[44] *PC* p. 76, n. 227. Since the man on the left in **11** is apparently not martial we should reconstruct him in the devotional attitude to give a scene like Nuzi 694.

[45] The rosette in **6**, though a Central symbol, also occurs occasionally in Northern: Ash 560, *PC* no. 88. For the goatfish in **5**, cf. Nuzi 696.

[46] Cf. especially PBS XIV 530; but there are exceptions, e.g. BN 300. Legrain saw **12** in a flounced dress and a horned headdress.

[47] Porada 1948, 64-5, s.v. no. 575; see also the Fribourg seal, FI 245.

bearded God. The arm posture with both hands at the waist does not usually occur in Kassite, except in the nude female (**11, 12**). There are, however, isolated cases in *PC* no. 118 and, more significantly, in FI 653 which belonged to a woman. Here an apparently female figure, beardless and with breasts (though without long hair) in the dress and headdress of the Interceding Goddess faces a seated God who holds a large corn ear. Except for the cup (**69, 70**, etc.) it is very rare for the Kassite God to hold anything at all[48] and there is no other case of a standard of this size in First Kassite.[49] The crescent-disk standard reminds me rather of some of the Nuzi impressions.[50] Fishmen are rare in First Kassite and normally occur singly (**55**, FI 236); the pair is comparable to Second Kassite usage[51] though there they form an integral part of the main design.

The long inscription dominates **18** and most other Central seals, while in Northern the design is usually more prominent (*PC* p. 79). There are several seals with nothing but the inscription (*PC* p. 86, C10B) but with the exception of **20**, which does seem to have no figures, it is impossible to say whether **19-24** belong to this type or are just fragments.[52] Likewise **25** has no main subject, only a couple of animal heads,[53] while **26-28** probably had a human figure as well as the surviving symbol.

With **29-56** we come to the most prominent series of Nippur designs, the single God, seated or standing (*PC* nos. 34-63). With many fragments the posture is uncertain,[54] but I guess that **43-48** are probably seated and **51-53** probably standing.[55] The seated God normally has his arm at a shallower angle (*PC* p. 77) and being shorter has room for more space at the top. The resulting proportion of about six seated figures to every standing one in these scenes is in contrast to the overall situation which is more like two to three.[56] This suggests that the seated God is a particular characteristic of the glyptic of Nippur, thus perhaps to be identified with Enlil. Another feature worth noting is the delineation of the back of the headdress with a pronounced re-entrant in **29, 31, 46** and **53**, also found in **18, 60, 61** and **62** - a high proportion of all of the seated and standing Gods where this area is preserved. Such a profile is known in some actual

---

[48] E.g. trident, Ash 559; branch, Southesk Qb 41, Marcopoli 135?

[49] Cf. **47** for 'trees'.

[50] HSS XIV 283, Nuzi 716, cf. CANES 1026.

[51] E.g. Thebes 27, 28, Ash 562, CANES 586.

[52] Also 14 N 246, to be published by R.L. Zettler.

[53] *PC* p. 86, C10A, nos. 67-70; cf. Nuzi 708, Louvre A597.

[54] Including 14 N 222, to be published by R.L. Zettler.

[55] R.L. Zettler will publish 14 N 247 which may also show a standing God.

[56] *PC* p. 86, C7:C9A, ratio of 23:33, not counting unusual cases.

seals[57] but, again, is not so common so this may be another mark of a Nippur provenance.

The tree or standard in **47** is most unusual in that First Kassite, unlike almost every other later second millennium style, shows virtually no interest in trees. There is, however, a good parallel in Wien-Graz 85, and it is possible that **34** should also be restored in this way.

The 'carrion-birds' motive in **48** formerly seemed most convincingly attached to Iranian connections.[58] It occurs both in First Kassite[59] and in pseudo-Kassite.[60] This variety of style, and of workshops within styles,[61] indicates that the birds are not a local peculiarity but are an integral part of the Kassite repertory; and the fact that Nippur is now the major source (though note that **69** has no provenance) makes it possible to suggest that it is an essentially Babylonian scene. It is, of course, my contention that pseudo-Kassite is a basically Babylonian, rather than as is usually supposed an Elamite style; but even leaving this aside it is perhaps significant that the pseudo-Kassite examples of the 'carrion-birds' are from Nippur and Subeidi in the Hamrin, not from Susa or Choga Zanbil. The accompanying main scenes both in First Kassite and in pseudo-Kassite show no regularity and yield no clue as to the meaning of the scene.

54 (like **69** and **70**) is an actual seal which was not found at Nippur. I include it because the publication in PBS XIV, no. 531, gives the photograph the wrong way round, producing an unusual case of this arm posture facing right. The true situation, facing left, corresponds to the other designs with the same theme.[62]

In **57-60** a standing or seated God is faced by a small kneeling figure,[63] either in normal devotional attitude (**58-60**) or with the arm on the right raised (**57**).[64] The dog is frequently shown together with the kneeling man.[65] The scene probably has the same meaning as the standing man in a devotional attitude facing the seated God (**61-65**)[66] - as explained above, the conventions of the Central group preclude a standing God if

---

[57] E.g. Wien-Graz 85, de Clercq 254, *PC* no. 36.

[58] Boehmer 1981, 73-4; Porada 1972, 174-5; *PC* p. 75.

[59] **48, 69**, *PC* no. 27.

[60] **76, 99**, Subeidi 19, 22, *PC* no. 241; Amiet (1990) *Marlik et Tchoga Zanbil* (*RA* 84), p. 46 fig. 1.

[61] Contrast the schematic design of **99** with the fine detail of *PC* no. 241.

[62] Louvre A601 and CANES 583, both crudely cut, are now the only cases facing right.

[63] *PC* nos. 14, 15, 26-29.

[64] A usage also known in *PC* nos. 15, 67, Marcopoli 135 and Southesk Qb 41.

[65] **57, 60**, *PC* nos. 15, 26, 27, Marcopoli 135, de Clercq 264, VR 554, Louvre A600.

[66] *PC* nos. 16-21. **64**, and 14 N 165 which may be another case, will be published by R.L. Zettler.

the worshipper is not on his knees. The God in **65** has, unusually, a flounced dress.[67] This is unlikely to have a great effect on the meaning since it corresponds to no other difference, and may be compared to some designs which show an isolated seated God in this dress.[68] In **66-68** the standing devotional figure is on his own (*PC* nos. 4-13). **66** is remarkably similar to (though not the same as) Brett 81, even down to some of the inscription, which allows us to reconstruct the line at the bottom as an animal's horn. In both designs the man wears a high hatched headdress, but there is no reason to suppose this implies divine status (*PC* p. 83, n. 315). The bird in **68** is unusual in First Kassite and it is possible that an elaborate Second Kassite tree should be reconstructed beneath it, as in **173**, **174**, 12 Glyptik 2, Thebes 32. The devotional arm posture is not otherwise known in Second Kassite, but the example of Thebes 29 (with the martial posture) demonstrates that that style can occasionally make use of the repertory of the Babylonian tradition.

2.4.3 *The seated figure with cup*

The last two First Kassite designs, **69** and **70**, are actual seals which were not found at Nippur, but I have included them because the published photographs are unclear. It was difficult in **70**, especially, to make out the arm posture of the worshipper or the symbols. They both show a seated figure with a cup, a standing beardless figure with the same unusual arm posture, and a fly and other symbols in the field. In **71-73** we have a pseudo-Kassite treatment of the same subject, this time from Nippur, and there are other (First Kassite) cases in CANES 575 and de Clercq 257.[69] The seated man with a cup is a common figure in the glyptic of this time, especially in the Middle Elamite 'Banqueting Scene' (Choga Zanbil 54-87, etc), but also in Assyrian and Mitannian seals.

There are three main threads in a very confusing network of relationships. First, in the Elamite scene, the man is accompanied by an attendant and neither figure shows any Babylonian attributes. The dresses have a fringe at the bottom and sometimes a diagonal band across the knees. The cup is tilted towards the man's lips. The attendant sometimes holds a fan. There is often a table between them[70] which may perhaps be compared to the object in **76**. Second, in the Babylonian scene, the man is accompanied by one of three figures: the King in a normal devotional

---

[67] The doubts I expressed in *PC* p. 86 on Legrain's drawing of the worshipper have turned out to be justified.

[68] *PC* nos. 45, 46; Walters Art Gallery 42.619 (described above).

[69] R.L. Zettler will publish 14 N 250 which may possibly show a similar scene. Turin 70028 (Bergamini 1987, 61) seems to be another.

[70] E.g. Choga Zanbil 55, 56, 59-68.

attitude,[71] the female attendant (**69-73**, etc) and a male attendant who bears a fan.[72] The first figure is always First Kassite and the last always pseudo-Kassite; the female attendant may be either. Dresses and symbols are as usual in First Kassite and pseudo-Kassite. The cup is normally vertical. Third, a seated man in Mitannian who drinks from a vase through a tube may be related to the Mitannian cases where he holds a cup.

The man with the drinking tube normally occurs in the crude hard stone Mitannian seals which have little or no trace of a Babylonian inheritance; he is often on his own and thus not in a scene which can be analysed.[73] He has various attendants[74] but the only important ones are the nude female[75] and the fan-bearer (*PC* nos. 538, 539). To make the connection between the nude female and the fan-bearer in this context even more evident, FI 270 seems to have been recut from the one to the other, the nude female receiving long hair and the man with the drinking tube a decorated stool, an Assyrian hairstyle and a mace held at the waist. Parker 1949 no. 122 may have been recut similarly, this time to replace the seated man's tube with a cup. The man with an Assyrian hairstyle and mace recurs, now holding a vessel, in Birmingham 58 and *PC* no. 514, the latter with a fan-bearer behind (cf. *PC* p. 112)

Turning now to the Mitannian seals with a seated figure bearing a cup, we find that the nude female occurs again in Thebes 22 and in a seal from the Uluburun shipwreck, KW 2159.[76] This is only limited evidence for the association of the two figures, but the other Mitannian cases of the seated man with a vessel show no consistency[77] except for some which may have Elamite connections.[78] It is important to bear in mind that with the exception of these latter, and of the crudest hard stone seals

---

[71] *PC* no. 26, de Clercq 258, perhaps **65**; cf. in Mitannian, 14 Glyptik 47, in Syrian, Ash 907.

[72] **74-76**, VR 555, *PC* no. 240.

[73] E.g. RS 17.024, Marcopoli 594, BM 89402, 103237, CANES 1036.

[74] Parker 1975 no. 31, BM 102456, Marcopoli 599, CANES 1037.

[75] BM 89855; Van Buren 1954b, no. 8 (winged); the drawing of 14 Glyptik 48 may, in my opinion, be understood in this way rather than as the figure seated on a horned animal, as it appears: the 'head' and 'horn' would make a good vase and tube.

[76] They also combine in Collon BAR 47, but not facing each other. I am indebted to Dominique Collon for showing me the Uluburun seal, which shows the seated person with cup combined with an intercessor, a nude female and a fourth figure. Stylistically it is comparable to another Uluburun seal, FI 570.

[77] Cf. Marcopoli 590, 651, Beyer 1980 no. 11, Nuzi 497, CANES 1027, 1028, Schaeffer-Forrer 1983, 62 (Chypre A8), Frankfort 1939 pl. 43a.

[78] Porada 1970, 12, figures annexes 8 (*PC* no. 543); Nuzi 895; Stein 1987 no. 78; 14 Glyptik 49.

(Marcopoli 590, etc), the Mitannian designs normally include figures which are clearly in the Babylonian tradition, such as the martial,[79] devotional[80] and interceding[81] arm positions, or figures derived from Old Babylonian which were not inherited in Kassite as well (e.g. Thebes 22, CANES 1027).

To summarise, the seated man with cup in Mitannian occurs in seals which, though not strongly patterned themselves, relate to two groups of seals which are. A few of them are comparable to the Elamite Banqueting Scene, which has no Babylonian connections. Most of the others are in a Babylonian tradition, and have some relationship to a series where the man has a drinking tube and is associated with a nude female. This series belongs to the crude hard stone Mitannian style which does not itself have much connection with the Babylonian tradition, but which is inextricably connected to the main more elaborate Mitannian style in hard stone, which has.[82] This much is reasonably clear, though ill-defined because of the many seals that do not conform to a recognisable pattern; but in the person of the fan-bearer there is real confusion because he is associated both with the drinking tube series and with the Elamite banqueting scene.

Our interest is in the Babylonian situation, where we have male and female attendants, and a version of the devotional *King-God* scene which we know from **59-64**. Indeed no difference can be detected between the examples of this scene where the seated figure holds a cup and those where he does not. The contrast between the female attendant of the Mitannian seals and the male Elamite attendant[83] is noteworthy, and may perhaps properly be compared with the female and male attendants found in our Kassite series. Is it too imaginative to see the female as the Kassite version of a Mitannian scene, and the male as the Kassite form of an Elamite scene?

2.4.4 *Pseudo-Kassite*

With the designs already mentioned, **71-76**,[84] we enter a world

---

[79] CANES 1028, Frankfort 1939 pl. 43a.

[80] 14 Glyptik 47, Ash 907.

[81] 14 Glyptik 47, Collon BAR 47.

[82] Cf. especially 14 Glyptik 48, Van Buren 1954b no. 8, BM 102456.

[83] The sex of the Elamite attendant is not marked clearly, but I take him to be male because of the lack of any visible distinction from the way in which the seated figure is depicted. In the Assyrian impression, Moortgat-Correns 1964 no. 2, the attendant has a beard; and although in some cases there is clearly no beard (e.g. Porada 1970, figures annexes 8 (*PC* no. 543); Stein 1987 no. 78), in them the seated figure is shown beardless as well.

[84] **76** appeared in *PC* as both no. 30 and no. 128: it was not possible to tell from the published photographs that they are the same design.

certainly related to, but rather different from First Kassite. Inscriptions are often now flanked by hatched bands (**72, 74**) or topped with a frieze (**76**, perhaps **75**), and are less carefully separated from the scene (**75, 76**); monsters appear (**71**), as do strongly hatched elements (**74**), a small volute tree (**71**) and a few new filling elements such as the circled dot (**75**). Most symbols, however, remain the same, even the most obviously First Kassite ones like the framed cross (**71, 85, 87, 125**), the locust (**85, 88, 138**) and the dog (**85, 86**). Likewise, the repertory of human figures is almost entirely the same as in First Kassite.

The Fan Scene (**74-76**), discussed above, has very complicated international relations (*PC* pp. 110-113). The pseudo-Kassite version almost always has a small animal in the field[85] and three cases[86] have a little table between the figures surmounted by a hatched object. The Elamite Banqueting Scene also normally has such a table, but with vases[87] or fish.[88] The Elamite seals normally have an animal in the field, but also often a rhomb, fly, vase or star, and sometimes even a monkey.[89] The pseudo-Kassite Fan Scenes do occasionally have a fly (*PC* no. 240), a monkey (**76**) or a vase (VR 555, **75**?) but not, for some reason (probably an accident in a small sample) a rhomb, even though it is, after the rosette, the most common pseudo-Kassite symbol.[90] Apart from the table, which is probably part of the main scene, I see no special significance in these symbols, which all occur elsewhere in pseudo-Kassite as well as here.[91]

There is no reason not to assign **77** to First Kassite,[92] but I have included it here because of the similarity of its syntax to **78**, with the seated man in the middle of a three-figure scene.[93] It cannot be readily understood because the arm types are not preserved and there are no other First Kassite three-figure scenes with the central figure seated (*PC* p. 78). **78**, though unusually exactly cut, should be counted as pseudo-Kassite because of the monster and volute tree(?) in the friezes above and below the main scene, like **71**. Its scene, like **79**, shows the pseudo-Kassite version of the devotional *King-God* scene which is familiar in First

---

[85] Not VR 555.

[86] VR 555, *PC* no. 240, and **76**, to be restored after them.

[87] E.g. Choga Zanbil 55, 56, 60, 61, 64.

[88] E.g. Choga Zanbil 59, 65, 66.

[89] Especially with a fish, e.g. Choga Zanbil 59, 65, 66.

[90] The star is not a normal First Kassite or pseudo-Kassite symbol.

[91] E.g. even the monkey in **97**.

[92] Indeed, as will be shown later, the cap is evidence that it is not pseudo-Kassite.

[93] Cf. Choga Zanbil 9, 10.

Kassite (**61-64**). The Intercessor is very rare in pseudo-Kassite, and normally appears, as here, on the edge of a two-figure scene. **84** is probably another example (cf. *PC* no. 231, VR 552).

The devotional arm posture is rare in pseudo-Kassite, and **80**, with its long inscription and First Kassite appearance (cf. **66-68**, etc), is very unusual. I place it here because of the artificial material. **81** and **82** have a more normal usage of this arm posture in combination with the martial attitude, also known in Choga Zanbil 1 and *PC* no. 241. Such an arrangement goes back to Old Babylonian prototypes (*PC* p. 36) and occurs occasionally in First Kassite, especially in the Northern group.[94] It probably represents a desire to illustrate the martial and devotional aspects of kingship together; but this does not explain the special distinction given to the flounced martial figure with a peaked headdress in **81**, **88**, **96-98**.

81 is an unusually handsome example of an extant pseudo-Kassite seal. Most of the surviving pieces are relatively crude, like **107** and **109**, but **81** is well laid out and fairly carefully engraved, though not as delicately as Choga Zanbil 1 or *PC* no. 241. **83** and **84** are not well preserved but seem to represent three-figure scenes like **88**. In **83** the central figure is martial while the one on the left seems not to be: the most likely possibility here would then be a devotional attitude as in **81** and **82**. I cannot guess the nature of the third figure without knowing its orientation. The little fillers are too faint to comprehend - perhaps animal heads, vases, or "insects" like **88**. **84** is rather clearer with, presumably, an Intercessor in a plain robe and a flounced martial figure facing the third person, who does not seem to have the projecting elbow of arms type 11 (as in **88**) and so should be another Intercessor. There is a comparable scene (though with different dresses) in PBS XIV 530.

85 and **86** have the standing God (*PC* nos. 242-248) combined with a rhomb and a dog. **85** with its elaborate inscription and detailed, exact engraving, is a much closer imitation of a Central First Kassite seal than is usual in pseudo-Kassite, even to the classic Central symbols, the framed cross, locust and rhomb, which are rare in the latter style.[95] It should, however, clearly be asssigned to pseudo-Kassite because of the circled dot, the double line delimiting the inscription behind the figure, and especially the guilloche, which is quite unknown in First Kassite.[96] **87** is an even better imitation of First Kassite as no extraneous traits are visible in the surviving fragment. The figure on the right must have arms type 11, yielding a standard *King-God* scene of the Northern/pseudo-Kassite type.[97]

---

[94]   *PC* nos. 87, 100, 108, de Clercq 228; cf. BN 300.

[95]   Cf. in First Kassite, especially Louvre A599, BM 119321.

[96]   Except in the Mitannian hybrid HSS XIV 293; in pseudo-Kassite cf. Choga Zanbil 7.

[97]   Cf. Choga Zanbil 2, Failaka 399.

COMMENTARY

Two details which have pseudo-Kassite parallels, the lack of a curved sword in the arm that hangs down (cf. **89**, **128**, Choga Zanbil 1), and the 'hood-like' appearance of the martial man's head[98] make me assign it to pseudo-Kassite; but the (presumably kneeling) small figure in the middle is unusual.[99] If not pseudo-Kassite, the scene should be Northern, as both figures are standing;[100] but the kneeling man is more typical of Central First Kassite than of Northern and this is also true of the framed cross.

88, as PBS XIV 562, has long been known, but the discovery of a new impression of it on UM 29-13-47 supplies significant new information, especially on the frieze of sphinxes flanking a little volute tree at the top. This makes it clear that it is a pseudo-Kassite design, which was not apparent from Legrain's drawing. The little volute tree is a recurrent feature of the finest pseudo-Kassite seals, as in **71**, **78**?, **90**.[101] It does not, interestingly enough, occur at Choga Zanbil, where it is replaced by the little twisted tree of Choga Zanbil 1, 13, Susa 2054,[102] which does not itself occur at Nippur. The larger version of this tree, which is found in the most typical and ornate pseudo-Kassite seals ("Elaborate Elamite" in Porada 1970), though not in the finest examples, occurs both at Nippur[103] and in Elam,[104] though not on Failaka.[105]

While I was studying the Assyrian impressions from Tell Billa in Philadelphia I came across the door sealing UM 33-58-84. The impression on it is very faint but agrees in every visible respect with our no. **88**: a man in a martial attitude with a high hat and a projecting flap just below the waist, facing a man with arms 11 and a round hat, possibly a third figure on the left, round symbols between their heads, frieze at top with winged monster and tree containing diagonal lines (Matthews forthcoming, no. 36). It is not certain that it was impressed by the same seal, and there may conceivably be some question of a confusion in the provenance at the time the number was assigned (though the bulla is not part of either of the Nippur fragments); but we may have here a remarkable instance of the same, or almost the same design attested both in Assyria and in

---

[98] Cf. **106**, Choga Zanbil 1. Porada noticed this feature (1970, 8), but it cannot now be considered a local feature of Choga Zanbil.

[99] Cf. *PC* no. 231, Choga Zanbil 8, Susa 2073.

[100] Cf. **9**, CANES 573, Nuzi 690, 691, 699.

[101] On this basis the aberrant seal VR 552, though in a hard stone, might be assigned to pseudo-Kassite; FI 653, on the other hand, though unusual, must be First Kassite.

[102] Cf. Porada 1970, 7, figures annexes 7; VR 562.

[103] **100**, **102**?, **116**, **118**, **119**.

[104] Choga Zanbil 15, 16, 20, Susa 2083, 2084.

[105] Failaka 405 is rather different and should be compared to the Kassite-Mitannian hybrids Subeidi 18, Brett 83, Louvre A603, Nuzi 704 etc (Boehmer 1981, 73).

Babylonia. On the whole, considering the freedom with which Common Mitannian seals circulated throughout the Near East at this time, the lack of cultural contact between Assyria and Babylonia is rather more remarkable than such connections as are attested. Assyrian seals, in particular, are extremely rare in the south (see below, p. 54, no. **207**).

89, like **87** and **88**, features the martial man with a mace held at his waist; like **87** and **128** the curved sword is not shown, and like **6** and **90** the dress is drawn up in front to show tassels between the feet.[106] The friezes with monsters above and below are like **71**, **78**, **88** and **90**.[107] The theme of a procession of martial men had an impact outside the realm of glyptic, in wall painting at Aqar Quf (Tomabechi 1983) and work in metal and glass found in Iran.[108] The dates of these are rather later, as is confirmed by the existence of a kudurru with this posture.[109] This is the most striking survival of the Babylonian convention after the thirteenth century, when almost everything in art was dependent on Assyria. The seal de Clercq 359, discussed by Porada (1972, 177), shows Assyrian influence in the altars and hairstyles, and probably belongs with these later pieces. The replication of the figure three times is rare in glyptic.[110]

90 is a similar design in the same delicate style with the frieze centred on a little volute tree underneath. The dress is raised in front to show tassels, as before, but in the middle figure it is also flounced. This may have been the situation with the middle figure of **88** as well, though the surface of the clay was too distorted there to be sure. This treatment of the flounced dress is unusual. **91-94** show a more normal form, though pairs of flounced martial figures without an accompanying one in a plain dress, as in **95-98**, are otherwise unknown. In **93** the curved sword seems to be replaced by a small animal. This is most peculiar and the only parallel I can suggest is from Cyprus, Southesk Qd 1.[111] These seals do not have special pseudo-Kassite features but I have placed them here because of **94**, which is made of glass. Its stag's head is a recurrent feature in pseudo-Kassite.[112]

---

[106]   Cf. Subeidi 6; in First Kassite CANES 574, FI 236, 462, PBS XIV 530; also FI 570.

[107]   Legrain seems to have seen the animal above the middle figure as a monster.

[108]   Porada 1972, 170; Amiet 1986, fig. 1.

[109]   King 1912, pl. XXI (Meli-Šipak).

[110]   **105/106**, UEX 579, Amiet 1986, no.1, Rimah 39, HSS XIV 292.

[111]   A curved sword would normally be expected here in Fine Cypriote, cf. RS 22.033.

[112]   **73**, **73**, **95**, **137**, *PC* no. 241: although it does not occur at Susa or at Choga Zanbil, there are stags in VR 562 and Porada 1970, figures annexes 7 which have the little twisted tree which occurs at Choga Zanbil but not at Nippur. Porada (1970, 10, nn. 3, 4) observes that stags are particularly prominent both in pseudo-Kassite and in the First Kassite of Nuzi, but not in the First Kassite of Babylonia.

COMMENTARY

Up to now, with few exceptions (**76**, **81**), the designs have been laid out in the First Kassite manner with each part of the scene in a rectangular box and the inscription quite separate from the figures. With **95** we encounter a different kind of layout, more typical of the 'Elaborate Elamite' group in Porada 1970, where the different parts of the design run into and overlap each other. This is, in terms of contemporary glyptic, a very singular method: in nearly every other style each design element is kept quite separate from all of the others except where some juncture is required (as in a hero grasping an animal) or a symmetric crossing over of the figures is depicted.[113] In the most common arrangement a hatched band above the inscription runs into a martial figure with a frieze of birds or symbols above.[114] The fact that half of the known cases are from Nippur must reduce the likelihood that this variant of pseudo-Kassite is essentially Elamite, as seemed probable previously on account of the cases from Choga Zanbil and Susa. **96-98** are further cases, where the martial figures are in both plain and flounced robes:[115] each of them has a clear pseudo-Kassite trait.[116]

In **99-108** we have the same scene, but with both martial figures in plain robes. The quality is now sometimes well below what we have been used to previously, for example **107**,[117] or the almost unrecognisably stylised 'carrion birds' in **99**.[118] This last makes it clear that glass was not necessarily a high prestige material, as is indeed implied by its common use in pseudo-Kassite, which has a much lower average quality of engraving than the contemporary First and Second Kassite seals in stone.[119] Inscriptions now tend to be short, generally only three lines, and standardised with the common phrases '[Marduk], great lord' and 'Show mercy!'[120] (Reiner 1970, 134 type II), unlike the longer more varied ones we had before.[121] Inscriptions of, or close to, the short type seem to be associated quite specifically with the overlapping layout, as is shown by **76** and **81**. Another striking trait of this group is the large elaborate volute tree of **100**, **102**, **116**, **118**, **119**, instead of the tiny one we had before in

---

[113] This convention occurs occasionally in pseudo-Kassite: *PC* no. 241, Choga Zanbil 16, Susa 2068.

[114] **81**, **95**, **100**, **101**, **119**, Choga Zanbil 16, 17, Susa 2068, 2071, FI 292.

[115] Cf. Choga Zanbil 4, Susa 2072.

[116] **96**: overlaps inscription; **97**: monster; **98**: made of glass.

[117] Also perhaps Nippur I pl. 120:14 (3D 205 from TA VIII, a Kassite level).

[118] Contrast **69**, **76**, *PC* no. 241, Subeidi 19.

[119] Though for high quality work in glass, cf. the perfect imitation of the fine thirteenth century Assyrian style in UEX 608.

[120] dDN umun gal, arḫuš tuku.a.

[121] E.g. **71**, **80**, **84**, **85**, **88**, **89**.

secondary scenes (**71** etc). This tree is found elsewhere in seals of this kind.[122] Elaborated volute trees are a feature of the new wave of seal styles that originated everywhere in the fourteenth century (*PC* p. 115 n. 8) and one is compelled to wonder, especially where the tree is topped by a bird,[123] whether pseudo-Kassite is here deliberately imitating Second Kassite.[124]

108, the last of the seals with two martial figures, has the restrained layout and less standardised inscription that are familiar to us from **80** and **94**: nothing in the design suggests that it is not a normal Northern First Kassite seal, except the material. In this, and in the subject, it closely resembles the seal from Megiddo (FI 246) which also has a horned animal as a filling motive[125] - Parker (1949, 6) recognised its pseudo-Kassite nature when she called it 'a copy of a Kassite seal'.

With **109**, **110** and **112**, on the other hand, we plumb a new depth of crudity, though other seals with a single martial figure (**113-119**) are fairly competently engraved. Indeed **109** is so coarse that the man's arms are not shown: nonetheless, the fact that he is facing right, and that the devotional posture is restricted to seals of rather better quality, indicate that he should be understood as martial. **112** cannot be interpreted with certainty but it seems at any rate possible that there is a curved sword on the right of the inscription and the diagonal body of a bird, animal or monster on the left: however this may be incorrect in which case the orientation of the design is unknown. The single figure with a column of small figures in front, usually including a bird or a winged monster, such as we have in **109** and **113** (and perhaps others)[126] is a typical arrangement in the coarser pseudo-Kassite seals, both with the martial figure[127] and with the standing God,[128] though the latter person only occurs at Nippur, Choga Zanbil and Susa in forms closer to First Kassite.[129]

120-126 are fragments of designs, which may be assigned to pseudo-Kassite because of their hatched bands, but whose arrangements remain obscure. **120** has a more rounded engraving than is usual is pseudo-Kassite but the tapering hatched member is like the stem of the large

---

[122] Choga Zanbil 15, 16, FI 292.

[123] **116**, Choga Zanbil 15, FI 292.

[124] **173**, **174**, 12 Glyptik 2, Thebes 32.

[125] For the closely similar inscriptions cf. *PC* p. 79 n. 261.

[126] Including 14 N 116, to be published by R.L. Zettler.

[127] Choga Zanbil 3, 17, FI 293, Subeidi 30, 42.

[128] Rimah 12, CANES 584, Guimet 94, *PC* no. 245.

[129] **85**, **86**, Choga Zanbil 7, 8, Susa 2069, 2073.

volute tree in **116** and **118**.[130] **121** evidently has an inscription under a frieze of birds, as in **81** and **95**, and a figure in a flounced dress, perhaps martial if the bottom right fragment can be interpreted as a corner of the inscription next to a hanging arm. In **124** the inscription is ruled across in an unusual way, like **19** in First Kassite. The objects in the panel are obscure: the upper one might be a tree or the thing with bulbous protrusions of **96, 101**, *PC* no. 260. **125** is also unusual with its rows of symbols between hatched bands.[131] Pseudo-Kassite inscriptions are nearly always in vertical columns, but there are a couple of exceptions[132] so the orientation may be wrong.

127-130 mark an almost complete break with the First Kassite tradition. The main figures are now monsters or contests in a manner more reminiscent of Mitannian than anything else. The style of **127** is not the same as the others and its ascription to pseudo-Kassite is doubtful. It does seem to show a man in martial posture and on that basis I have placed it next to **128**. Here the man in his open dress and without a curved sword is close to **89**. The hero dominating a bull, on the other hand, a very ancient motive, was only preserved in our period in Mitannian.[133] This impression is also related to the actual seal Subeidi 19 (which I described previously, rather doubtfully, as Second Kassite: *PC* p. 63). Here the bull is attacked by two heroes with the 'carrion birds' (which do not occur in Second Kassite) above. The pair of bullmen with a standard in **129** is another ancient motive preserved in Mitannian.[134] **130**, with its pair of sphinxes[135] belongs to a small series with a pair of winged monsters[136] - unless it is just a frieze above the main design, like **88**. Such designs are common enough in Mitannian,[137] but as with the bird above

---

[130] Also 14 N 330, to be published by R.L. Zettler.

[131] Cf. in First Kassite, *PC* no. 35 for the crosses in panels.

[132] Choga Zanbil 20, *PC* no. 260.

[133] Cf. 14 Glyptik 58, BN 440, *PC* no. 602, Frankfort 1939 pl. 43a, Nuzi 671, 714, Newell 357.

[134] E.g. 14 Glyptik 87, Offner 1950 fig. 1 (Qatna), Frankfort 1939 pl. 42 o (Tiryns), Thebes 19, Nuzi 661, 777, *PC* no. 472.

[135] Although Legrain's drawing of this impression in PBS XIV is not a bad one it somehow conveys the idea that the monsters are centaurs (cf. the griffin in Nuzi 134: *PC* p. 82 n. 298) - though Porada interprets it correctly (1970, 13). The only non-Assyrian centaur on a cylinder seal of this period known to me is **158** (*PC* p. 98 nn. 117, 118).

[136] Choga Zanbil 13, Subeidi 45.

[137] E.g. **191**?, HSS XIV 284, 303; cf. Ash 916, Newell 551, Louvre A943, 944, Marcopoli 627, 628. Pairs of sphinxes occur more frequently, however, in secondary scenes: e.g. 13 Glyptik 76; 14 Glyptik 53, 90; Nuzi 653; Enkomi 2; Collon AOAT 189.

the tree mentioned above it is also possible that the reference is to Second Kassite (cf. FI 241, VR 559).

In **131-134** we have archery scenes. **131** has long been known from a photograph in BE XIV, but this gave no hint of the nature of the design. Chariot scenes are rare in this period[138] and ours has no similarity to any of the others. Since it is not demonstrably foreign, I take it to be Babylonian; and there it can only be pseudo-Kassite on account of its simplified linear engraving. But it has no specific relationship to pseudo-Kassite, and the star, in particular, is uncommon there (cf. **137**). Another couple of chariot scenes is known in pseudo-Kassite.[139]

132-134 show a kneeling archer, a large winged creature, horned animals and a rhomb in the field. **132** and **133** may possibly be impressions of the same seal.[140] The kneeling archer is characteristic of a special group of pseudo-Kassite seals, Susa 2082-2084, Choga Zanbil 19, 20, Moortgat-Correns 1969, Marlik 6 and *PC* no. 260.[141] The four Nippur cases do not, however, belong to this group as they lack the distinctive composition in small rectangular panels divided by hatched bands[142] and some typical features such as short inscriptions, the elaborate volute tree or the animal with its body at right angles.[143] Although *PC* no. 260 was acquired in Iraq the simplest explanation may be that the panelled group is an Elamite variant; or it may be just a freak of discovery as the constituent elements of the panelled group are known at Nippur.[144] The archer is not known in First Kassite and is fairly rare in Mitannian: it may be that these seals are reflecting the new ideas in Second Kassite (**157, 158**) and Assyria (*PC* p. 116 n. 20).

An important series of pseudo-Kassite and Elamite seals shows horizontal rows of animals and symbols (e.g. Choga Zanbil 88-105). Because they do not include humans it is difficult to assign a boundary between the two styles, as elsewhere, with reference to Babylonian

---

[138] Some examples: 12 Glyptik 39, Rimah 26 (Assyrian); VR 563 (Third Kassite); Thebes 37, 38 (Second Kassite?); Nuzi 527, 910-912 (Mitannian); de Clercq 310, Moore 179, Nimrud ND 5363 (Parker 1962 pl. XIII.6), Collon BAR 119, Amiet 1973 no. 428 (Levantine); Ash 965, CANES 1099, Kenna 1971, nos. 88, 91 (Cypriote); Frankfort 1939 text fig. 107 (Astrakous), Louvre A955 (Aegeanising).

[139] VR 562: Porada 1970, 7, *PC* p. 68-9; Amiet (1990) *Marlik et Tchoga Zanbil* (*RA* 84) pp. 46-7, fig. 3; Amiet (1973) *Glyptique élamite à propos de documents nouveaux* (*Arts Asiatiques* 26) pl. XV:65 may be better classed as Elamite.

[140] An actual seal 14 N 33 with an archer and an animal will be published by R.L. Zettler.

[141] *PC* nos. 259-265; also the Drouot sale catalogue 30 Mars 1981, no. 57.

[142] Cf. perhaps **123, 124** and **126**; but this arrangement always has the archer.

[143] Cf. perhaps Choga Zanbil 38 (Porada 1970, 21).

[144] Even the animal at right angles possibly in **126** and **139**.

conventions. A few of them may thus be assigned to pseudo-Kassite because of the presence of particular elements (*PC* p. 68). **135-139** are of this type and, being from Nippur, are no doubt pseudo-Kassite: we may note especially the locust in **138**.[145] **136** is such a small fragment that it may be a secondary part of a design that had a more important theme, like VR 562. **137** is the only well preserved case and is also the only known pseudo-Kassite impression of a seal which had metal caps, though imitations of the typical granulated triangles are occasionally found engraved into the material of the seal,[146] as in First and Second Kassite[147] and more often in Third Kassite.[148] The fox or jackal occurs occasionally in Third Kassite[149] and also in Assyrian,[150] but we should prefer the comparison with Choga Zanbil 91 which, like **138**, has a row of rhombs in its top register.[151] The stag heads in **137** are a recurrent pseudo-Kassite filler.[152] **139** is clearly laid out in horizontal registers, but is so badly preserved that little else can be seen: it is perhaps comparable to Choga Zanbil 103.

2.5 Pseudo-Kassite workshops

The 70 or so pseudo-Kassite designs presented here are now the largest source for this style, far exceeding those from Choga Zanbil and Failaka (about twenty each), and indeed coming not far short of half of all of the known examples.[153] We should therefore undertake a brief study of the different types of pseudo-Kassite seal, the more so as our material has, for our period, quite a good geographical distribution, with four main sources.[154] Failaka and Choga Zanbil have only produced actual seals, while Susa and Subeidi have mostly yielded impressions: we have both

---

[145] Cf. **72**?, **85**, **88**, Choga Zanbil 105, Porada 1970 figures annexes 18.

[146] **123**, **125**?, Choga Zanbil 14, *PC* no. 245, Failaka 417, Subeidi 1, 30; also 13 N 412, to be published by R.L. Zettler. Cf. Porada 1970, 13, 127-8; but the evidence of this and the next footnote makes it unlikely that the practice was restricted to the time of Third Kassite.

[147] CANES 580, *PC* no. 136.

[148] E.g. VR 560, 561, 563, 688. See Trokay 1981, 21, 28.

[149] Geneva 58, Frankfort 1939 pl. 32a.

[150] 14 Glyptik 29, VR 592.

[151] As does 13 N 556, to be published by R.L. Zettler.

[152] **72**, **73**, **94**, **95**, *PC* no. 241.

[153] There are about ten each from Susa and Subeidi, and some thirty from all other sources, giving a total of about 90 (listed in *PC* p. 69-70) - the numbers are vague because of uncertainties in the style of some pieces.

[154] Contrast First Kassite, very rare except at Nuzi and Nippur; Second Kassite: Nippur and Thebes; Assyrian: Assur, Rimah, Fakhariyah and soon Billa (Matthews forthcoming) and Sheikh Hamad.

from Nippur. The general rule with cylinder seals is that there is very little correspondence between the actual seals and the impressions from the same site, the impressions normally being of much higher quality (Collon 1982a, 1); but though we should bear this in mind its effects do not seem to be as severe in pseudo-Kassite as usual. The phenomenon does apply at Nippur in that the high quality impressions are First and Second Kassite which are almost unknown as actual seals. It is because pseudo-Kassite is a low-grade style that, for once, we get a degree of correspondence between the seals and the impressions.

We have already noticed a basic difference in quality between **71-98** and **99-126**, with a few exceptions. The order of the catalogue was defined by the subjects of the principal scene, so this means that the better quality group includes seated figures, devotional figures, the standing God, and martial figures in open or flounced dresses, while the coarser group concentrates on the martial figure in a plain dress. The features that are especially reminiscent of Central First Kassite are most prominent in the former group: inscriptions with four or more lines, the framed cross, dog, locust, kneeling man, rhomb and rosette, and the layout of the surface in rectangular compartments. These features only occur sporadically in the latter group.[155] The second group has its own peculiarities in the large hatched volute tree, birds, a profusion of hatched bands and the layout where parts of the design run into and overlap each other. These in turn are rare in the first group.[156]

At Failaka the seals have quite a well defined character, different from both of our groups. Like our first group, the seals are laid out in a restrained and fairly geometrical way with little use of hatched bands,[157] apart from a group with a basically horizontal geometry which should be compared to the last pieces in our catalogue.[158] Like our second group, there is a heavy emphasis on the martial figure in a plain robe[159] - indeed Failaka 402 (with flounced dress and Intercessor(?)) and 417 seem to be the only cases there where there is a reasonably clear Babylonianising scene which does not have him. Inscriptions are only three or four lines long.

---

[155] Inscription with more than three lines: **108**; rosette: **104**. **125** with its rosette and framed cross may, when complete, have belonged to the first group.

[156] **81**, **95** and **96** are laid out in the latter fashion: apart from these, there are hatched bands in **72**, **73**, **74** and **79**; and birds in **72**, **81** and **95**. The 'carrion birds' in **76** and **99** are a separate phenomenon.

[157] Except Failaka 400, 418, 419, but these do not show the hatched bands and overlapping together.

[158] Failaka 404, 409, 410, 417, 422.

[159] Failaka 398, 399, 400, 401?, 418, 419 - Failaka 421 apparently imitates the shorter dress of the Old Babylonian 'King with mace'.

COMMENTARY

These are minimal attributes of our two groups, and Failaka conspicuously lacks their more distinctive features. Apart from Failaka 402 and 417, there are no examples of the rarer Babylonian figures that tend to appear in our first group - the seated God, the devotional King, the Intercessor, or either of the attendants in **71-76**, and none of the Central First Kassite symbols, except for a rosette in Failaka 404. In the same way we miss the exuberance of the second group, the birds, the large volute tree and the hatched bands (only used horizontally at Failaka, with the rather miserable exception of Failaka 418). Indeed only one aspect of the Failaka glyptic is striking: the boats in Failaka 404 and 422, which have no parallel in Babylonia, but which occur in Elam in Choga Zanbil 127 and Louvre S466.

It is possible that these characteristics are partly due to the difference between seals and impressions alluded to above, since the actual seals from Nippur[160] share them more fully than the impressions do. Again we find restrained layouts without use of hatched bands, the almost universal presence of the martial figure, and the lack of Central symbols or the elaborate tree; though the flounced dress, devotional posture and longer inscriptions are not under-represented.

The other main source of actual seals is Choga Zanbil, and here we have roughly equal representation of the two groups, as described by Porada (1970: "Pseudo-Kassite" and "Elaborate Elamite"). Choga Zanbil 1, 7 and 8 in particular have long inscriptions, Babylonian scenes and symbols and, like all of the first twelve seals in Porada's catalogue, a lack of the attributes of the second group. Choga Zanbil 15-20 have the profusion of hatched bands, martial figures, trees, birds, overlapping and short inscriptions that we expect in the second group. Unlike Failaka, this is not a minimal similarity - special First Kassite figures and symbols do occur in the first group, and so do all of the elaborations of the second group. The greater simplicity of the actual seals in Babylonia thus does not apply to Elam, perhaps because of a difference in the archaeological contexts, as the Choga Zanbil seals were ritually deposited. Such more elaborate seals are known from elsewhere in Babylonia.[161]

Susa, though not as rich a source as Choga Zanbil, produces closely similar results. Susa 2069, 2070 and 2073 belong to the first group or are possibly even impressions of First Kassite seals, so close are they to the type with the standing God, framed cross, dog and the kneeling man. Susa 2074, though somewhat unusual, belongs with them. On the other side, Susa 2068, 2071, 2072, 2082-2084 are classic cases of the second group.

---

[160] **80, 81, 94, 98, 107-109**.

[161] *PC* no. 241 (Warka?), UEX 579; cf. Amiet 1986, nos. 1-3, acquired in Iraq.

Subeidi, however, does not fit well into this scheme. Hatched bands are rare in the intelligible designs[162] and, where they do occur (Subeidi 6, 40), they do not coincide with the large tree (Subeidi 45) or the overlapping layout (Subeidi 30). Subeidi 19, with a long inscription, does not have a Kassite design; Subeidi 40, with a framed Kassite cross, has a short inscription and a hatched band.

In looking for a more detailed classification, the most interesting scheme, or key, will be the one in which divisions made according to one criterion are confirmed by those resulting from another. Here the groups should have had some meaning in antiquity, and are not merely a modern convenience - in other words their value should be not only descriptive, but also analytical. I have tried to find the best criteria for this, and the discussion is intended to explore how far the distinctions really are inherent in the material, and not just imposed from outside. Since the criteria and the number of groups are thus chosen according to the results they produce the analysis is circular and 'grammatical' rather than experimental and 'scientific', which I do not consider to be appropriate where there is no means of repeating or extending the observations.[163] I am deliberately not guessing at what level to apply words such as 'workshop' which imply some knowledge of what the groups meant in human terms. We have no evidence bearing on that.

The designs combine a subject with a manner of depiction. The most obvious difference in the latter is between the simple seals that resemble First Kassite and the ones with elaborate hatching and extra detail, as observed by Porada (1970, Groups I and II) and described above. However this distinction does not exactly conform to the differences in subject which are utilised in the scheme in eight groups below. This more complicated typology to some extent corresponds to Porada's but some of the groups contain both simple and elaborate examples, so the arrangement, though more detailed than Porada's, is not quite so satisfactory.

Most, but not all, pseudo-Kassite seals have an inscription in vertical columns. The first two groups are defined by its absence: *(i)* the 'archery' group[164] and *(ii)* the group in horizontal bands. It is unclear which should include the archery designs from Nippur (**131-134**, 14 N 33) as they have the archer but not the regular panelled design with hatched bands which

---

[162] Subeidi 1, 6, 19, 30, 40, 42, 45: I am ignoring the most fragmentary ones and the ones in horizontal bands.

[163] For the theoretical background, cf. *PC* pp. 12-14.

[164] Susa 2082-4, Marlik 6, Moortgat-Correns 1969, Drouot 1981 no. 57, Choga Zanbil 19, 20, *PC* no. 260: note the short horizontal inscription in the last two.

COMMENTARY

divides these two groups.[165] In almost all of the remaining pseudo-Kassite seals there is both an inscription and a main design on Babylonian lines. The absence of both here shows the integral relation between the Babylonian scene type and the presence of the inscription, both of which are almost universal in First Kassite.

Most pseudo-Kassite inscriptions are between two and four lines long, but in the next two groups there are five or more. One group has several main figures, while the other only has one. In the former case *(iii)*[166] the designs are delicately and precisely engraved, unlike other pseudo-Kassite seals. The layout normally has a main scene with a frieze above or below it, not impinging on the inscription.[167] This frieze generally includes monsters and a little tree, either, at Nippur, with volutes (**71**, **88**, **90**) or, in the east, a small twisted tree (Choga Zanbil 1, 13, Subeidi 6). The main scene, with the exception of Choga Zanbil 13 and Subeidi 19, is in the First Kassite form, normally a pair of figures facing each other, sometimes with a third figure on the left. The most common figure, as in pseudo-Kassite generally, is martial, but the open dress showing tassels between the legs and the mace at the waist[168] does not occur elsewhere in pseudo-Kassite.[169] The standing God faces the martial figure in **87**, **88**, Choga Zanbil 1 and Subeidi 6. Other figures are similar to First Kassite and are generally rare in pseudo-Kassite.[170] Central First Kassite symbols often occur.[171] There are some flounced dresses, but like the rosette and the rhomb this also occurs elsewhere in pseudo-Kassite. Birds, hatched bands and circled dots, however, are very rare here,[172] though very common in general; and in only one instance (**79**) does a design with a long inscription fail to conform generally to type. The devotional *King-*

---

[165] Cf. Subeidi 45, also not panelled and without an archer, but with the typical monster and tree of the archery seals.

[166] **71**, **84**, **88**, **89**, Choga Zanbil 1, 13, Subeidi 6, 19, *PC* no. 231, together with **78**, **87** and **90** which are similar but the length of the inscription in unknown.

[167] Choga Zanbil 1 has a frieze running over the inscription, but it is not interrupted by the main scene as in the normal pseudo-Kassite arrangement (**99**-**101**, etc). It should rather be compared to the group Subeidi 18, Brett 83, Louvre A603, Failaka 405 (Porada 1970, 8 n. 2), though these are not pseudo-Kassite.

[168] **87**-**90**, Choga Zanbil 1, Subeidi 6; Abdul Kerim 1987, 127 fig. 13 (Tell Sa'ud, Eski Mosul area).

[169] **128** should probably also be assigned to this group because of this figure together with a contest comparable with Subeidi 19.

[170] Seated figure: **71**, **78**; devotional (**78**, Choga Zanbil 1, *PC* no. 231) and interceding (**78**, **84**, *PC* no. 231, Abdul Kerim 1987 fig. 13) arms; kneeling man: **87**, *PC* no. 231.

[171] Framed cross: **71**, **87**, Choga Zanbil 1; locust: **88**, Choga Zanbil 1, Abdul Kerim 1987 fig. 13; dog: *PC* no. 231.

[172] Choga Zanbil 1, Subeidi 6, *PC* no. 231.

God scene in this design would not be at home in any of the other groups, but the conspicuous hatched bands interrupting the inscription and the circled dots are not what we expect in this group. Amiet 1986, no.1 and **105/106** probably belong here. The little tree, open dress and delicate engraving of the former are distinctive, despite only having four lines of inscription; the length of the latter's inscription is unknown but there does, again, seem to be a small tree.

The examples with only one figure *(iv)* have a somewhat different character, though they remain closer to First Kassite than elsewhere.[173] Apart from **80**, they all show a standing God, usually with Central First Kassite symbols, the framed cross (**85**, Susa 2073), locust (**85**, UET VII 1?), dog (**85**, Choga Zanbil 8, Susa 2073) and corn ear (Choga Zanbil 8). The kneeling man (Choga Zanbil 8, Susa 2073) and the devotional arm posture in **80** are other distinctive Central First Kassite attributes. Most seals, as in pseudo-Kassite generally, have an animal or an animal head in the field. All the recurrent features apply to group *(iii)* also, but here the engraving is less delicate and the features which were not normal in First Kassite, the special type of martial figure, the monsters and the small trees, are not present. Indeed there are very few traits which might not occur in First Kassite - only the circled dot and the double line in **85**, and the guilloche in **85** and Choga Zanbil 7. As in the previous group, the more elaborate pseudo-Kassite forms do not appear, except in **86**, which despite its hatched band should probably be understood in relation to **85**, Choga Zanbil 8 and Susa 2073 which all have the standing God, dog and rhomb.

The remaining four groups have short vertical inscriptions and are not so close to First Kassite. As before, scenes with single figures may be divided from those with multiple figures; and again those with martial figures from those without. Having defined the four groups in this way, further confirming differences between them may be observed. In group *(v)*[174] there is a standing God in a coarse style, quite unlike the previous group, accompanied generally by a monster, an animal and a rhomb.[175] A rosette in Guimet 94 and whatever the minor fillers are in Rimah 12 are the only deviations from this. The layout is very simple, with no friezes or hatched bands, except for the horizontal ones round the rim in *PC* no. 245, which are a different phenomenon. They go with the hatched

---

[173] **80**, **85**, Choga Zanbil 7, 8, probably BM 123288, Subeidi 1, UET VII 1, Susa 2073; perhaps Susa 2069, but the metal cap, as explained below, is evidence that it is First Kassite. It is possible that some of the other impressions in this group should be assigned to First Kassite.

[174] Guimet 94, Rimah 12, CANES 584 and *PC* no. 245 (Nemrik).

[175] It is possible that BM 123288, with its coarse style, should be assigned here, despite the long inscription.

COMMENTARY

triangles and imitate the herringbone filigree bands on metal caps.[176] The only seal with a short inscription and a different single non-martial figure is Louvre A605, where he is seated. This design evidently belongs elsewhere on account of the frieze of circled dots above the inscription.

The seals with multiple non-martial figures *(vi)* all have a seated figure, usually holding a cup.[177] There is little unity in the manner of depiction. Some seals are elaborated with the inscription interrupted by a frieze,[178] others have a very restrained layout (Choga Zanbil 10, 11), though we may observe one detail, the row of vases in the upper field, both in elaborate and in plain designs.[179] Although seated figures are very rare outside this group[180] the variation in style makes it necessary to consider whether it is significant. Central First Kassite symbols are rare[181] but this is most economically associated with inscription length: such symbols are common in the two groups with long inscriptions *(iii, iv)*, rare elsewhere. The presence of the seated figure results from the general repertory of pseudo-Kassite. Scenes with martial figures are excluded from this group by definition, and it happens that pseudo-Kassite includes almost no scenes which do not include either a martial figure or a seated one.[182] The only exceptions to this are the two groups *(iv, v)* described above which feature a standing God; and this underlines the point in that in pseudo-Kassite the expansion of this one-figure scene to two figures always adds a martial figure.[183] Our group *(vi)* thus has no internal cohesion that is not accounted for by the general conditions of the pseudo-Kassite style.

The last two groups then have short inscriptions and martial figures, either *(vii)* with one figure or *(viii)* with more. With the exception of the three seals just mentioned where the martial figure faces a standing God, martial scenes with multiple figures always duplicate the martial person, as was also the case in Northern First Kassite. This convention occurred before in the finely engraved group *(iii)*[184] but there a standing God is

---

176   Also Choga Zanbil 14, Failaka 417.

177   **72-76**, Choga Zanbil 9-11, *PC* no. 240, Susa 2074, VR 555, probably also Failaka 417.

178   **76**, VR 555, *PC* no. 240, Choga Zanbil 9.

179   Choga Zanbil 10, Failaka 417, VR 555; cf. Porada 1970, 11.

180   **71, 78, 79**, Louvre A605.

181   There is a framed cross in Susa 2074.

182   **80**, *PC* no. 231, not counting the two groups *(i, ii)* without inscriptions at the beginning.

183   Louvre A604, Failaka 399, Choga Zanbil 2.

184   **89, 90, 105, 106**, Amiet 1986, no.1.

normally placed on the right as well,[185] while here with the short inscription there are normally only two figures, and if there are three they all face the same way.[186] *PC* no. 241, however, despite its fine detail and the devotional figure on the left like Choga Zanbil 1, is not a member of the fine group *(iii)*. The dresses are not drawn up in front, there are no Central First Kassite symbols[187] and the inscription, or rather pseudo-inscription, is short and surmounted by a frieze. **81** and probably **82** show the same characteristics.

A distinction can thus be maintained between the fine group *(iii)* and group *(viii)* with multiple martial figures, both in inscription length (by definition) and in other respects. It is also possible to distinguish between the group with one martial figure *(vii)*[188] and the group with two or three *(viii)*,[189] though only in general terms - the confirming traits do not occur in every case and there are some exceptions. The former group *(vii)* is elaborated, especially with the circled dot and the large volute tree which are rare elsewhere in pseudo-Kassite, except in the 'archery' group *(i)*. In the latter group *(viii)* where the martial figure is duplicated they only occur in **100-102** and Choga Zanbil 18. One person or both is often given a flounced dress. This only occurs in group *(vii)* in Choga Zanbil 16 and, possibly, in Susa 2070.

The most striking difference, however, is in the birds. Nearly all of the ornate designs in group *(vii)* with one martial figure have a single bird, generally placed in the field beside the human, most typically on top of the elaborated tree.[190] The only case of such a bird in group *(viii)* is **108**, which has a quite different (Mitannianising) stylisation. Birds are less common in these seals, and normally take the form of a row of birds or other bird frieze (such as the 'carrion birds') placed above the inscription.[191] Such a row does not occur in group *(vii)*, with one martial figure, except conceivably in **119**.[192] In this group the rule is a row of

---

[185]   **88**, Choga Zanbil 1, Subeidi 6.

[186]   UEX 579; the inscription is lost in **98**.

[187]   Note the *unframed* cross.

[188]   **109**, **113-119**, Choga Zanbil 3, 6, 12?, 15-17, Subeidi 30, 40, 42, Susa 2068, 2070, Failaka 419, FI 292, 293.

[189]   **81**, **82**, **91-104**, **107**, **108**, Choga Zanbil 4, 5?, 18, Failaka 400, 401, 418, *PC* no. 241, UEX 579, Susa 2071, 2072.

[190]   **114?**, **116**, **117?**, Choga Zanbil 15, FI 292.

[191]   **81**, **95**, **99**, **101**, **121**, *PC* no. 241, Susa 2071.

[192]   Choga Zanbil 16 has crossed birds whose stylisation is more like the single birds than the birds in rows.

circled dots[193] or rhombs.[194] These only occur with two figures in **100** and Choga Zanbil 18. This distinction is an important one because it is not dependent in any way on the definition of the groups. The elaborated tree, for example, may be more common with one martial figure than with two because it occupies space which would otherwise be taken up by the second human; but in both groups the inscription is often interrupted by a frieze and there is no restraint either in the mode of description or in the artistic situation on what is placed there. In addition, all the bird friezes, except Susa 2071, are from Babylonia, and all the circled dot or rhomb friezes, except **100** and possibly **118**, are from the east. Both the designs with single martial figures *(vii)* and those with multiple martial figures *(viii)* are common at Nippur, and the reason for the shortage of circled dot or rhomb friezes there may simply be that the friezes are often not preserved **(114-117)**. Multiple martial figures are, on the other hand, undoubtably rare in Elam and at Subeidi.[195] There thus seems to be a tendency towards single martial figures in the east and multiple ones in Babylonia, and a rather stronger difference between friezes of rhombs and circled dots in the east and of birds in Babylonia. Failaka is closer to the Nippur situation but does not have friezes at all, except the row of circled dots in Failaka 404, a boating scene with parallels in Elam but not at Nippur.

Seals with these friezes nearly always have martial figures, though there are some Fan Scenes with bird friezes.[196] Louvre A604 has rosettes, but this seal is atypical in every respect. Louvre A605 has the circled dots, again with a unique scene. It is worth noting that the 'archery' series *(i)*, which is known in Elam but not, in the standard form, in Babylonia, includes friezes of circled dots (Susa 2082) and rhombs (*PC* no. 262).

---

[193] **118?**, Choga Zanbil 15-17, Subeidi 40, FI 292. Porada (1970, 10, 21 n. 2) ingeniously suggested that the circled dots represent the heads of 'wall-nails', which are common in Elamite architecture; but note that they do occur, if not in rows, at Nippur, e.g. **75**, **79**, **85**, **126**.

[194] FI 293, Susa 2068, (Subeidi 30).

[195] Choga Zanbil 4, 18, Susa 2072, presumably 2071: there are nine with single martial figures though the proportions in pseudo-Kassite overall are about three multiple cases to two single.

[196] **76**, *PC* no. 240, VR 555. This suggests that VR 555 may have travelled to Assur from Babylonia.

3. The Second Kassite style

3.1 Survey of the designs

The most distinctive and characteristic scene in the Second Kassite style shows a mountain god flanked by streams of flowing water.[197] **140** is a simple case of a water scene, with a fishman, streams and fish only. Legrain's drawing is misleading with its restored upper edge: in fact there is certainly another scene above the preserved one, but it is unclear wheher it is just a narrow frieze containing fish or another full-size panel with a second fishman, to give a layout like VR 556. Like that Berlin seal, the attribution to Second, rather than to First Kassite is in doubt, as the same elements occur, in a secondary position, in the First Kassite seal FI 236.[198] **141**, another simple water scene, is on the other hand without question Second Kassite. Instead of the ambiguous rectilinear layout of **140**, we now have an arrangement in horizontal registers which would be impossible in First Kassite, and the eye is drawn along the flowing lines from one main figure to the next in a manner foreign to the older tradition, where each element occupies its own proper space. The strange undulating quantity above is almost unique, but must be the same as the one in **161**;[199] its appearance in a water scene makes it more credible that it represents clouds in the sky (Porada 1952, 181). While it is not unknown for the streams to centre on a kneeling man (**148**, FI 236, CANES 586) the scene here with the men in a row only otherwise occurs in an Elamite seal, Choga Zanbil 26, which has no Babylonian elements. **142** was made with a delicately carved seal which apparently included the naked leg of a man and flowing waters. This could yield a scene like Thebes 28, but the state of the impression does not permit any further understanding. **143** is still less well preserved. The fine curvature of a profile, which alone remains of the design, is most likely Second Kassite, and there is an inscription. The cap has each triangle granulated instead of every other one, as is normal. **142** has the same cap, but there is no other reason to suppose that the designs are the same.

The mountain god rises up out of the ground in a tapering form which becomes human above the waist. The lower form normally has an undulating profile, presumably meant to indicate mountains,[200] and plants or other hills may grow from the slope.[201] **144**, which is very badly

---

[197] See *PC* pp. 60-61 for non-Kassite representations of the mountain god and a discussion of its significance.

[198] Cf. **18**, **55**, CANES 581, 586, *PC* no. 428.

[199] Cf. also Thebes 31.

[200] **144?**, **145**, **147?**, **148**, **149**, Subeidi 2, Ash 562, *PC* no. 133.

[201] Thebes 26, 27, *PC* no. 133.

damaged, may possibly be restored thus. The god holds his hands at the waist, which is the standard position in the water scene for holding a vase from which streams may flow over both shoulders and down each side.[202] Sometimes the water also runs down from a source in the sky, such as a large bird.[203] **145** is unusual in having two birds in the sky, one for each stream, but this arrangement does occur in **146** and perhaps also in *PC* no. 136. The water flows down to two fishmen, who grasp it to one side, as in Thebes 27, rather than holding a vase in front, which is more common. The body of the mountain god is textured with wavy lines curving over at the top, exactly as in Subeidi 2: in other cases cross-hatching (Thebes 27, Ash 562, *PC* no. 136) or dots (UET VII 9) are used for the same purpose. The intention must be to portray a hilly landscape, most explicitly in the little triangles of **148**, but perhaps also to indicate streams running down from the hills.[204] The god often has a tall horned headdress[205] which in **146** is unusually rigidly stylised.

147 is probably another scene with a mountain god but I was unable to form a satisfactory composite from the traces. I have combined two undulating profiles to form the mountain body, apparently with internal hatching similar to Thebes 26. The mountain god never has wings, so the traces of wings at the top of the scene must represent one or conceivably two birds.[206] A trace on the right may represent water flowing down from the bird, but I can make no sense of the area where the god's head should be. He seems to hold his arms outstretched on either side, which normally denotes the mastery of rampant animals or monsters,[207] but we already have a suggestion of flowing water and in Thebes 26 the outstretched arms are used to hold pots. If it is a water scene, then the figures on either side should be fishmen, which is possible; but a different interpretation, such as rampant animals, cannot be excluded.

With **148** and **149** we come to the most splendid expressions of the mountain god. **148**, the seal of Rimutu, was published forty years ago by Porada (1952, no. 5) and the drawing given here from the Philadelphia impressions differs little from her version based on the Istanbul tablets. On investigating the list of tablet numbers given by Porada I found that their dates in Brinkman (1976) fell into two groups, one in the early

---

[202] **145, 146**, Thebes 27, 28, UET VII 9, Ash 562, *PC* no. 136.

[203] Thebes 27, Ash 562, **147**?

[204] Cf. Thebes 27, and the reliefs of the Kara-indash temple which show alternate female water deities, with wavy lines down the body, and male water deities, with 'mountain scales' (Basmachi 1976, fig. 127).

[205] **145, 148, 149**, Thebes 27, Ash 562; but apparently not Thebes 26.

[206] **145, 146**, Thebes 27, Ash 562.

[207] **148, 149**, Subeidi 2, *PC* no. 133.

thirteenth century and the other fifty years later. On consulting Professor Brinkman it became evident that the later group of tablets bear the seal of Amil-Marduk, the governor of Nippur under Šagarakti-Šuriaš, here no. **149**.[208] That such a confusion is possible underlines the very close similarity between the two designs. The Rimutu impressions are for the most part on small tablets and rather faint, while the Amil-Marduk impressions, though on larger tablets, are normally indistinct and poorly preserved. The caps are quite different, Amil-Marduk's being much more elaborate, but a smudged impression of a part of the design cannot be assigned definitely to one or the other without careful study.[209]

148 and **149** are not just two treatments of the same subject, like **145** and **146**, but are alike to such a degree that it is necessary to demonstrate that they are not in fact the same. They are the only Kassite examples of a Janus-headed figure[210] and, except for **159** and perhaps **150**, the only Second Kassite cases of the griffin. They are the only designs with a flock of birds and the only ones with a scatter of cuneiform signs all over the field. **148** has the only mountain god with a scene engraved on his body: the lines in **149** could be just striations, as in **145**, but could be interpreted as part of a similar scene. Both designs have an irregularity among the birds at the upper right, a little animal in **148** and an unclear object in **149**. A pair of birds in a tree, generally identical, is a common feature of Second Kassite seals.[211] In **149**, however, the bird on the left has its head up and the bird on the right has its head down. The situation in **148** is unclear, but the raised neck indicated in the drawing is no more than a guess and it is possible that the same unusual configuration occurred there as in **149**.

Given these similarities, it might be suggested that all of the impressions are in fact of the same seal, perhaps a little recut in the later period; but this is not possible. The row of three birds at the top of **148** could not be recut into **149**'s five; the trees have leaves of different shapes; and **148** has no room for the inscription at the top. The lower edge of **148** is attested several times, while there is only one impression of that of **149**, but it shows what are probably flowing waters at the root of the tree, like Thebes 27, which are certainly not present in **148**. But

---

[208] For details, see the Catalogue.

[209] The disparity in overall size shown in my drawings should be treated with some caution. Both drawings are composites from small fragments and cumulative errors of scale due to distortion cannot be ruled out. The horizontal scale is more reliable than the vertical. Compare the scale of Porada's drawing.

[210] In other styles, cf. Kenna 1971 no. 71, Louvre A1191, 1196, FI 323, 327, Newell 359, VR 584 (Fine Cypriote); Nuzi 505, FI 267 (Mitannian); FI 868; *PC* no. 146 has separate heads.

[211] **175**, Geneva 56, Copenhagen 109, Thebes 29, BN 299, *PC* no. 133.

given the extraordinary similarity between the two designs I think it is not unreasonable to propose that **149** is a deliberate copy of **148**. Rimutu and Amil-Marduk were both officials in the temple of Nippur, so it is not improbable that Amil-Marduk knew of Rimutu, though without further knowledge of their family relationship, if any, and of Rimutu's career, I cannot guess in what precise context the imitation was made.[212] I shall propose another case of deliberate imitation below (**155** and **156**), in that instance in contemporary impressions.

150 is another design that I cannot reconstruct properly. There is a bird at the top and probably a scene of mastery of animals, perhaps yielding a scene like BN 301 with a hero flanked by small trees or rosettes. Second Kassite designs nearly always have a terminal, a neutral element marking the end of the scene, either a tree[213] or an inscription.[214] Both trees and inscriptions are easily recognisable in small fragments and given the extensive surviving traces of **150** it is unlikely that it had either. This would release part of the seal's surface for other treatment. In Ash 562 such a space is occupied by a large bird and a network of streams; UEX 607 has a bird and a fish; CANES 593 a leaping animal. FI 961 is a particularly interesting case as it was evidently intended to insert a tree into the cut-out in the horizontal inscription at the top, in the manner of **162**, Thebes 31, UEX 577 and *PC* no. 146. Instead, a wide design of two lions attacking two animals was engraved without reference to the axis of the inscription. It is possible that a similar solution was adopted for **150**. The main scene of a Second Kassite seal usually consists of a vertical member, either a dominating figure (**145-153**) or a tree (**167-172**) with flanking elements on either side, giving a tripartite structure with the terminal at the end. FI 961 has four, rather than three main elements, with no terminal. It is possible that in **150** the terminal was replaced by two additional elements, conceivably a griffin and a lion menacing the dominated animals; but the traces are uncertain.

As is demonstrated by Thebes 28 and 31, the two contexts of the mountain god, the water scene and the mastery of animals, can also surround a nude hero or, in Thebes 30, a winged demon. **142** may show a nude hero in a water scene; **152**, a seal in Chicago which is not from Nippur, is a handsome example of the latter situation. The exact form of

---

212 Dr Oelsner and Dr Dalley inform me that Rimutu's title given in BE XIV 87a (Clay 1906, 8-9, 14 '*rab riqqu*') should now be read *sirāšu* 'brewer'. See below, p. 58-9 for a further discussion.

213 **146, 148, 149, 151, 153, 158, 161, 162, 169**.

214 **145, 147, 168, 170**. Note how **155** and **167** have both a tree and an inscription as a terminal.

the demon varies from seal to seal. He always has wings and there is usually a human head, though not in **153** or *PC* no. 146. His feet, where marked, resemble the talons of a bird (**152**, UEX 607). In UEX 607 he has a tail. He usually dominates herbivorous animals, though in CANES 593 they have wings. In **152** alone he looks back over his shoulder. The rather tentative, scratchy engraving is reminiscent of *PC* no. 146, which has a 'pseudo-inscription' comparable to the apparently unfinished foliage of **152**'s tree. **151** had the same kind of tree and the large wing above the body of an animal is most easily understood as the same kind of scene. In **153** the demon's legs are clearly not human and he is apparently standing on two animals. This configuration, which as discussed by Moortgat (1970), also occurs in Geneva 56, CANES 593 and UEX 607. I had the opportunity of making a drawing of the latter seal while I was in Philadelphia which I have included here though it is from Ur, not from Nippur.

154-166 are scenes which do not have a vertical element. This is not certain in **154** as it is possible that the lions are rampant on either side of such a member - there is no impression across the middle of the design. However the insertion of a tree or a dominating figure would cause an improbable elongation of the bird at the top, and I would prefer to reconstruct a more upright version of FI 961, with two lions, each dominating an animal. There may be traces of such animals under the lions' hindlegs. Although no cuneiform is preserved it is likely that the vertical lines behind each lion are the edges of an inscription.

155, the seal of Ninurta-ken-pišu, is an altogether more interesting design whose nature and subtlety were unrecognisable from the photographs published in BE XIV. The main figure is a demon, similar to the one in UEX 607 with wings, a human head, animal legs, tail, and perhaps talons. Unlike all other Second Kassite designs, however, he is in smiting posture, raising a club. The asymmetrical scheme with him grasping a winged bull by the tail is quite unlike the previous arrangements. The smiting posture was common in Syrian, Hittite and Assyrian seals (*PC* p. 22), though not in this kind of scene.[215] Indeed I was in some doubt over the seal's classification until I found an impression of the little volute tree which is clearly a minute example of the typical Second Kassite type. The frieze of little animals and sphinxes at the bottom, though otherwise only known in **141**, is evidently related to the animals under the demons' feet in **153** and UEX 607. The vertical and horizontal inscriptions, also, are normal for this style. The artist made use

---

[215] Matthews forthcoming, no. 16, from Tell Billa, shows a smiting hero grasping a winged bull by the tail; but this scene belongs to the 'Bull of Heaven' series (14 Glyptik 40, Nuzi 774, Geneva 62: Lambert 1987).

of these standard elements in a remarkable and ingenious way, exploiting the different centres of gravity of the demon's wings and of the seal as a whole to provide two terminal elements - the tree and the inscription - on different axes, and tying the three horizontal pictorial registers together naturally by means of the vertical body of the demon. This kind of agility in providing a mobile and balanced layout is normally obtained in this style by means of rigid symmetry.[216] **155** is more adventurous than this, and only in the rather unnatural appearance of the little tree above the bull's head does it fail to match the perfection of composition of **189**.

Given this uniqueness it is astonishing to find exactly the same arrangement - so far as one can tell in a less fully preserved design - in **156**. There is the same scene of smiting demon and winged bull, the same vertical inscription, and even the same curly tail, which is otherwise unknown in seals of this period.[217] The object above the winged bull seemed to me to resemble the Assyrian animal head found in VR 579 and FI 963, but the example of **155** clearly identifies it as another small volute tree. These similarities are too close for coincidence, as in **148** and **149**, and once again it is necessary to demonstrate that the two designs are not in fact the same. In **155** the line running over the vertical inscription is extended beneath the little tree and above the winged bull's head. No such line is visible in **156** and even if it were just not preserved, and allowing for the possibility of distortion, it would be impossible to construct such a line across the traces of **156** without cutting the animal's head. Moreover the engraving is coarser and the composition less perfect in **156**, so it should be seen as a deliberate copy of **155**. Unlike **148** and **149**, however, the two impressions are not separated in time by half a century, but are both dated to the reign of Nazi-Maruttaš. In the other case, we can speculate that Amil-Marduk wished to perpetuate the use of Rimutu's seal, which was perhaps lost (or buried?), for family or official reasons; but this will not do here. Kings had multiple dynastic seals, especially that of Ugarit which was deliberately copied,[218] but it is not easy to see why an individual should have the requirement for duplication which we can readily understand in a large bureaucracy. There is evidence from Assyria in the thirteenth century for multiple seal ownership in a very high official (Röllig 1980) and there are instances of high Babylonian officials with more than one seal (*PC* p. 58). In these cases, however, the seals are not identical and had special functions. We have no evidence, moreover, that

---

[216] **141, 167**, Ash 562, UEX 607, CANES 593.

[217] There is a similar tail on a bullman on the kudurru Seidl 1968, 40 no. 63, abb. 9; and as Dominique Collon pointed out to me, on a scorpion-man(?) in an (Old Babylonian?) relief from Tell al Rimah, Oates 1966, pl. XXXIV:b.

[218] Collon 1987, 128-130; *PC* p. 11 n. 88.

156 belonged to the same man as **155**.

157 and **158** are exquisitely engraved seals featuring archery. **157** is poorly preserved and uncertainly reconstructed, but it may possibly be that elusive creation, the Second Kassite chariot scene. It seems unlikely that this scene did not exist, given the prominence of chariots in the world of international connections to which the style belongs (Smith 1965, 22-37), but examples are hard to find (*PC* p. 62 n. 73). Thebes 37 is the best candidate, for the reasons given by Porada (1981-2, 65-6); but the star is unusual in Second Kassite and it has no traits that are unequivocally Babylonian. On the other hand, the lion in the upper field is comparable to **157**. The slain animal in **157** has an almost Aegean perfection in its contorted stance and is a masterpiece of Babylonian modelling.

158 has, since its original publication by Clay, been known as the most finely worked piece of Babylonian sculpture of the second millennium, and its importance was underlined by Porada.[219] The drawing presented here shows a number of features, such as the centaur's head and rear-projecting wing, which have not been recognised before. Although it only survives, heavily overrolled, on one envelope, the impressions are fortunately very sharp and, unlike **157**, easily combined. The centaur did not have a fixed canonical form at this time and the particular combination of parts here is unique. The complete fish, with fins and tail, which is laid over the body is especially interesting. There may be some connection with the fish-cloaked man who originated in Babylonia at this time (*PC* nos. 142-144), or with the later Nimrud winged bulls with fishy features behind their heads and along their bellies (Mallowan 1966, 194 fig. 50). The crook across the waist is somewhat reminiscent of Egypt. The large wing projecting from the rump is most peculiar and has no parallels. The split end of the animal's horn is a feature of some of the best Second Kassite and Middle Assyrian designs (*PC* p. 116 n. 19). The tree rises from among the mountains rather than from the top of a hill in the Assyrian manner.

159 is only known to me from a photograph, and it is unclear whether the parts of a monster visible on either side of the cross belong to the same creature. Griffins do not otherwise occur in Second Kassite, except for **148** and **149**, and the general appearance of the scene is very Assyrian, if it is understood as a griffin menacing an animal beneath it;[220] but the framed cross and the rosette shaped like a doughnut leave no doubt that it is Babylonian. **160** is unfortunately only preserved in a blurred impression and I cannot make sense of the traces beneath the

---

[219] 1952, no. 2. She pointed out that it cannot be the same design as **161**, as Herzfeld had proposed, despite having the same tree and minute perfection.

[220] 14 Glyptik 36, 39, Rimah 10, 36, Fakhariyah XVII.

monster. The object above is presumably a bird. **161** shows another single monster, probably a winged bull, under the same "clouds" representation as in **141**. The composition appears a little strange with the large Egyptianising bird beside the top of the tree, but it may have made more sense when the picture was complete. There are similar birds in **179** and *PC* no. 176, as well as in Syrian seals such as Collon AOAT 3 which no doubt derived it from Egypt independently. In **162** the monster is a human-headed winged lion, again more familiar in Assyrian designs such as VR 580. The impression is dated to Nazi-Maruttaš, much earlier than VR 580 which is probably late thirteenth century or later (Moortgat 1944, 33). As in several other instances, traits that we tend to think of as Assyrian are actually attested earlier in Babylonia (*PC* pp. 92, 115, 116). **163** may be a trace of a similar design.

164 has long been well known for its excellent representation of a seeder plough. The drawing given here which utilises evidence from published Jena photographs, adds a few details such as the goad held by the man on the left, like the one in *PC* no. 155, and the second line of the inscription. The first line, which would give the owner's name, is unfortunately not visible. The cap is unique with its row of rosettes (misunderstood in the drawing in Clay 1912 due to overrolling). The details of the heads and feet of the oxen are finely rendered. A ploughing scene naturally occupies a longer space than is provided by a normal cylinder seal. **164** solves this problem by giving half of the seal's height to the inscription. In *PC* no. 155 there are two registers, and this may also be the solution in **165** which, though badly preserved, certainly has a main scene too short to constitute the entire design. One impression shows the bottom of the seal at a credible distance below to allow another register, but it is just as likely that this is due to overrolling and that no trace survives of the rest of the design. **166**, known only from a Jena photograph, is hard to understand, as the arm positions are so rare in Second Kassite, but the similarity with the figures in **164** is sufficient to propose another ploughing scene here.

In **167-172** we return to axial designs, this time with a central tree. **167** is the most interesting of them with a subtle design in two registers centred on two trees at different levels. The inscription in the upper register with a small globular tree underneath is similar to Subeidi 2, and we may also compare Geneva 66 which is much more pedestrian. In this series the animals are either bulls[221] or caprids,[222] and they are sometimes winged (FI 241, VR 559) though this is not attested at Nippur. The tree in the middle is nearly always of the globular type with a twisted trunk and

[221] **167**, **171**, FI 241, VR 559, Geneva 66, Southesk Qc 10.
[222] **168**, CANES 587, *PC* no. 176.

the animals lean right over it with folded forelegs, as in **167-170**. Louvre A695 is an exception. There is often a terminal tree, either a volute tree[223] or a palm,[224] or there may be an inscription.[225] Most of these seals are formulaic with the different possible combinations occurring in turn, but there are sometimes special features such as the sphinx(?) and monkey(??) of **167**.[226] The palm tree of **169** has the tripartite form familiar in Thebes 29 and Geneva 56 (*PC* p. 61 n. 60). The bird above the tree in **171** is another standard feature.[227]

172 forms a bridge to the next series, where there is a single human and a tree. 12 Glyptik 3 and *PC* no. 176 are similar designs where the human accompanies a pair of animals flanking a tree. This scene also occurs in the Middle Assyrian impression 13 Glyptik 53 which can be dated to the reign of Adad-nirari I in the early thirteenth century (*PC* p. 92 n. 39). The globular twisted tree was an innovation at that time in Assyria but originated in Babylonia a couple of generations earlier (Thebes 26, FI 241). For this reason it seems likely that the influence here ran northward.

The man in these seals usually stands in the attitude of the First Kassite God.[228] He is accompanied by a tree, a rampant animal, or a corn ear. There may be a globular twisted tree,[229] a volute tree,[230] or a palm.[231] Apart from the birds perched on the tree there is often a larger bird at the top with outspread wings.[232] First Kassite symbols are common, such as the framed cross, rhomb, locust, rosette and dog. In **175, 177?**, Thebes 29 and BN 299 a pair of birds perch on the branches of the tree. **176** is probably an impression from the same seal as **175** (see the Catalogue).

177 is only preserved in fragments, but if my reconstruction is correct it is a Babylonian member of a remarkable series of seals better known further to the north and east. A man sits on a backed chair with a mace(?) at his waist and holds a flower(?). In FI 297 there is a man on a backed

---

[223] **167**, Southesk Qc 10, Copenhagen 109.

[224] **169**, VR 559.

[225] **168, 170**, FI 241, CANES 587, Louvre A695.

[226] Monkeys are rare in Second Kassite but there are cases in Thebes 28, Ash. supp. 39, *PC* no. 185. Cf. sphinxes and monkeys beside trees in late fourteenth and early thirteenth century Assyrian seals: CANES 592, 596, Newell 450, de Clercq 285, FI 963, *PC* no. 475.

[227] **173, 174**, 12 Glyptik 2, Thebes 32, Subeidi 2, *PC* no. 162.

[228] **177, 178**, 12 Glyptik 3, Geneva 55, Thebes 29, 33, BN 299 are exceptions.

[229] **172-174**, 12 Glyptik 2, *PC* no. 176.

[230] **175**, Thebes 32, 33, *PC* no. 187, cf. VR 556.

[231] **177**, Thebes 29, *PC* no. 181.

[232] **173**, Geneva 55, *PC* nos. 176-181, 183, 185.

chair holding a flower. Although the style there is not Babylonian, there is clear Kassite influence in the globular twisted tree and the dog. As I have tried to show elsewhere (*PC* pp. 112-3, no. 542) this seal has connections with a wide range of Elamite, Mitannian and Assyrian designs which often feature a seated man with a mace at his waist and an attendant with a fan. In Porada's (1986) article on FI 297 she proposes that a flower with two leaves, which probably occurs in our **177**, has Elamite connections over a very long period of time. Whether **177** is aptly compared to these foreign designs, it is at any rate, as I have reconstructed it, quite unlike the other Second Kassite impressions from Nippur.

178, which shows a man or woman with long hair holding a staff, with a strange winged object in front, is also different from the others. The arm posture is like Geneva 55 and Thebes 33, which are both unusual. The staff may be compared to a seal from Ur, UEX 578.[233] There are also some kudurrus that are comparable (Seidl 1968, nos. 98, 102, 105, 110) but these are dated several centuries later. **179** has a finely drawn Egyptianising bird but the main part of the design is lost.

3.2 Analysis of Second Kassite

The prospects for analysing the Second Kassite style into coherent groups which can then be assigned temporal or spatial significance appear to be good, with about fifty designs from Nippur and another fifty from other sources,[234] and with dated pieces over a period of one hundred and fifty years. Such an analysis should be based on fundamental structural distinctions rather than on citation of a few apparently diagnostic traits;[235] but I have to say at once that despite much effort I have not succeeded in applying such an analysis to Second Kassite. What follows here should be regarded merely as suggestive, and I am still unable to estimate the date of a Second Kassite seal at a glance as can be done with Middle Assyrian seals.

In my earlier work (*PC* p. 63), following Collon (1987, 61) and Porada (1981-2, 69), I mentioned two styles, one hard and flat, the other delicate and modelled. In particular, the former group included a small series of seals which all have the same inscription,[236] which I suggested might date

---

[233] The present whereabouts of this seal are not given in Legrain's publication, but I came across it in the University Museum, Philadelphia, UM 87-28-1. I did not have time to make a drawing but the staff runs right down from the man's hand to the ground.

[234] I illustrated nearly all of the seals known to me in *PC* nos. 129-195, though I would now describe no. 152 (Subeidi 19) as pseudo-Kassite.

[235] For example the analysis of animals and trees in Middle Assyrian reveals a clear structural division irrespective of the actual forms involved: *PC* p. 94.

[236] Louvre A620, Ash. supp. 39, *PC* no. 155.

to the beginning of the thirteenth century because of a similarity with **164** and because of similar developments in Assyria at that time (*PC* p. 62 n. 76).

The two Nippur impressions, **148** and **149**, seem to give us a good opportunity to make further progress, because they show exactly the same subject but are dated fifty years apart. **148** is a perfect example of the more delicate style. The expression of the mountain-god theme is adventurous and fluid with a riot of tiny detail which does not overwhelm the whole conception. The design, particularly of the birds, is mobile without being chaotic. In **149** there is a very different treatment of the birds. They are separated out from each other to form two rigid rows, wing-tip to wing-tip like an air-display team. The griffins are larger and more formal and the whole scene has a more heraldic impact, attained by the loss of the spontaneity and imagination of the earlier version.

On this basis we may propose that Second Kassite underwent a formalisation and standardisation in the thirteenth century, which must not, however, be confused with the restrained composition of the 'flat' style which is known to have existed already in the reign of Burnaburiaš II (FI 241). Since **148** and **149** are unique pieces without symbols or many features known elsewhere, and since restraint and formality thus did not originate in the later period, it is difficult to build on this foundation.

Another approach, investigating alternative ways of depicting the same element, is also disappointing. The elaborate Second Kassite volute tree appears in a wide variety of forms, including three main types of leaf. In **148** the leaf is hatched to give a serrated profile, and this also occurs in Thebes 27 and 32, which both have much delicate detail like **148**.[237] However the Aqar Quf impression, *PC* no. 157, which should be dated late (*PC* p. 63 n. 88), reminds us that such serrated leaves are also typical of Third Kassite seals and cannot be taken as an early trait. **158** and **161**, which are the most delicately detailed of all Second Kassite designs, render the leaves (or fruits) with dots - and so does VR 556, which has a hard flat style indistinguishable from First Kassite. In **149** the leaves are given a plain outline (though this may be misleading in an unclear impression), which also occurs in **155** and **162** which date to Nazi-Maruttaš.

Another possibility lies in the splendid birds which often adorn the upper field in Second Kassite seals. There are five types, as found in **145**, **148**, **161**, UEX 607 and Thebes 27 respectively; but most of them occur too rarely for analysis. The type of **148** might be supposed to occur in **149** only through imitation, were it not also known in the Peiser impression P117 (*PC* no. 183) which dates to Šagarakti-Šuriaš. The type

---

[237] Cf. also **188**.

of UEX 607 is also known to be late (**154**), but it occurs in Southesk Qc 10, which has a tripartite tree which I shall suggest is an early trait. Forms of inscription are also unhelpful - continuous horizontal bands occur both early (**164**) and late (**146**), and so do vertical inscriptions (Thebes 26, **147**).

It appears, in short, that the Second Kassite repertory was established early and maintained largely intact, stylistic change being confined to some area where this kind of investigation is not very helpful. The indications given below are mutually consistent but not comprehensive. One problem is in the definition of the terms 'early' and 'late'. Although the Second Kassite style existed in the mid fourteenth century only three designs are dated before Nazi-Maruttaš (**164**, Thebes 26, FI 241). Of the remainder, a third date to the reign of Nazi-Maruttaš in the early thirteenth century, which must be included in the 'early' period for lack of earlier evidence; but it seems probable that some of the 'late' features were already in use by then.

There may be a guide in the treatment of the rhomb, which occurs in many Second Kassite seals. In **145**, **164** and BN 301 it is placed in opposition to a framed cross, and they are adjacent in **163** and VR 556. These are well composed and restrained designs without extraneous elements, although the style varies from the hard VR 556 to the delicate BN 301. A firm outline and clear composition, as in **164**, together with the date of that impression, suggest that a fourteenth century date alongside First Kassite is reasonable for this group.

In several of the Thebes seals (Thebes 27, 28, 29, 31) the rhomb is duplicated and scattered carelessly around the field. As Porada has noted (1981-2, 69) some of the Thebes seals have particular common features, and in these we may observe the fine detail and imagination of the more delicate Second Kassite style without the discipline and balance of the harder group. While I thus agree with Porada on the special nature of this 'Thebes group' and on the distinction betwen them and Thebes 26, I do not explain the difference chronologically as they include seals with most of my 'early' features.

In **147**, **154** and the Ur impression UET VII 9 there is a third way of using rhombs. Here they are duplicated again but are now placed in rigid rows at the edges of the scenes. These impressions have late dates[238] and I take this 'heraldic' use of rhombs as definitive for the late group - other cases are **175**, CANES 587, Louvre A620, Thebes 33 and BN 299. In *PC* nos. 185, 190 and Subeidi 2 there is a special kind of formal rhomb arrangement in which four of them make up a cross. Another usage is to lay them out in horizontal bands (Geneva 55, 66, *PC* no. 136).

---

[238]   For UET VII 9, Gurney 1983, 46: Adad-šuma-uṣur year 7, c. 1209 B.C.

The close similarity between FI 241, dated to the late fourteenth century, and CANES 587, which I have just assigned to a period a century later, underlines the problems of this scheme. The scene of two antithetic rampant creatures did, however, certainly exist in the late thirteenth century, as is demonstrated by **168**. **167** is probably another instance, as its elaborate layout in two registers is like that of Subeidi 2, which has the formal arrangement of rhombs just mentioned. BN 299 and UET VII 9 have similar compositions, and so does **189** which is dated to the mid thirteenth century. *PC* no. 155, however, has the same composition but cannot easily be divided from **164**.

We may nonetheless notice two differences between FI 241 and CANES 587. The earlier seal features winged animals, while the later one is naturalistic; and in FI 241 the monsters' wings overlap the inscription in a way unknown in the more rigidly organised late group.[239] FI 241 thus, despite its rigid and spare composition, partakes to an extent in the fantasy and lack of inhibition that characterised Second Kassite in its first two generations. Indeed - with the possible exception of **157** with its mid thirteenth century date - one may propose that all of the most lively and exquisite Second Kassite seals date to the reign of Nazi-Maruttaš or earlier. A useful little criterion is the splitting or doubling of animals' horns, which was also used in Assyria at this time (e.g. CANES 595). It occurs in BN 301 which had the rhomb opposed to a framed cross, and in Thebes 30 and 31 which have the typical outlined heads of the 'Thebes group' (Porada 1981-2, 57-8).

Even more striking is its occurrence in **158** and **161** - it is an almost infallible mark of the very best Second Kassite engraving. These impressions are dated to unnamed kings, but are likely to be relatively early. The latest tablets in the Kassite archives from Nippur belong to the reign of Kaštiliaš IV, but no Kassite king between Kadašman-Enlil II and Adad-šuma-uṣur (who reigned after the end of the Nippur archives) lasted for more than thirteen years. **158** and **161**, which belong to the fifteenth and the seventeenth year respectively, should thus be dated to Kadašman-Turgu or earlier.[240] The only case of a split horn in a seal which I think may be late is *PC* no. 179, which is generally similar to *PC* nos. 183, 185 and 190 which were mentioned above.

The Iraq Museum seal, *PC* no. 133, is a fine example of a design with split horns, comparable in its scene to **148** (Porada 1952, nos. 4, 5). The palm tree with three main branches is another early trait. We have seen it

---

[239] Cf. in contemporary Assyria, 14 Glyptik 17, 19.

[240] As Kadašman-Turgu reigned for 18 years, this argument places **142** and **160** (years 22 and 21) in the time of Nazi-Maruttaš or earlier. For the distribution of reigns and texts, see Brinkman 1976.

already in UEX 577, which had a single rhomb and framed cross, and in the exuberant 'Thebes group' seal, Thebes 29. It occurs at Nippur in **169**, which has a similar scene to Southesk Qc 10 where it is a twisted tree that is tripartite. But although the palm tree is an early trait in Assyria (*PC* pp. 92-95) it appears in the Second Kassite late group[241] and in Third Kassite.[242]

Geneva 56, which has a splendid tripartite palm tree, introduces three more early conventions, all of them reflecting the style's original flexible imagination and disregard for rigid tradition. The inscription is built around, or rather (to judge from FI 961) 'cut-out' in anticipation of the form of the main vertical element. This is evidently an alternative to the overlapping of the inscription that we observed in FI 241. In the Thebes group, it occurs in Thebes 27 and 31 - I am not here counting more ad-hoc fitting of the inscription to the design as in Thebes 26 or 29. UEX 577 is another case with a tripartite palm tree, while *PC* no. 146 has a winged demon like Geneva 56.[243] At Nippur, **162** and **163** demonstrate another aspect of these seals: their interest in fantastic demons and monsters. Such creatures, though occasionally present in the later period,[244] are less common and tend to be less prominent in the scene.

Third, the demon in Geneva 56 is standing on two monsters, introducing a vertical dimension to the scene which is rare in Mesopotamian glyptic where figures are normally at the same level. Such a composition is not restricted to Second Kassite (Moortgat 1970, cf. **210**), but belongs there in a fairly coherent group with demons.[245] **167** is an exception, with its well-conceived juxtaposition of antithetic animals on two levels. As I suggested above, this is best compared to the late compositions in registers like Subeidi 2.

The finest of these early two-level designs is the seal of Ninurta-ken-pišu, **155**, where the Second Kassite conventions are manipulated with remarkable freedom and originality. It is dated to Nazi-Maruttaš in the early thirteenth century. The demon, the winged bull and the two little sphinxes are typical of the fantastic repertory of the era, while the frieze of small animals recalls **141**, whose 'clouds' motive brings us back to **161**, the winged monster with doubled horn.

---

[241] Louvre A620, Geneva 66, *PC* no. 136. An impression 14 N 249 with palms, illustrated by Porada (1981-2, 55-56 fig. p), will be published by R.L. Zettler. It is not dated itself though the context is loosely attached to the mid thirteenth century.

[242] VR 688, CANES 591 - but not with the three branches.

[243] Note especially the way the animals' heads are turned right round: *PC* p. 61.

[244] **149**, Subeidi 2, UET VII 9.

[245] **155**, UEX 607, CANES 593.

I have tried in this sketch of possible early features to show that although I cannot describe the essential principles which were changed over time, nonetheless the 'early traits' are not just piecemeal aspects of the designs for which we happen to have early dates. They frequently combine with each other and there is a certain rationale behind their adoption. Turning now to the later group, recognition becomes more difficult because there was virtually no innovation, the emphasis being on the standardisation of the inheritance and the rejection of the more extraneous byways that the style had entered in its younger days. Rhombs are no longer scattered around promiscuously, horns are not untidily divided, palms are restricted to one stem, inscriptions are kept in neat rectangular boxes, birds are regimented in correct order. The best of the new work - **146**, **149**, Subeidi 2 - remains very handsome, but like the equally magnificent glyptic being made at the same time in Assyria, the reign of Tukulti-Ninurta I, it is no longer transcendent.[246] There is evidence for the survival of most of the scene types in use previously, such as water scenes (**146**, **147**, UET VII 9), contests (**154**, Louvre A620, UET VII 9), animals and trees (**168**, CANES 587), though not apparently scenes with demons - at any rate none of those designs show any distinctive late traits.[247]

The Peiser impression P117 (*PC* no. 183) is dated to Šagarakti-Šuriaš and is a typical member of a group of seals which can be assigned to the later period (*PC* nos. 178-180, 183-185, 189, 190). The impression on the Louvre tablet AO 21.381 (Amiet 1980) is comparable, though unlike the others its terminal is a palm tree, not an inscription. It is dated to Shalmaneser I in the mid thirteenth century.[248] These seals include formal

---

[246] The more limited repertory and smaller surviving corpus of Second Kassite seals means that I have not been able to investigate whether the increased formalism of the later thirteenth century in Babylonia carried with it the loss of meaning that I have suggested for Assyria at that time: *PC* p. 106. If so, this might explain why Second Kassite was not extensively drawn on in the following century when a very specifically referential art was required for the kudurrus.

[247] There is a puzzle in the four seals found in a deposit at Ur (Woolley 1939, 90): UEX 577, 607, 608, *PC* no. 190 (Porada 1981-2, 61 fig. r). The last of these belongs to the late group, because of the formation of four rhombs in a cross (which is quite clear on the original seal, if not even in the good photograph published by Porada - the seal is of fractured glass and cannot take the strain of a sharp impression). UEX 608 is an excellent imitation of contemporary Middle Assyrian work (*PC* pp. 90 n.12, 103; no. 376). UEX 577 and 607, however, belong to my early group, one with a tripartite palm and cut-out inscription, the other a two-level scene with a demon. If my scheme is not wrong, then this may - like the Thebes hoard - be an accumulation of votive material over a long period.

[248] *Limu* Aššur-ketti-ide: Saporetti 1979, 76.

arrangements of rhombs.[249] In each case there is a single human figure, usually standing, with a tree or a column of small objects in front of him in the First Kassite manner. These objects include classic First Kassite symbols, the framed cross, corn ear and dog. There is often an elaborate Second Kassite bird at the top. In the Assur impression, 12 Glyptik 2 (*PC* no. 184) the space available is effectively utilised with the same elements by placing the bird on top of the tree. This also occurs in the late impression Subeidi 2.

At Nippur, **173-176** belong to this group. **173** and **174** have the bird on a tree, while **173** has the elaborate bird above as well. The rhombs are in an orderly row in **175/176**. The scene of **179** has disappeared, but it is a fairly narrow space, like the others, and has the bird at the top.

Although all this makes quite good sense, seals of this type are not restricted to the later period. **173** is dated to Kadašman-Turgu, relatively early in that era, and **174** is earlier still (Nazi-Maruttaš). **177**, which is also dated to Nazi-Maruttaš, has a resemblance to the series, with a single human, a locust and a tree; but its spreading feathery palm interlocked with the inscription is most reminiscent of Thebes 29, which I have counted in the earlier group because of the tripartite palm and scattered rhombs. Thebes 32 is another case, with a single human, tree and bird, but it is difficult to separate its abundant linear detail and serrated leaves from earlier designs such as **148** and Thebes 27. The motive of the bird on a tree occurs in *PC* no. 162 whose beautiful composition and engraving are reminiscent of **158**.

In conclusion, we should try to visualise an overall picture of the Second Kassite seals. They originated probably in the second half of the fourteenth century and the three designs we can date to that period[250] have a firm well defined style with a strong outline. The scenes are adventurously and imaginatively composed, but the design is kept well in hand and there is no loose detail or excessive filling of empty space. **164** has a single rhomb and a cross in the field in opposition to each other, and the other two only have elements that are required by the scene.

By the time of Nazi-Maruttaš at the beginning of the thirteenth century Second Kassite had developed into an explosion of different styles and subjects. If we suppose that split horns are restricted to this time, then three simultaneous trends can be suggested, though in all of them the engraving was softer and more modelled than before. BN 301 is a continuation of the previous type, perfectly composed, restrained in concept, but with the new delicate cutting.[251] The 'Thebes group' on the

---

[249] Geneva 55, Thebes 33, *PC* nos. 185, 190.

[250] **164**, Thebes 26, FI 241; also **188**, if *Kurigalzu* is correctly restored in the inscription.

[251] See the good photograph in Porada 1981-2, 59 fig. q.

other hand combined the new engraving with a lack of restraint in detail, cluttering beautiful compositions with excessive rhombs and other fillers (e.g. Thebes 27, 29). The period is characterised by the free exploration of the limits of the new conventions, with imaginative ways of composing both figures, such as experimental new monsters, and whole scenes, with the inscriptions and pictures interacting in a manner not seen since the Old Akkadian period. The very best of these seals represent, perhaps, the finest glyptic in the whole history of Babylonia, and there is reason to think that they were made at Nippur itself (**141**, **148**, **155**, **157**, **158**, **161**). The 'Thebes group', on the other hand, is not attested at Nippur, and probably came from some other source, such as the Marduk temple at Babylon, as Porada has suggested (1981-2, 68-70).

At the same time the First Kassite style came to an end - the latest Nippur impressions date to Nazi-Maruttaš (**48**, **55**, **57**, **61**). The formula which already existed in Second Kassite of a single human and a tree (**177**, Thebes 29) was adapted in the later period into a group of fairly stiff designs with a single human which now often included First Kassite symbols. The more typically Second Kassite series, except for the demon dominating animals, also continued in the later period, but in a more rigid, formal and constrained way, yielding magnificent pieces such as **149**, but not the very finest work that had existed in the former age.

This progression, from a classic fourteenth century beginning, through a vibrant chaos of invention at the beginning of the thirteenth century, to a formal heraldic end phase, is, though not so well grounded, strikingly similar to the sequence I proposed for the Middle Assyrian seals (*PC* pp. 105-6). This similarity in the development of the two countries is matched by close resemblances in many of the particular design elements (*PC* pp. 115-6). But the evidence is still not yet sufficiently clear to allow us to estimate which way the influences flowed.

4. Minor groups

4.1 Second Kassite derivatives

The title of this section is somewhat misleading as the designs are not all necessarily derived from Second Kassite: they are like it but differ in some respect. **180** and **181** are impressions of caps where no part of the design survived. Most impressions with caps are First or Second Kassite, not pseudo-Kassite or Mitannian.

182-186 are impressions of ring stamps. It would be premature to discuss these fully before **183** and **184** have been published by R.L. Zettler. The subject has been extensively treated by Beyer (1982) who suggested that the well-known 'Luristan' ring stamps (cf. *PC* p. 64 n. 94) derive from shell rings which he dates to the early twelfth century on account of a ring which was found at Mari in association with an Egyptian scarab (Beyer 1982, 181). For the most part the stylistic relations of the ring stamps are with the Third Kassite cylinders, and Beyer's dating of them with Third Kassite in the twelfth century (1982, 188-9) is sound. In particular, the trees (e.g. Beyer 1982, 170 fig. 1) have the distinctive Third Kassite form with serrated leaves and a straight trunk. Beyer pointed out (1982, 179, figs. 21, 22) that ring impressions were found at Ur (UET VII 26, 69) and demonstrated (1982, 180) that UET VII 26 is similar to the other ring stamps such as his fig. 20 from Emar. UET VII 69, however, is rather different. On the face of it the tree seems to be typically globular and serrated like Beyer's other examples, but comparison with **182** shows that it is better restored as a little twisted tree with a characteristic pear-shaped head. UET VII 69 is possibly dated to Adad-šuma-uṣur at the end of the thirteenth century[252] and a similar date can be proposed for the Aqar Quf impression, *PC* no. 157 (*PC* p. 63 n. 88), which has the same twisted tree. Now the twisted tree does not occur in Third Kassite or in the other rings discussed by Beyer, so this gives us a rather exact period of only twenty years or so for the beginning of Third Kassite (cf. Beyer 1982, 181-4) - the twisted tree was probably still current c. 1210 B.C., and was probably extinct by 1190 B.C. Such a time makes good sense as it was precisely during the reign of Meli-Šipak (1186-1172 B.C.) that the art of the kudurrus underwent its most important development and attained its classic form (Seidl 1968, 93). A change in glyptic art at the same time is thus not surprising. As the Nippur impressions came to an end in the reign of Kaštiliaš IV, c. 1230 B.C., with the Second Kassite style still in full flow, we cannot yet build a bridge between the Second Kassite style on cylinders and these 'Second Kassite' ring stamps. However the fishmen and mountain god (?)[253] on two of the shell rings (Beyer 1982, 170 figs. 2, 5) are reminiscent of Second Kassite, and the eagle with lamb of **186** may be compared to the cylinder BM 89214 (*PC* no. 177).

187 and **188** have variations on the Second Kassite volute tree. **187** is unusually crude for a style which rarely descends below perfection: we might perhaps compare *PC* no. 136. **188** is a very finely engraved seal, but with a curiously clumsy composition. Indeed Clay thought (1906, 15), presumably, that the human and inscription belonged to a second seal

---

[252] Gurney 1983, 172. Note that UET VII 26 is significantly later, Marduk-apla-iddina year 5, c. 1166 B.C. (Gurney 1983, 87).

[253] Beyer 1982, 177. The creature has wings, which would be impossible in Second Kassite, but otherwise resembles **149** or *PC* no. 133. There may be a similar creature in Nuzi 815.

impressed on the same tablet, and did not include them in his drawing. The fact that exactly the same juxtaposition occurs in both examples shows, however, that it is all one design. My first thought, as with **189**, was that it is an Ur III seal later recut with the Second Kassite tree. However such a composition of human and inscription is not normal for that period,[254] and having, with the help of Hermann Behrens, identified the name *Kurigalzu* in the inscription, I am inclined now to think that the whole design was engraved at the same time. It is, however, unrelated to the other Second Kassite seals, except in the form of the tree, and the seated goddess is particularly puzzling. In Kassite seals with a seated figure, the elbow behind the body is always rendered with a single angle (e.g. **29-35**). In both **188** and **189** there is a double curve to indicate the folding of the cloth over the elbow. This feature, and the very fine detail of the hands, heads and headdresses in both **188** and **189** is far closer to the Ur III - Old Babylonian tradition than to Kassite.

188, despite its fine engraving, is not a classic composition. **189**, on the other hand, while showing no specifically Kassite traits like **188**'s tree, applies the Second Kassite genius for composition to elements unquestionably derived from the Ur III period. The seated god in a flounced robe, the leading and interceding goddesses, and the worshipper with his bald head and fringed garment are all taken directly from one of the very best Ur III seals, such as BM II 437, 469, FI 531. The subtlety of the composition in staggered registers whereby the eye is led from the small figure of the mortal, past the taller figure of the leading goddess, to the elevated majesty of the seated god above, is surely Kassite. Such staggered inscriptions are known in UET VII 9, BN 299 and the Princeton seal, Ward 517 (van Buren 1954a, fig. 15), and there are several other examples in registers with the inscription only in the upper half.[255] Ingenious exploitation of the possibilities of more than one level is a feature of a few of the best Second Kassite seals, such as **155** and **167**. Thus, although there is no trace of Kassite convention in the elements of **189**, its conceptual framework is within the known capability of the style.

190 appears to be a fairly standard variation on Second Kassite, with its two registers of animals flanking trees (cf. **167**, Geneva 66). The tree, however, is a relative of the Mitannian volute tree which does not occur in Second Kassite, except for Thebes 33. On the other hand, I do not know of any close Mitannian parallels - the long tendrils ending in three

---

[254] I have to thank Professor Porada for her opinion, that both **188** and **189** are 'archaeology', deliberate Kassite imitation of a former age. Dr. Braun-Holzinger, whose experience of the third millennium is much greater than mine, also rejected my suggestion that they are Ur III.

[255] **167**, Subeidi 2, *PC* no. 155.

leaves each are most unusual.[256]

4.2 Mitannian

The Mitannian style, or rather styles, for its variants are endless, may be divided most conveniently into Common Mitannian, which is a fairly coherent style, and the remainder, which is not. Common Mitannian is the principal style in actual seals found in excavations, including most of the Mitannian seals found outside the area of the Mitanni kingdom; the other Mitannian styles are known mainly from impressions, and from actual seals in collections whose provenance is unknown (see *PC* pp. 4-9). There is no reason to suppose that Mitannian seals were made at Nippur, or anywhere south of Assur, but Common Mitannian comprises a large proportion of the actual seals found at the site. The other Mitannian styles, however, are represented only by the impressions **191** and **192**. **191** is only a small fragment, with the typical efficiently engraved, but simplified cutting of the better and more elaborate Mitannian seals in hard stone. The two small monsters, back to back, are probably a secondary scene in some much larger conception.[257]

192 is a quite different kind of design with its loose careless engraving and chaotic composition. If the contorted body of the human is correctly understood, it may belong to a class of seals known at Nuzi;[258] or, alternatively, the monster, scorpion and rampant lion may be best compared to crude drilled Mitannian seals such as CANES 1046, Ash 916 or Marcopoli 608.[259]

193-203 are Common Mitannian designs. **193**, with its fragment of an interceding figure and narrow tree or standard, is similar to some Nuzi impressions (e.g. Nuzi 318-335). **194**, however, is unusual as it is rare to see nude females duplicated.[260] **195** belongs to a series which is common all over the Mitannian world, accounting for about 5% of Common Mitannian everywhere (Matthews 1988, 109). **196** is a rare case of a 'grill-pattern' in a design in horizontal registers - it is more normal to find a lattice or a guilloche in such seals (cf. Palestine 82, 115, Marcopoli 583, Failaka 389).

---

[256] Cf. perhaps Choga Zanbil 42, 43; for the tendrils cf. Frankfort 1939, text fig. 88 (*PC* no. 608); Surkh Dum 39; Schaeffer-Forrer 1983, Chypre A19; *PC* nos. 286, 287, 290, 291.

[257] Cf. 13 Glyptik 76; 14 Glyptik 53, 88, 90; Nuzi 648, 649, 653.

[258] Porada 1947, Group XII: cf. Contenau 1926, figs. 125, 127, Nuzi 518-527.

[259] Cf. Nuzi 587-591.

[260] Cf. Nuzi 181, 264, 291, Marcopoli 587. Such duplication does occur in Schematic Elamite (*PC* p. 46 n. 125) but with a stylisation absent here.

197, 198, 200-202 belong to the 'Stag Group' which I described in my thesis (1988, 119-125). This group is characterised by a restricted repertory of elements and a quadripartite structure. Animals are normally either stags (**197, 200, 201?**) or bulls (**198, 199**) and either stand looking backward, often in crossed pairs (**197, 198**), or adopt a distinctive posture with their bodies at right angles (**199-201**). Lions do not occur but there are occasional sphinxes. Humans can occur either standing alone or horizontal in threes, the latter sometimes represented only by the heads (**197**). Geometrical panels include the grill pattern (**198**) and a double zig-zag hatching (**197**) which does not occur elsewhere in Common Mitannian, but never the guilloche. The Stag Group is particularly common in Palestine, where it accounts for about 20% of the Common Mitannian seals,[261] but there are other cases from Mesopotamia proper.[262] It is not, however, much at home at Nuzi where there are atypical variations (Matthews 1988, 124). Particularly close comparisons for the Nippur examples may be found, as is usual in Common Mitannian, all over the Mitannian world (Matthews 1988, 109-112). The crossed stags and panel of **197** recur in Palestine 127 and RS 22.37; in RS 11.194 there are two animals, three human heads and a hatched panel. The double grill pattern in **198** may be seen again, with a single animal at right angles, in Pini 1983, N23, which comes from Stavros in Greece. The pair of stags at right angles in **200** also occurs in Yadin 1961 pl. 321:7 (Hazor), RS 24.140, Ash 944, Adana 35 (Tarsus), Palestine 73, 92 and BM 123347 (Nineveh). The three "winged disks" in **201** and **202** have an unusual form quite unlike the "winged disk" found in other Common Mitannian seals mounted on a pole (e.g. Collon BAR 75, RS 8.448) where there are two branches, each with short downward strokes. As winged disks, where indisputably present, are almost never duplicated, it seems likely that we are dealing here with some different object. 14 Glyptik 92 is another eastern case, from Assur, but there is an example from Hazor (Yadin 1961 pl. 321:3) and possibly one from Ugarit (RS 17.265), though conceivably there the saltires should be understood as bodies going with the three human heads.

199 belongs to a small group where the animal at right angles appears in a secondary scene (cf. RS 5.065, Palestine 78, Choga Zanbil 111) - the parallels suggest that the tree on the left was originally grasped by a human figure, whether kneeling or sitting. When duplicated, the animals at right angles nearly always face in the same direction if they form the

---

[261] Matthews 1988, 109-110; see especially the most typical examples of all, Kenna 1971 no. 58 (Enkomi) and its twin, Yadin 1961 pl. 320:2 (Hazor).

[262] VR 572 (Assur); Nuzi 87, 212, 407, 409, 410, 554; BM 123347 (Nineveh); Failaka 378; Parker 1975, nos. 21, 24, 47 (Rimah); Susa 2051.

COMMENTARY

main scene;[263] while in a secondary scene they normally face each other.[264] Finally **203** is a standard case of a Common Mitannian seal in horizontal registers: the combination of fish and lattice is particularly frequent.[265]

4.3 Levantine and various

I use 'Levantine' to refer to the formless seals which are particularly common in the west during this period,[266] but this does not imply that seals such as **204** and **205** must be imports, as they do not belong to any recognisable group. **206**, on the other hand, is a member of a very distinctive group which, though known from widely scattered sites,[267] is primarily attested at Ugarit where it accounts for a significant proportion of the whole.[268] The style occasionally appears on unprovenanced seals.[269] Our seal from Nippur is almost identical to one from Palestine, Beck 1967 fig. 189:2, and one from Ugarit, RS 19.188.

207 is a Middle Assyrian impression generally similar to designs of the early thirteenth century (cf. *PC* nos. 312-324). It is unusual to have a herbivore and a lion facing each other across the tree - the lion is normally rampant and behind the animal (*PC* nos. 317, 318). Fakhariyah XV has a comparable form of lion, though facing the other way. Considering the substantial penetration of Babylonian seals northward[270] there are surprisingly few Assyrian seals from Babylonia: the only ones known to me are from Ur, UEX 589 and 608. Since the objects in the N collection do not have individual provenances the possibility cannot be excluded that our impression was acquired by the Nippur expedition elsewhere; but it was not usual for isolated impressions not on tablets to

---

[263] **200** etc: Collon BAR 44 is an exception.

[264] Cf. Nuzi 199A, 215, 247, 318, 320, 321, RS 8.349, Palestine 113, Collon BAR 67.

[265] Collon AOAT 232, Collon BAR 33, Nuzi 83, Palestine 63, RS 9.140, 23.11, 24.227, Ash 951, CANES 1066, Brussels 190:4.

[266] Cf. Ash 1000-1029, Marcopoli 648-675.

[267] Palestine 146 (Beth Shan); Kenna 1971 no. 112 (Hala Sultan Tekké); Schaeffer-Forrer 1983, 164 (Enkomi 4.108 and Idalion 1294), 168 fig. 3 (Mycenae); Beck 1967 fig. 189:2 (Tell Artal); Matthews forthcoming no. 38 (Tell Billa); and possibly Mohammed Arab 1.

[268] 8 seals are listed in Schaeffer-Forrer 1983, 167, but to these should be added RS 8.152, 8.262, 17.161, 19.191, 23.17, 24.02, 24.46, 24.362, 25.248, 30.255 on account of the connections shown in the diagram Matthews 1988, pl. IX.

[269] Aleppo 267, Seidl 1985 fig. 1. Apart from the literature just cited, cf. Collon 1987, 62-5, Workshops C and D (these workshops should not be separated); and Mazzoni 1986, 173 nos. 13-15.

[270] 12 Glyptik 1-3, 33?; 14 Glyptik 103, 104?, VR 555 (Assur); Matthews forthcoming nos. 36, 37 (Tell Billa); Nimrud ND 1681 (Parker 1955 pl. X.2), ND 5374 (Parker 1962 pl. XIII.1); *PC* no. 245 (Nemrik); Rimah 12.

circulate in the antiquities market then.[271]

Finally **208-210** are designs belonging to styles unknown to me. I guess that **208** is rather earlier than the other Nippur designs. Seated figures are common in the Old Babylonian period and there are squatting animals at that time.[272] The heavy drilled style is not, however, typical of Old Babylonian[273] and may possibly be compared to some Syro-Cappadocian designs;[274] but there is no specific link with that style and I have not been able to find comparisons for the hatched bands.

209 and **210** I suppose to be later than the other impressions. I do not understand the design in **209** but the herringbone band above occurs in the neo-Assyrian Linear style,[275] though also in a few Levantine seals.[276] The smooth rounded style of cutting does not fit well into either context. **210** evidently shows a bird-footed demon standing on two animals holding two more animals upside down, like **153**, but the engraving style is quite unlike Second Kassite.[277] Elaborate compositions on two levels are known in seals whose origin is unknown but which probably belong to the early first millennium, such as Louvre A607 and de Clercq 357,[278] and the composition was certainly current in the Achaemenid period,[279] so **210** probably stands in the middle of a long development.

5. Seal use

The simultaneous existence of three main Babylonian styles, certainly for at least the latter half of the fourteenth century, is strange; but the problem can be explored by considering the usage of the seals. Here we are only concerned with ancient impressions. The factors are the seal's style, what it was impressed on, and whether it was given a metal cap. These are in principle independent of each other so patterns in their relative distributions may be assumed to be significant. In the statistics given here I have counted each design once, so for those where several impressions exist a notional typical case is used.

---

[271] Cf. perhaps the fine Second Kassite impression, Beran 1957-8 fig. 12 (Meissner 1934, A77).

[272] Cf. BM III 132, 135, 138, FI 164.

[273] It is not the same as the late style with small drillings.

[274] E.g. CCT VI 17, 19, 42, Marcopoli 416.

[275] E.g. Marcopoli 201, 203, 204, VR 668, 672.

[276] Kenna 1971 no. 89, Louvre A1199: see Opificius 1969, 97.

[277] It reminds me rather of neo-Babylonian modelled seals, e.g. VR 610; but Dominique Collon does not think that it belongs there.

[278] Cf. also Susa 2092.

[279] E.g. VR 762, 763, CANES 824, 825.

COMMENTARY

About 19% of the seals had metal caps. We may expect that some seals had caps which do not show in the available impressions, but this distortion should apply equally to all of the styles. Impressions were made normally on tablets (47%) or bullae (41%), by which I mean any lump of clay not in the form of a tablet or envelope.[280] Envelopes are less common (12%): this may be because they do not survive well, as is evident from the many extant unsealed inner tablets. Envelopes are almost always sealed, and inner tablets almost always unsealed.[281] This is clearly a great loss to us, as some of the most important designs are only known from tiny envelopes (e.g. **158**, **161**). Caps are relatively more common on envelopes (39% of sealed envelopes show caps) and less common on bullae (11%).

We may divide the impressions into four groups, First Kassite (35%), pseudo-Kassite (32%), Second Kassite (22%), and Other, including ring-stamps (11%). The only envelope with a non-Kassite design is **190**; otherwise there are several cases of each style on a tablet, bulla and envelope. The pseudo-Kassite style is, however, underrepresented on tablets[282] and overrepresented on bullae, while Second Kassite has the opposite distribution (28 cases on tablets, where 20 are expected). The strongest patterning, however, appears when comparing the style with the presence of a cap. **137** is the only case of a pseudo-Kassite seal with a cap, and there are no caps on the non-Kassite seals. Second Kassite is heavily overrepresented here. Given an average frequency of 19% with caps, we expect about 8 Second Kassite impressions to have them: in fact there are 18 cases, or 43%.

On this basis an explanation for the coexistence of the styles can be suggested. Gold caps were no doubt a sign of wealth, and were perhaps no more than that. The caps are extremely stereotyped, unlike the designs, and contain no figures or symbols which might carry some more specific meaning. Precisely the same metalwork can be seen in other Kassite artefacts.[283] The First and Second Kassite styles were thus preferred by rich people, while the poor used pseudo-Kassite or other styles. This makes excellent sense in that the pseudo-Kassite designs are artistically impoverished, imitative, structurally simple, coarsely engraved, and cut

---

[280] Some bullae bear short inscriptions, e.g. **16**, **182**, **189** (CBS 3818).

[281] Except **85**. Clay 1906, 12.

[282] We expect 187 impressions × 32% pseudo-Kassite × 47% tablets = 28 cases; but actually there are 18.

[283] Such as the Aqar Quf ring Baqir 1946, pl. XV:8, pl. XXI:16 (top left), or an object from Susa, Maxwell-Hyslop 1971, pl. 128; see also the gold band M.M.A. 62.253 (C.K. Wilkinson (1975) *Ivories from Ziwiye* p. 70 fig. 39b).

into 'fake' materials, composition and glass.[284] Much the same goes for the Common Mitannian seals which form the bulk of the 'Other' category.

First Kassite seals occur in all contexts, while Second Kassite ones are particularly fond of caps and envelopes and particularly unlikely to be on bullae - **140, 144, 151, 171** and **172** are the only examples.[285] On the face of it, bullae require a lower level of professional expertise than tablets, as they can be used by illiterate persons. We may therefore propose that the Second Kassite seals tended to be used by scribes or, better, that they were used for some special function that was almost always carried out in writing. This is confirmed by the prevalence of this style on envelopes, which were only applied to special categories of tablets, especially receipts and salary payments. Kidin-Marduk, the *ša rēši* official of Burnaburiaš II had two seals, one First Kassite (VR 554) and the other Second (Thebes 26), and it is possible that this was a normal pattern for wealthy Babylonians who would have one, First Kassite, seal for general use, and another, Second Kassite one for the special function. A common man would just have a pseudo-Kassite seal. It is interesting to note that the ring-stamps, whose style resembles Second Kassite, most commonly occur on bullae (**182, 185, 186**): perhaps this was a third type of seal occasionally owned by the wealthy in the thirteenth century for use in lower status contexts where an ordinary person would employ a First Kassite or pseudo-Kassite seal.

Further progress can certainly be made by a study of the text types of the sealed tablets and envelopes, but this can only be done here on a very rough and ready basis as the archival studies which are a necessary preliminary to approaching it properly have not yet been done. The computer lists in the University Museum provide a summary classification which gives an indication of what is going on, but it should be stressed that these are not infallible and that with broken tablets in particular it may have been difficult to recognise the true nature of the text in the time available to the cataloguers - a list, for example, may occur within the framework of many types of text. Oelsner (1980, 89 n.2) distinguishes legal documents from administrative ones on the basis of the presence of witnesses; but as he says there are difficulties here and in any case the

---

[284] Dominique Collon reminds me that different media (stone, glass, ivory etc.) required different kinds of technical expertise and may therefore have been carved in different workshops with their own traditions which did not necessarily develop at the same rate or in the same way. It is possible that the difference between First Kassite and pseudo-Kassite, i.e. between stone and composition, should be understood in this sense and not just in terms of the wealth of their clientele.

[285] Cf. Beran 1957-8, fig. 12 (Meissner 1934 pl. XI: A77; *PC* no. 162). This exceptionally fine Second Kassite impression has no provenance but bullae do not usually circulate in the art market and Hilprecht may have obtained it from Nippur.

presence or absence of witnesses is not known to me.[286]

There are 112 designs sealed onto a tablet or envelope. In 33 cases the text type is unknown.[287] A number of text types, such as letters (**35**, **153**, **167**) are rare and even the most common types, receipts and contracts, only occur fifteen times each. Combining rare types to obtain larger numbers is problematic, but even so, the creation of larger units, such as 26 'business' texts (legal, loans, debts, economic, contracts), or the 28 'administration' texts (records, lists, temple payments and accounts, ledgers), is not helpful as the distribution of the styles is almost exactly what would be expected in random circumstances. Only in one instance is there a clear pattern: all of the "salary" texts except **61** are Second Kassite. This surely gives us an indication that the authorisation of "salary" payments was part of the special responsibilities that were connected with the use of this style. Moreover, all the seals used on "salaries" have caps, against a general proportion of caps on 26% of designs used on tablets or envelopes. It is then interesting that it is receipts and salaries which account for nearly all of the envelopes with known text types.[288]

The term "salary" used here and in the Catalogue is taken from Clay but may not now be considered appropriate for the particular administrative transaction involved. The word is *aklum*, which according to *CAD* A/1 is used for beer products received by a person, perhaps better described as an 'expenditure'. The archive of Rimutu (**148**) is especially illuminating here. Rimutu is described as the *sirāšu* or brewer in the *aklum* text BE XIV 87a. Although the impression on this tablet was made with the same seal which is used elsewhere by Rimutu, it is here described as the seal of Ninurta-KI-pišu. Dr. Dalley tells me that this could be the same name as that of the owner of **155**, who was also authorising *aklum*-expenditures at this time. Why he borrowed Rimutu's seal is obscure, but Dr. Oelsner informs me that he did bear the same title (EAH 194 l. 4). The Rimutu seal is attested between year 5 of Nazi-Maruttaš (CBS 13352) and Kadašman-Turgu year 15, and is known to have been used by Rimutu at least between Nazi-Maruttaš year 15 (Ni 7835, 12216) and Kadašman-Turgu year 13 (Ni 2253). BE XIV 87a is dated to Nazi-Maruttaš, year unknown. Seal **155** existed by Nazi-Maruttaš year 11 (BE XIV 53), though use by Ninurta-ken-pišu is first attested in

---

[286] There is a good discussion of the texts and sealing practices in Clay 1906, 5-16.

[287] Note these statistics are confused where the same design, e.g. **189**, is attested on several different text types.

[288] Except **84** (account), **123** (list), **167** (letter). Clay (1906, 10) says that envelopes were used on records of debts paid out and receipts paid in to the storehouse, and salary payments.

year 24. But as this is in the middle of the spread of Rimutu dates, one cannot assume that one official had inherited seal **148** (either personally or with the office) from the other.

It seems most likely that the seals - and by extension perhaps all Second Kassite seals - were official seals used only in the course of special official business. Since Second Kassite seals often give an owner's name in the inscription, and since the annotations on the tablets known to me almost always give the same owner's name for the same seal, it is probable that they were personal seals owned by the individual for use in his official capacity;[289] but this does not seem to have precluded some use by other people. So in BE XIV 87a the *aklum*-expenditure of Rimutu is sealed (using Rimutu's seal!) by Ninurta-KI-pišu, while in BE XIV 87 the *aklum*-expenditure of Ba'erum is sealed by Rimutu.[290] It should be clear from this that a full archival study of the *aklum*-texts, taking the sealings into account, is required; but we may now expect such a study to illuminate our knowledge of the sealing practices which were specifically associated with the Second Kassite style.[291]

Turning now to impressions on clay lumps, it is hard to provide a sound and consistent classification, despite occasional marks of baskets (**25**) or jars (**31**). The only type which really stands out is the 'door sealing', where the clay shows the impression of string wrapped round a peg projecting from a surface. Of the 79 designs on clay lumps, 13 are on door sealings, with a heavy preponderance in favour of the Northern group of First Kassite (**3, 7, 10, 11**) and pseudo-Kassite (**71, 72, 76, 88, 93, 130**). These are 57% and 17% respectively of all the designs of these styles on bullae, compared to an overall proportion of 16%. Although there are only three Central First Kassite examples (**29, 65, 67**) this is the expected number given that Central is impressed on bullae much less frequently than pseudo-Kassite. In other words, given that Central is less, and pseudo-Kassite more common on bullae than on texts, there is no further preference within that for or against door sealings. It is more significant that none of the 8 cases of Second Kassite cylinders or stamps impressed on bullae is on a door sealing. Evidently the special function associated with this style did not include safeguarding storerooms.

In the pseudo-Kassite discussion the style was divided into several groups (see above, p. 27-32), of which three were prominent in the Nippur impressions, the group *(iii)* with fine detail, long inscriptions and

---

[289] Compare for instance business cards.

[290] Cf. *CAD* A/1 s.v. *aklu*: '... *aklu* received by a person .... while another person seals the receipt.'

[291] See the Catalogue entries for **148** and **155**. I am indebted to Dr Oelsner and Dr. Dalley for their help with the Rimutu archive. See further Petschow 1974.

no hatched bands **(71, 78, 84, 87-90, 105, 106)**; the group *(viii)* with bird friezes **(76, 81, 95, 99, 101, 121)**; and the group *(vii)* with single birds and friezes of rhombs or circled dots **(100, 109, 113-119)**. All three occur on bullae but it is interesting that group *(vii)* does not occur on door sealings though the others do **(71, 76, 88)**. The other cases in door sealings **(72, 93, 130)** are also relatively well designed with fine detail and do not correspond to the coarser group *(vii)*, despite the (single) circled dot in **130**. Door sealings indicate above all *local use* (see below), so this - admittedly rather weak - evidence might suggest either that group *(vii)* is foreign, for which we found some evidence above (p. 32), or that the different seal types were used for different functions. There is already reason to suppose that the Second Kassite style was used for a particular function involving written documents, which was certainly of very high status, and that pseudo-Kassite seals, which do not normally have caps, are of lower status. But if group *(vii)* had relatively low status within pseudo-Kassite, as is suggested by its very poor quality of engraving, then it may be that sealing up storerooms was a relatively responsible task which would not be entrusted to someone who possessed such a seal.[292]

This suggestion however is not supported by the pseudo-Kassite designs impressed on tablets. There is no instance of a design with a bird frieze (group *(viii)*) - thought to be generally rather higher in quality than group *(vii)* - impressed on a written text. Both of the other groups do occur on tablets and envelopes with no visible difference in text type - **78** and **117** are both on contracts, **84** and **116** both on accounts. Indeed the majority of the designs in group *(vii)* are impressed on tablets or envelopes **(114-119)**, while group *(iii)* with its fine engraving has roughly equal numbers on tablets and on bullae. There is thus no question of the coarsest pseudo-Kassite seals being relegated to contexts outside the area of written administration,[293] and if there is a bias against them in the sealing of doors it is due to some distinction more subtle then merely one of status.

The particular importance of door sealings lies in that, unlike other kinds of bulla, they must have been sealed at the same site as that in which they were found, and cannot therefore represent an intrusion of foreign glyptic unless the foreign seal was itself imported. This evidence then proves that pseudo-Kassite was used at Nippur, as is confirmed by the finds of actual seals, and suggests that Northern First Kassite was also a local style, though four cases is perhaps not quite enough to exclude

---

[292] This at once raises the question: how far down the ladder of society does seal ownership go? There is little evidence on this, but we may note the extensive use of nailmarks instead of seals in the Kassite period (Oelsner 1980).

[293] Though this could be proposed for Mitannian: in **191-205** only **194** is on a tablet.

some statistical freak. The implication is that the difference between Central and Northern is primarily chronological, not geographical, with the apparent geographical distinction being supplied by the chronological difference between the Nuzi and Nippur archives, combined with the rarity of actual provenanced First Kassite seals.

The contrary to this argument does not, however, seem to hold. I prefer to explain the absence of Second Kassite door sealings by a functional difference, not by proposing that all the bullae and tablets sealed with this style were imported. Mitannian is a more tricky case. The six bullae, none of them a door sealing, with Mitannian impressions (**191**, **192**, **193**, **197**, **199**, **203**) could easily have been imported, since this style, though conceivably made in Babylonia, was not really at home there; and so could the six actual Mitannian seals (**195**, **196**, **198**, **200**, **201**, **202**). But it remains paradoxical to assert the local character of First Kassite, which is *not* certainly attested in an actual seal from Nippur, and of Second Kassite, whose only case is **145**, while denying that of Mitannian which does occur both in seals and in impressions.

6. Endpiece

We have investigated the various Kassite styles, First Kassite, pseudo-Kassite and Second Kassite, from different angles, chronological, typological and functional. A combined picture can be outlined from these, but the evidence remains too partial to have confidence that it will not subsequently require basic revision.

The first phase, ending c. 1350 B.C., is virtually unattested at Nippur; but the Kassite impressions at Nuzi belong to it. This is the Northern tradition of First Kassite, and it remains possible that it was the only style throughout the Kassite area then. In the mid fourteenth century two new styles arose, Second Kassite and pseudo-Kassite, while First Kassite adopted the conventions of the Central tradition. Second Kassite was a Babylonian style used by wealthy individuals for some special function which included some aspects of temple administration. At the beginning it was quite different from First Kassite, having much more in common with the new style that was developing at the same time in Assyria. It had a profusion of new forms and several engraving styles.

Pseudo-Kassite was a Babylonian style probably derived from Northern First Kassite which was also probably made in Elam where it was used for ritual deposition at Choga Zanbil and for sealing at Susa. There are slight traces of regional differentiation within the style, but the functional significance of the subgroups remains obscure. Pseudo-Kassite was an imitation style coarsely engraved onto an imitation material, and was used by a lower social class than Second Kassite, though unlike Common

Mitannian one not outside the sphere of written culture.[294] At the same time the Central First Kassite style flourished. This was an upper class style, like Second Kassite; but it was not restricted in its context of use. Central had a subtle pictorial syntax and added the classic Kassite symbols and a rich inventiveness in the inscriptions to the impoverished remnant of the Old Babylonian tradition which survived in Northern First Kassite and pseudo-Kassite.

In the reign of Nazi-Maruttaš, c. 1300 B.C., these styles were at their height. Subsequently Kassite culture declined. The styles in the Babylonian tradition, Central First Kassite and pseudo-Kassite, may have come to an end in a generation or so. Second Kassite continued until at least the end of the Nippur archives about 1230 B.C., but it became more stiff and formal and seems to have subsumed First Kassite within it. The growth in the use of fingernail marks (Oelsner 1980) may mean that the lower class clientele which used pseudo-Kassite in the fourteenth century now ceased to possess seals.

Ring stamps were very occasionally used in the thirteenth century, and still retained a Second Kassite character c. 1210 B.C. By 1190 B.C. Third Kassite seems to have taken over in them, and presumably also in the cylinders. The era in which Babylonia gave the lead to Mesopotamian artistic development had at last come to an end.[295]

---

[294] Cf. the role of Common Mitannian in contemporary Assyria: Nissen 1967.

[295] Matthews 1990, 64-6, 115-117.

II. CATALOGUE

Catalogue entries are arranged in two parts, the first one describing the object, and the second the design. As an impression may occur several times the first part may have multiple entries.

Sigla:
Museum numbers are given first wherever possible and, if not, field numbers. Nearly all of the material is in the University Museum, Philadelphia, and the greater part of it from the earlier excavations (cf. Gerardi 1984, ix):

CBS: Material catalogued soon after the excavations.

UM: Numbers assigned later.

N: The N collection was discovered in the Museum some decades after the earlier excavations at Nippur. It is believed to derive entirely from them but there are no individual object records and it is possible that some of the pieces were acquired by the expedition elsewhere.

B: The archaeological collections have been separated from the tablets and the original CBS numbers were replaced with B numbers, usually with the same number (see **185** for an exception).

L-29- : The Hilprecht Collection was acquired by Hilprecht during the earlier excavations at Nippur and included some excavated material given to Hilprecht by the Sultan.

HS: Hilprecht-Sammlung, Friedrich-Schiller-Universität, Jena. This material is only known to me from published photographs.

Ni. : The Nippur material in Istanbul is only known to me at second hand, through the casts of Istanbul tablets in Philadelphia, from Porada 1952, and from information kindly given to me from his notes by J.A. Brinkman.

The material from the more recent excavations is in Chicago, Philadelphia and Baghdad, the Philadelphia objects having UM numbers.

A: Oriental Institute Museum, Chicago.

IM: Iraq Museum, Baghdad.

Original objects are not now given to foreign museums but through the kindness of Professor Zettler and Professor Gibson I have been able to see excellent casts of the most recent discoveries. Here, and in some other cases where the present location of the object is uncertain, I have used Field numbers:

D, 2D, 3D, 2N, 3N: see Nippur I.

12 N, 13 N, 14 N, 15 N: material courtesy of R.L. Zettler or McG. Gibson.

CATALOGUE

Object information:

Information about objects is derived either from my own observation, or from museum records, or from publications. My own observations, generally descriptions of bullae, are given immediately after the object number; other information is given after the citation of the source, which ceases to apply after the first full stop.

L: Philadelphia museum records, usually from the computer printouts in the Tablet Room. This information is copied from the ledger and file cards originally made out by hand (sometimes referred to as the 'old records'), and suffers from the same problems of outdated knowledge; but it also includes much extra information added recently. The descriptions of text types in the records are based on an informed look at the object but, as is inevitable when cataloguing thousands of texts, they are not infallible, especially where the text is not published.

M: information from Brinkman (1976), which is a guide to the dated Kassite tablets. In a few cases dates are given from other sources, but these are less reliable. Many Kassite tablets, especially those published in BE XV, give a date but not the name of the king; in other cases the king's name or the date may be damaged. The number following the king's name is the regnal year.

For publication abbreviations, see the Bibliography.

Provenance: nearly all the material is from, or is believed to be from, Nippur. I have explicitly cited this wherever it is given in museum records or publications, and it is implicit in all cases with an N number or a Nippur field number. The only cases which I do not believe are from Nippur are **9, 54, 69?, 70, 152**. It is impossible to tell whether the Hilprecht seals (**80, 81, 87, 94, 97, 108**) are from Nippur or elsewhere unless it is so stated. I have given such further information on provenance as is available, usually in the case of the earlier excavations a source west of the Shatt an-Nil which divides the city in two; but I have not tried to assess the significance of this. A number of provenances given in Nippur I are unlikely or incredible (cf. **76, 113, 125, 128, 135, 197, 200**), but this is normal for small objects in the old-style large scale excavations.

Design descriptions:

These are introduced, after a space, by the dimensions in millimetres. For impressions, these are height × width (i.e. circumference), for actual seals height × seal diameter, marked 'diam.'. Dimensions always refer to the ideal cylindrical design, never to the object impressed onto or to the size of the impressed area. If the ideal rectangle round the cylinder cannot be reconstructed the damaged dimension is marked '(ext)'; '?' usually means that the dimension is estimated from a bad composite. 'Composite' means that the drawing combines evidence from several impressions, which can be misleading as drastic distortions are common and can be difficult to compensate for. In most cases, I have assumed that the ruled lines in the design are rectilinear and have used them as axes, but this approach is not always possible (e.g. **5, 74, 121, 129, 139**). I have always combined fragments wherever possible, even where the reconstruction is not certain. Cases where there is serious uncertainty are marked '*'. In some cases (**117, 126, 139, 142, 143, 147, 150**) I was unable to form a basic mental image of the design and the drawing is wholly unreliable. Nonetheless, substantial traces survive and I think it useful to provide a sketch of some sort. These are marked '**'. I have included drawings of some designs which are made from photographs, marked '†'. These should all be considered unreliable and they are not to scale. '(†)' means the drawing includes some details from photographs.

An integral part of my drawing method is to form a mental image of what is in the design and to use that to distinguish between the significant and insignificant traces which are visible. I do not believe that it is useful to draw 'what is there' rather than to interpret; but there is unquestionably scope for self-delusion. The descriptions are essentially meant to summarise how I see the design and are thus rather more interpretive discussions, especially where there is uncertainty, than plain lists of items. Restorations are sometimes suggested but the meaning of the design is not considered. 'Man', 'human', 'person' and 'figure' are formal terms, with the same meaning, and are applied without respect to whether the figure was mortal or divine; 'god' and 'goddess' are used as rarely as possible. Likewise the human arm posture terms, 'interceding', 'martial' and 'devotional' are all merely code words, describing a form, with no more meaning than 'arms 11', which is used for the most common arm type (for which I could not think of a suitable word).

Caps:

Many impressions include traces of metal caps and these are described in abbreviated form after the design descriptions. The caps consist of bands of decoration which were remarkably stereotyped, and are listed in order from the end of the object towards the middle (the caps were identical at either end):

triangles: a wide band, with triangles formed from granulations attached to a plain backing plate. This yielded an alternation of granulated and plain triangles, except for a few cases (e.g. **35, 142, 143**) where the whole band was granulated and the triangles marked out with wire.

diamonds: same as above, but the triangles were smaller and a symmetric band was placed below them, to yield a diamond pattern. Less common.

twist: a broad guilloche band made of filigree.

CATALOGUE

hbone: narrow filigree bands twisted to give a diagonal pattern, normally in opposed pairs to yield a herringbone, occasionally a third band as well (e.g. **156**).

gran: a row of granulations round the cap.

plate: I think all the decorative bands were fixed to a plain backing plate. In some cases this plate projects below the last decorative row to give a plain band between the elaboration of the cap and the engraved design on the seal stone.

rosettes: **164** only.

King List.

This is a simplified list adapted from Brinkman 1976, 31:

Kara-indaš	c. 1413
Kadašman-Ḫarbe I	
Kurigalzu I	
Kadašman-Enlil I	(1374)-1360
Burnaburiaš II	1359-1333
Kurigalzu II	1332-1308
Nazi-Maruttaš	1307-1282
Kadašman-Turgu	1281-1264
Kadašman-Enlil II	1263-1255
Kudur-Enlil	1254-1246
Šagarakti-Šuriaš	1245-1246
Kaštiliaš IV	1232-1225
Adad-šuma-iddina	1222-1217
Adad-šuma-uṣur	1216-1187
Meli-Šipak	1186-1172

The drawings

The drawings are reproduced at a scale of about 140%, except for **158** and **161** which are at about 180% because of their exceptionally fine detail. Drawings which were made from photographs, marked † in the caption, are not to scale. Areas of uncertainly are not shaded so as not to obscure such traces as are visible: it may be assumed that the absence of some feature is never certain. The designs come from Nippur unless otherwise stated in the caption. In a few cases no drawing is given because others have prior publication rights.

The Inscriptions

The transliterations and translations of the inscriptions in the Catalogue, together with the immediately following comments, if any, are the work of W.G. Lambert. A few of them have also been treated by Limet (1971) and by Legrain in PBS XIV. Nos. **61** and **164** are also given in Matthews and Brinkman (forthcoming). The drawings of cuneiform are not copies in the conventional sense, which I could not do without knowledge of the signs, but are rather an attempt to resolve what was visible into a pattern of wedges. It is likely that there are obvious errors; but I was unable to re-check without knowledge of what would be improbable. Epigraphic conventions are not used, in particular no distinction is made between 'no sign present' and 'uncertain area'. This is partly because I felt that shading such areas would obscure the traces, and partly because in the nature of impressions one is almost never sure that no sign was present. Column rulings are generally more clearly engraved and more easily seen than signs, so drawings showing columns without signs should not be taken to mean that the area was clearly preserved. Composites of inscriptions were particularly difficult to make up from small fragments and the results, mentioned as such in the catalogue, are most uncertain.

The following section has been contributed by W.G. Lambert:

* * * * * * *

The inscriptions of Cassite seals can be extremely difficult. Many of them are written in a corrupted form of Sumerian, and can only be understood with the help of the underlying Akkadian. In addition many seem to have been engraved by illiterate craftsmen who frequently introduced corruptions, both in the shapes of the signs and in more serious ways. For the present volume it seemed best not to present a full critical study. First, this would involve use of the whole corpus of these short texts, and get involved in all kinds of philological intricacies which are inappropriate to what is primarily an art-historical study. Secondly, the editor of these texts has not himself seen more than the drawings of D.M. Matthews and what else is already published. In general he is very impressed with the obvious accuracy of most of the drawings of the inscriptions, but a trained cuneiformist's eye might here and there see more. Another difficulty is that in making the drawings it proved impossible to mark where the surface is missing or damaged, so that more signs may have been present. Accordingly it was decided to offer a transliteration and translation of those inscriptions and parts of inscriptions which can be translated with a reasonable measure of certainty. When only an odd phrase that provides no light on the context remains, it has been ignored. The editor of these texts has been involved in a study of this genre for many years, and has given a survey of the problems in his review of H. Limet's *Les légendes des sceaux cassites* in BiOr 32 (1975) 219-223.

This new material provides surprises. A totally new type of such inscription occurs in no. **94**, but the writer does not understand a single line! Also there are inscriptions arranged in grids (nos. **19, 124**), but not adequately preserved even to begin to work on their decipherment. Also there are corrupted inscriptions, nos. **80, 99, 107, 109** and **152**. Previously one had hoped that such work originated from peripheral areas where cuneiform was less well known than in Nippur. Interestingly, two of them are glass (**107, 109**), and one (**80**) is frit. Glass cylinder seals of the same period from Susa and Choga Zanbil also commonly attest corrupted inscriptions of the types well known in Babylonia, which may be significant.

*   *   *   *   *   *   *

1   UM 29-15-189. **L** Nippur tablet, record of the verdict in a lawsuit.
       M p. 144, J.5.5, Kadašman-x; use of a year name and archaic sign forms suggest a date prior to Burnaburiaš II, i.e. as presently known Kadašman-Enlil I or Kadašman-Ḫarbe I.
       Translation **M** p. 391, text no. 23, includes "Seal of Ili-rabi. Seal of Ekur-[ ]"

       29 × 38(ext).
       One end of the tablet is broken off and there is only one intelligible impression, on the reverse. The cap impression on the edge very likely belongs to a different seal since there is no sign of it on the face impression which has clear upper and lower edges.
       Inscription in at least two vertical lines, faced by an interceding goddess (?) in a flounced dress with a horned headdress. Large space behind her probably unengraved.
       Cap (another seal?): gran-gran-twist-?-hbone-gran-gran.

2   CBS 15041. Tablet (no old record).

13(ext) × 27(ext). Composite.
Inscription in at least four vertical lines. A man in martial attitude in a long robe, vessel in field.

3   UM 51-6-355. Probably door sealing, mark of cloth on surface over figure.
Nippur, 2D 588a.
Nippur I pl. 121:3, from TA 117 VI, room opening off paved courtyard (pl. 74A).

29(ext) × 39(ext). Composite.
Inscription in five vertical lines. Man in martial attitude holding mace. Topline over inscription.

Inscription:

d[.....]	[.....],
dingir a.r[a.zu] giš.tu[k]	The god who hears prayer,
ì[r ní.tuk]u.za.a[š]?	On the servant who reverences you
igi.zi.bar.ra.n[a]	Look with steadfast favour,
a[rḫuš] tuku.na.a[b]	Show [mercy] to him.

4   CBS 14240. Irregular bulla, stringmarks on back. **L** Nippur.

24 (caps?) × 38(ext).
Inscription in at least four vertical lines. A man in an open dress, probably martial, holding a curved sword (?) faces a person in a flounced robe and a person in a plain robe. The orientation of the central figure is uncertain; the one on the right faces left. Fine engraving. Plain caps?

Inscription: remains of three lines and final line:

[ì]r ní.tuku.z[a]?   The servant who reverences you.

The preceding line may contain the owner's name.

5   A29624. Clay lump with flat face and irregular back, poor surface.
Nippur, 3D 32.
Nippur I pl. 120:18, from TA VII 2, Kassite level (p. 68).

33(ext) × 35(ext).

There are certainly two rollings and I suspect these may be of two seals. The upper rolling shows a topline and traces perhaps of Common Mitannian character, e.g. two human heads - animal - tree? The lower rolling is of a Babylonian seal: inscription in at least four vertical lines, man facing right with arms 11, fish and goatfish behind him, trace in front.

6   N2257. **L** Tablet, marriage contract.
M p. 144, J.5.7, *ṭuppi aḫuzati* text, date MU.10.KAM.MA ᵐ*Ka-*⌈*da*⌉-[ ] of type presently attested only in Kurigalzu II and earlier; and as ᵐ before RN is not known at Nippur after Nazi-Maruttaš the tablet may belong to the time of Kadašman-Enlil I.

32(ext) × 40(ext). Composite.

Inscription in at least four vertical lines; the first three lines seem to show the same signs. Man in martial posture holding mace at waist, perhaps tassels between legs, facing man with arms 11, object between them. Frieze below with rosette. Topline.

Inscription:

[ka]r lú [ᵈutu]	Saving is the sphere of [Shamash],
[ka]r lú [ᵈmarduk]	Rescuing is the sphere of [Marduk],
[ka]r lú [ᵈ...]	Helping is the sphere of [...],
[x] x x [..]	. . . . . .

Cf. no. 10. A few lines probably missing, with traces of the last.

7   A29627. Door sealing.
Nippur, 3D 50.
Nippur I pl. 120:15, from TA VII 2, Kassite level (p. 68).

24(ext) × 30(ext). Composite.

A man in martial posture with a curved sword faces a man with arms 11, both in ladder-patterned robes. The lower part of their bodies is conjectural. Inscription in at least two vertical lines. Crude engraving.

8   N1672. Irregular bulla.

36 × 34(ext). Composite.

Inscription in seven vertical lines. A man with a curved sword, doubtless in martial attitude, faces a man in a tall hat, probably standing; cross? in field.

9   B 14442. Seal, red jasper.
PBS XIV p. 297 no. 566, Maxwell Somerville coll. (**not from Nippur**).
Limet 1971, 7.2.

24 × diam. 14.

Inscription in four vertical lines with topline; man in martial attitude and curved sword faces man with arms 11, groundline beneath.

Legrain's transliteration of the last line *Ni-pu-ur* should, as E. Leichty confirmed for me, be rejected in favour of *lí-bu-ur*.

Inscription:

šá-ki-in	May he equipped
na₄kunukki	with this seal
an-ni-i	be
lí-bu-ur	confirmed.

10   12 N 691 d. Faceted bulla.
12 N 691 e. Flattish clay lump.
OIC 23 fig. 48:5d,e, fig. 92:2; pp. 62, 65, 67: Nippur, area WB, Level III beneath lowest floor of locus 12, the room next to the courtyard in the Level II Kassite palace (fig. 46), and above floor 1 of locus 25, which is outside the OB house (fig. 40). Same provenance as **71, 129**.

27(ext) × 42. Composite.

Drawn from cast shown to me by McG. Gibson. Inscription in seven vertical lines. Man in flounced dress and martial attitude with curved sword faces female in pointed headdress and flounced dress, to be restored with interceding arms. Between them, small creature (lizard? insect?); topline over inscription. Civil, OIC 23 p. 125, refers to the unusual phraseology of the inscription; (n.b. not fig. 92:1 = **71**).

Inscription:

[k]ar lú [^d]u[tu]   Saving is the sphere of [Shamash],
[k]ar lú [^dmarduk]   Rescuing is the sphere of [Marduk].
[k]i dùg.ga [ka eme]   How good are [(the divine) mouth
                              and tongue].

a.ba x.[sá.sá]   Who can [rival you],
^dnin.é.[an.na]   Nin-Eanna?
x [x] x x [...]   . . . . .
x x x [...]   . . . . .

The last two lines probably gave the owner's name and title or father's name.

11   CBS 14237. Door sealing.
       CBS 14285. Approximately cylindrical bulla with stringmarks, sealing on curved surface and end.
       PBS XIV p. 292, no. 542, Nippur.

       30(ext) × 50. Composite.
       Inscription in five vertical lines. A person in a plain robe, arms and head missing, faces(?) an interceding female in a plain robe, a small long-haired nude female between them. Topline.

       Inscription:

[^dn]anna u₄.sakar an   Nanna, crescent of the sky,
[dumu sa]g ^dEn-líl-l[á]   Prime [son] of Enlil,
[z]à?.zà.bi nu.bal   Whose rules are not transgressed,
lú.sum ka.aš.bar zi   Who gives firm decisions
kisal dingir.gal.gal.e.n[e] In the courtyard of the great gods.

12   CBS 8276. Approximately cylindrical bulla with stringmarks, sealed on curved surface and end.
       PBS XIV p. 292 no. 543, Nippur bulla fragment.

       24 × 38. Composite.
       Inscription in six vertical lines. A nude female and an interceding person in a plain robe at a slightly larger scale. Contrary to Legrain's description the head of the nude female is not preserved.

       Inscription:

^dmes umun gal   Marduk, great lord,

lú.kar zi.a?	Who saves life,
[za].e me-en	Are you.
[x] (x) x x	. . . . .
x [x] x **ti**	. . . . .
[arḫ]uš tuku.a.[(x)]	Show mercy.

13 CBS 11626. **L** Nippur tablet, W side of Shatt; unknown MB king, year 22; seal of son of A-gi-ia.

21(ext) × 40. Composite.

Inscription in six vertical lines - the three last lines are much wider than the others, suggesting that they were added. Interceding figure in plain robe. Topline, at least over inscription.

Inscription:

[t]a-ri-ba-t[um]	Tarībatum,
dumu.munus x x [..]	Daughter of ..[..].
re-me-[ni]	Merciful
^dut[u]	Is Shamash,
za-qí-i[p]	Who plants.
[ku]r-b[a-šu]	Bless him!

14 UM 29-16-688. **L** Nippur tablet, contract.
M p. 301, V.2.10.232, Šagarakti-Šuriaš 12.

6(ext) × 35(ext). Composite.

Inscription in four vertical lines. Curve, perhaps animal horn? Human face, traces in front conceivably interceding hands? Very faint and unintelligible.

15 CBS 13712. **L** Nippur envelope frag, W side of Shatt, temple archives, contract.
M p. 114, E.2.25.60, Burnaburiaš 21.

20(ext) × 47?(ext). Composite.

Inscription in five vertical lines. Interceding goddess in flounced robe facing unclear traces, conceivably a seated man.

16 CBS 14247. Irregular bulla, stringmarks on back.
PBS XIV p. 294 no. 552. Nippur.

UM 29-16-380. Fragment of cylindrical bulla with stringmarks, sealed on curved surface and ends. There are four lines of inscription on the bulla in which E. Leichty kindly read *Kurigalzu*. L Nippur.

32? (caps) × 39? Composite.
    Inscription, possibly in six vertical lines. An interceding goddess in a flounced robe faces a seated man, rosette and locust in field between them.
Cap: trace of twist.

17   2D 213. Clay lump.
    Nippur I pl. 121:4, from Nippur, TB 62 B dump, open area? (pl. 65).

    †
Interceding figure in flounced dress faces seated person, cross between them.
Plain cap?

    Inscription: last line only:

d_{iškur} d_{ša.la.bi.[da]}   (of) Adad and Shala.

18   CBS 3116. L Nippur envelope, W side of Shatt.
    BE XIV pl. XV:48.9b.
    BE XV 38, pl. III:4, p. 59 receipt; unnamed king, yr. 13.
    CBS 3454. L Nippur envelope, W. side of Shatt.
    BE XIV pl. XV:48.9a.
    BE XV 20, p. 58 receipt, trans. p. 18; unnamed king, yr. 18 (BE XIV and XV in error).
    CBS 9846. L Nippur, W side of Shatt, MB envelope corner.

35 (caps) × 47. Composite.
    Inscription, apparently in eight vertical lines. A standing person, arms joined at waist, faces a seated man who grasps a crescent-disk standard. Underneath, three rhombs around antithetic fishmen.
Caps: Triangles-hbone-hbone-gran-plate.

    Inscription:

d_{DUMU}.**gal dingir** x x x (x) God ...., the .... god,

x.**bi diri.ga**   Whose ... excels,
(four illegible lines)
[**îr**] *ka-dáš-man!-[*^d*en-líl]*   [Servant] of Kadashman-[Enlil],
[**lugal**] **zag n[u.sá.(a)]**   The [king] without rival.

19   UM 29-15-653. **L** Nippur tablet, contract for *rimutim* gift of Warad-
Šamaš.
M p. 270, U.2.24.93, Nazi-Maruttaš 8.

29(ext) × 15(ext).
Faint trace of inscription lines ruled across at least twice.

20   CBS 3002. **L** Nippur tablet, W side of Shatt.
M p. 269, U.2.24.56, Nazi-Maruttaš 5.
BE XIV 48, trans. p. 27; Clay notes (p. 26) that it is probably a
rent of temple property as no creditor is named.

18(ext) × 45. Composite.
Seven vertical inscription lines, one apparently not used.
There is ample space for a design but it seems to be empty.

Inscription: the third line appears to consist of a personal
name:

[^d*]nin-urta-ap-lam-i-[din-nam]*
Ninurta-aplam-iddinam.

21   CBS 6730. Approximately conical bulla frag. with smooth top,
sealing on curved surface, stringmarks. **L** Nippur.

15(ext) × 20(ext).
At least five vertical inscription lines. Topline.

Inscription:

^d**marduk** *[bēlu rabû]*   Marduk, great lord,
dingir šà.l[á.sù]   Merciful god,
níg.b[a ti.la]   Who grants [life],
KIN/LUGA[L ...]   . . . . .

22   CBS 11767. **L** Nippur tablet, MB accounts.

Ht. 20(ext).
Fragments of inscription lines, topline above them.

23 CBS 14238. Approximately conical bulla with smooth top, sealing on curved surface. L Nippur.

Fragments of inscription.

24 12 N 295. Tablet fragment.
OIC 23 fig. 48:3, p. 66-7: Nippur, area WB level II, locus 12, room next to courtyard of large Kassite palace (fig. 46).

Trace of inscription lines.

25 A 29648. Clay lump with basket? impression on back, surface cracked.
Nippur, 3D 175.
Nippur I pl. 120:13, from TA VIII, Kassite level (p. 68).

23 × 27(ext).
Inscription in at least four vertical lines. Two panels, each including a raised pillow-shaped area containing an animal's head, conceivably with antlers. Unclear and distorted.

26 CBS 3136. L Nippur, MB tablet, W side of Shatt.

35(ext) × 28(ext). Composite.
Inscription in probably seven or more vertical lines. Locust. A faint trace unattachable to the rest could be part of a seated man, another trace might show feet. Very faint, patchy, and badly overrolled.

27 CBS 14602. L Nippur tablet, unnamed MB? king, yr. 1? Receipt.

29(ext) × 30(ext). Composite.
Inscription in at least four lines; cross.

28 N 4257. L envelope of MB receipt for barley rations.

8(ext) × 35(ext).

Inscription in at least three vertical lines; cross. Very faint. Trace of cap granulations.

29 CBS 6743. Approximately cylindrical bulla with stringmarks, sealing on curved surface and end.
PBS XIV p. 297 no. 565, drawn pl. LIII, Nippur bulla.
The 'flounced dress' in Legrain's drawing is due to a superimposed ridged fingerprint.
CBS 6746.
PBS XIV p. 297 no. 565, Nippur bulla. Legrain's drawing shows CBS 6743 only.
CBS 14239. Irregular bulla, reed? marks on back. **L** Nippur.
CBS 14243. Irregular bulla, reed marks on back. **L** Nippur.
CBS 14262, joins N2602. Irregular bulla, reed impression on back.
PBS XIV p. 291 no. 541, Nippur.
This is the best impression of the inscription. Legrain's drawing (PBS XIV pl. LXIII) does not include the join. CBS 14262 consists of two rollings at a slight angle to one another, which Legrain correctly combined. He did not notice that one of the rollings is itself overrolled in such a way that the lines of the two parts almost exactly coincide. The first four lines of his copy are in fact part of the last four lines of the inscription, and his fifth line is the true first line. In addition there is a small overrolling of the man's arm in Legrain's seventh line, on the right (though not recognisable as such on his copy).
CBS 14269. Door sealing. **L** Nippur.
CBS 14270. Irregular bulla.
PBS XIV p. 297 no. 564, Nippur.
CBS 14273A. Irregular bulla with stringmarks.
There are two bullae with the number 14273, but as the old records say it is black they evidently refer to the other one, here no. **72**.
CBS 14277. Approximately cylindrical bulla with stringmarks, sealing on curved surface and end. Cap impression, apparently the same as the others here. **L** Nippur.
CBS 14284. Approximately cylindrical bulla with stringmarks, sealing on curved surface and end. **L** Nippur.

33 (caps) × 46. Composite. *
Inscription in nine vertical lines. A seated man, cross and rhomb above.
Cap: gran-hbone?-twist?-hbone?-diamonds-hbone-twist-hbone-

gran.

Inscription:

^dnin.ísina x x x (x)	To Nin-isina . . . .
é.kur gi.en?.na.aš	Who ... Ekur,
giš lá x x x	Into whose hand is put
šu.na.aš [í]b.sá.[x]	. . . . .
níg.gál ú gi₄ gar x [(x)]	. . . . .
sag/KA in.ši.x.(x).**aš**	. . . . .
lūṣâ(è)-a-na-nūr(**ud**)-^d*nin-kar-r[a-ak]?*	
	Luṣa-ana-nur-Ninkarrak(?)
[dum]u UD.x.ḪI-^d**mard[uk]?**	
	Son of ....Marduk(?),
máš.šu.gíd.gíd	The seer.

30 CBS 14246, joins CBS 14282. Irregular bulla, stringmarks on back. **L** Nippur.

25(ext) × 50?(ext). Composite.
Inscription in at least four vertical lines. Seated man with rosette, cross, rhomb and locust in field.

31 CBS 6738.
PBS XIV p. 291 no. 540, bulla with stringmarks, Nippur.
CBS 6740. Jar sealing?
PBS XIV p. 297 no. 563, bulla with stringmarks, Nippur.
CBS 14244. Irregular bulla, jar sealing? **L** Nippur.
PBS XIV p. 291 no. 540.
Limet 1971, 9.3.

39 × 41. Composite. *
Inscription in six vertical lines. A seated man with dog, rhomb and rosette above. There is no good impression of the upper field and due to overrolling it is not clear whether the rosette is at the same level as the rhomb, as shown in Legrain's drawing, or higher. There is also an unclear linear object. Topline, interrupted probably by chip on the original seal; bottom line.
Lambert 1970, 46 and Limet 1971, 110 (9.3) note that PBS XIV 540 is the same design as no. 563.

Inscription:

[a]k-pu-ud lu né-me-lu   I have made the effort, let there
                                           be profit,

ú-tu-lu du-um-qu   flocks, divine favour.
su-pe-e ša ^{d}*nin-urta*   I have addressed prayers
ù ^{d}*gu-la*   to Ninurta
aṣ-ṣa-ba-at   and Gula,
da-ma-qa lu-mur   may I experience a blessing!

32   CBS 3098. **L** MB tablet, Nippur, W side of Shatt.

24(ext) × 45. Composite from small fragments. *
Seated man, rhomb; inscription in nine vertical lines, signs as drawn unreliable.

Inscription: the first line addresses [^{d}**Nin].ísina dumu an.na** "Nin-isina, daughter of Anu," but the remainder is not understood.

33   CBS 3126. **L** Nippur envelope, W side of Shatt.
BE XV 129, p. 64 receipt, unnamed king, yr. 22.
CBS 3154. **L** Nippur envelope, W side of Shatt.
BE XV 118, p. 63 receipt, unnamed king yr. 22 (BE XV in error).
The defective DINGIR sign in the first line proves these impressions are of the same seal.

26(ext) × 30(ext). Composite.
Inscription in at least six vertical lines. Seated man, walking animal on groundline, rosette in upper field.

34   CBS 3233. **L** Nippur tablet, W side of Shatt, temple archives.
BE XIV pl. XIV:46-7.
BE XV 189, p. 67 payments.

23 (ext, cap) × 35. Composite. *
Inscription in four vertical lines. Seated man with objects in front of him (bird??). A thick vertical line behind him is probably part of a standard rather than a fifth, blank inscription line. Topline, at least over inscription. The DINGIR and DUMU signs shown in the first two lines may be misplaced. Faint.

Cap: triangles-hbone-twist-hbone-gran-plate.

Inscription:

anu/ilu-muš-tál	Anu/Ilu-mushtal,
dumu x x **ša?**	son of ....
[x] x [(x)] x	. . . . .
[x] x [(x)] x [(x)]	. . . . .

Name of owner.

35 UM 29-15-3. **L** Nippur tablet, MB letter?

25(cap) × 44. Composite.
Probably six vertical inscription lines: the first one is apparently empty and there may be two lines in the third. Seated man.
Cap: triangles-hbone-twist-hbone-gran; all the triangles are granulated instead of alternate ones as usual.

Inscription: the first line mentions the person Enlil-shemi (^{d}*en-líl*-**še**), and seems to relate him to a deity in the following line.

36 UM 51-6-344. Shapeless lump.
Nippur, D 553 from TB 34 B.

22(ext) × 35(ext). Composite. *
Inscription in at least six vertical lines. Seated man on groundline - there is no direct connection between his upper and lower parts. The clumsiness of his 'hand' suggests that the form may be the product of overrolling.

Inscription: the penultimate preserved line names the goddess Nin-Eanna, (*[^{d}]nin-é-an-[na]*). The next line might be restored: *[bu]r-na-bu-r[i?-aš?]* "Burnaburiash."

37 CBS 9894. **L** Nippur, MB tablet, W side of Shatt.

27 (ext, cap) × 26(ext). Composite. *
Inscription in at least four vertical lines - I am unable to combine all of the fragments. Seated man, possibly symbol in

upper field.
Cap: triangles-hbone-twist-hbone-gran-plate.

38 N 1702. Fragment, unclear whether of tablet or of bulla.

21(ext) × 18(ext).
Seated man, corn ear? and other traces behind him. Baseline.

39 N 2711. **L** Tablet, MB ledger: barley, emmer and other commodities.

16(ext) × 20(ext).
Seated man, locust behind, perhaps trace of inscription line behind that.

40 CBS 3455. **L** MB envelope, Nippur, W side of Shatt. Receipt, unnamed king, yr. 21.

Ht. at least 52. *
Inscription in vertical lines. A seated man above a groundline with a peaked hat. Topline, at least above design. Unidentifiable traces in upper field, almost certainly overrolled.

41 N 6359. **L** Tablet.

31 × 28(ext).
Inscription in at least five vertical lines; seated man, trace behind him.

42 CBS 14263. Roughly conical bulla with smooth top, sealing on curved surface. **L** Nippur.

12 (ext, cap) × 24(ext).
Inscription in at least three vertical lines, seated man in a ladder-patterned? robe. Very faint.
Cap: trace of triangles.

43 N 865. **L** MB tablet, account of commodities.

16(ext) × 30(ext).

Inscription in at least four vertical lines. Man in tall hat.

44 CBS 9895. **L** Nippur, MB tablet, W side of Shatt.

22 (caps) × 29(ext).

Inscription in at least three vertical lines. Man, the lower part of his body obscured by the cap. Even so, unless the seal was cut down before being capped, there is probably only room for a seated figure.

Cap: gran-hbone-diamonds-hbone-gran-plate.

Inscription:

^den.líl.lá dingir [šà.lá.sù]	Enlil, [merciful] god,
[k]a.ta.è.[a.ni]	[Whose] command
[lú].na me šu.nu?.[bal.(le)]	No one can [frustrate].

45 UM 29-13-912. **L** Nippur, legal tablet; *Ka*-[ ], yr. 6.

J.A. Brinkman tells me this is a legal text with witnesses concerning a slave woman.

7(ext) × 11(ext).

Trace of man with arms 1î, the angle of the arm being normal for a seated figure; cap triangles.

46 CBS 13142. **L** MB envelope, Nippur, W side of Shatt.

23 (ext, cap) × 17(ext).

Inscription in at least two vertical lines. A man facing left, standing or more probably (from the height of the field above) seated. In upper field, rosette and probably cross.

Cap: gran-hbone-diamonds-hbone in three rows-gran.

47 UM 29-13-38. **L** Nippur. Bulla with stringmarks.

32(ext) × 33(ext). Composite.

Inscription in at least six vertical lines, perhaps no line between the last line and the scene. Trace of a tall hat; tree or standard with kite-shaped top.

48 CBS 7242. **L** Nippur tablet, contract.
M p. 271, U.2.24.108, Nazi-Maruttaš 10.

18(ext) × 45. Composite.
Inscription in eight vertical lines, the sixth line unreliable.
Man, in pointed hat, probably seated (from the height of the
frieze above), unclear object before him. Above groundline,
carrion birds peck at an inverted horned animal. Probably capped.

Inscription: this might begin with an address to a deity, or
might name a human. The last two lines might be restored:

dumu *ku-r[i-gal-zu]*   Son of Kuri-[galzu]
[lu]gal [kiši]   King of the world.

49 CBS 11450. **L** Nippur, W side of Shatt; MB tablet, accounts;
unnamed king, yr. 12.

20(ext) × 47? Composite. *
Inscription, apparently in six vertical lines. Trace of a man,
facing left, probably seated as there is a frieze above, containing
an animal and a rhomb? In the field below the frieze, a locust
and perhaps a cross; but I am unable to match the fragments in a
satisfactory way and I am especially puzzled by a vertical line to
the right of the locust. The pictorial field should not include such
a line; while if the last inscription line was used for symbols it is
strange that the upper fragment shows it containing cuneiform. It
may be most probable that it is just an effect of overrolling.
Faint.

50 CBS 10946. **L** Nippur, MB tablet, W slope of Tablet Hill.

20(ext) × 9(ext).
Inscription in at least two vertical lines. Trace of a man,
facing left, unclear whether seated or standing. Topline, at least
over inscription.

51 CBS 3094. **L** Nippur tablet, W side of Shatt.
BE XV 94, p. 62 record of payments; unnamed king, yr. 19.

12(ext) × 36. Composite.

Inscription in six vertical lines, the last one perhaps not used. A man, possibly standing as seated men normally have the arm at a shallower angle. Locust and rosette.

52 N 913. **L** tablet.

16(ext) × 19(ext).
Inscription in at least two vertical lines. Man, probably standing, arms 11. Cross.

53 CBS 13321. **L** Nippur tablet, MB temple record.

17(ext) × 38(ext). Composite. *
Inscription probably in at least seven vertical lines, but faint and badly overrolled. Standing(?) man facing left, arms 11.

54 B1062. Seal, pink banded agate, chipped.
PBS XIV p. 289-90, no. 531; bought Baghdad 1889 (**not from Nippur**); photograph published in reverse.
Limet 1971, 6.20.

32 × diam. 14.
Inscription in eight vertical lines; man facing left, arms 11, on groundline; cross, rhombs and locust. Topline over inscription.

Inscription:

mu.pà.da dingir.bi ḫé.gi/zi May he be established as one
chosen by his god,
ká lugal.a.ni.ta ḫé.nir.gál May he be (considered) noble
in the gate of his king,
giš.šub.ba.bi ḫé.nun níg.tuku

As his lot may abundance, wealth,
ti.la ud sù ḫé.nam.bi And a life of long days be decreed
for him,
pir-ḫi-^d**mar.dú** Pir'i-Amurru,
gal ukkin.na gal sag.d[ùn] Chief of the Assembly, Chief
Surveyor
ku-ri-gal-zu Of Kurigalzu,
lugal ki.šár.ra King of the world.

55 CBS 6646. L Nippur tablet.
M p. 273, U.2.24.179, Nazi-Maruttaš 14.
Powdery surface, very faint.
CBS 11542. L Nippur tablet, economic text.
M p. 274, U.2.24.200, Nazi-Maruttaš 15.

24(ext) × 36. Composite.
Inscription in six vertical lines. Standing man, arms 11; fishman, cross and rhomb in field.

56 UM 29-15-719. L Nippur tablet, loan with interest.
M p. 238, Q.2.115.134, Kurigalzu 21.

16(ext) × 33?(ext). Composite.
Inscription in at least five vertical lines. Standing man, corn ear and dog.

57 CBS 12928. L Nippur tablet, W side of Shatt.
M p. 272, U.2.24.150, Nazi-Maruttaš 12.
PBS II/2 27.

24(ext) × 45. Composite.
Inscription in seven vertical lines. Standing man, bordered robe, arms 11? In field, small kneeling man above dog.

58 CBS 3350. L Nippur tablet, W side of Shatt, unnamed king yr. 24.

27(ext) × 41(ext). Composite.
Inscription in at least six vertical lines. A standing man, arms 11, with streamer behind his back. In front of him, two(?) rhombs, a kneeling man with devotional arms, and probably another symbol above.

59 CBS 3127. L Nippur envelope, W side of Shatt.
BE XIV pl.XV:48.7.
BE XV 138, p. 64 receipt; unnamed king, yr. 24.

32(ext) × 20(ext). Composite.
Although there is no trace of an inscription the surviving traces leave plenty of room for one, and they are of completely First Kassite character. In the upper field a kneeling man on a

groundline, devotional arms, faces animal on groundline, cross, rhomb and rosette. A man underneath is probably seated unless the seal was unusually tall. Hard linear engraving, somewhat careless (especially in the cross). Topline.

There seems to be a separate trace of two circled dots near a line. If these are correctly understood (and are not e.g. components of some larger object) they would be most comfortable in a pseudo-Kassite design.

60   CBS 3045. **L** Nippur tablet, **W** side of Shatt.
   M p. 233, Q.2.115.11, Kurigalzu 5.
   BE XIV 13, p. 62 receipt for wool.
   Mentioned by Porada 1970, 11 n. 1.

   20(ext) × 42.
   Inscription in eight vertical lines, the last one apparently not used. Seated man; before him kneeling man, devotional arms, on a double baseline above a dog. Rhomb and perhaps cross in field.

61   CBS 3015. **L** Nippur envelope, **W** side of Shatt.
   M p. 268, U.2.24.50, Nazi-Maruttaš 4.
   CBS 3022. Impression on envelope fragment adhering to one end of tablet.
   L Nippur, **W** side of Shatt.
   BE XV 23, p. 58 official's salary; unnamed king yr. 9.
   CBS 3107. **L** Nippur envelope, **W** side of Shatt.
   BE XV 15, p. 58 official's salary; unnamed king yr. 4 (trans. p. 18).
   CBS 3153. **L** Nippur envelope, **W** side of Shatt.
   BE XIV pl. 15:48.1.
   BE XV 25, p. 58 official's salary; unnamed king yr. 10.
   CBS 3165. **L** Nippur envelope, **W** side of Shatt.
   BE XIV pl. XV:48.2.
   BE XV 31, p. 59 official's salary; unnamed king yr. 12 (trans. p. 20).
   CBS 3197. **L** Nippur envelope, **W** side of Shatt.
   BE XV 18, p. 58 official's salary; unnamed king yr. 7.
   CBS 8872. **L** Nippur tablet, temple record.

   There is a commentary on the inscription in Matthews and Brinkman (forthcoming).

30(caps) × 40. Composite.

Eight-line inscription in vertical lines: two of the lines are in a single wide line. A man, devotional arms, faces a seated man, locust between them, rhomb and cross above. Linear engraving of details. Faint (guide-?)line under upper symbols. Topline.
Cap (unclear, ext): triangles-twist-hbone-gran-plate.

Inscription:

[be]-la-ṇu-um	Belanum,
[n]u.èš ^den.líl	Prelate of Enlil,
[dumu] *ka-da-aš-ma-an-^den-líl*	
	[Son] of Kadashman-Enlil,
[du]mu.dumu *ku-ri-gal-zu*	Grandson of Kurigalzu,
lugal kiši	King of the world,
ìr ^dnusk[a]	Servant of Nuska
ù ^dun.gal.nibru^{ki}	And Šarrat-Nippuri.

62   CBS 11455. **L** Nippur tablet, accounts.

28(ext) × 42(ext). Composite.
Inscription in at least five vertical lines. A standing man, devotional arms, faces a seated man, probably cross between them. Frieze above of three rosettes. Very faint.

63   CBS 8250.
PBS XIV p. 295 no. 554; Nippur, bulla fragment.

25(ext) × 25(ext).
Inscription in at least two vertical lines. Standing man, devotional arms, faces a seated man, cross and rhomb in field. Topline (interrupted by chip on original seal?).

64   13 N 592.

Impression with inscription and two(?) persons, to be published by R.L. Zettler.

65   CBS 6729. Door sealing. **L** Nippur, MB bulla.
PBS XIV p. 295 no. 557.

27(ext) × 48?(ext). Composite.

Inscription in at least two vertical lines. Man, devotional arms, faces seated figure in flounced robe who may be holding a vessel; locust between them. Legrain thought the locust was a kid held by the first man but the 'extended arm' is an imperfection in the clay. Bottom line? Coarse linear engraving.

66 N1069. About a quarter of a cylindrical bulla tied round a knot.

28(ext) × 39(ext).

Inscription in at least five vertical lines. Man in hatched headdress and devotional attitude, cross, rhomb and line perhaps to be restored as an animal head after Brett 81. Topline, interrupted by chips on the original seal.

Inscription:

ᵈšà.zu umun g[al]	Marduk, great lord,
dingir šà.lá.[sù]	Merciful god,
giš.tuku š[ùd]	Who hears prayer,
níg.ba ti.[la]	Who grants life,
x AN x [x]	. . . . .

67 N720. Door sealing.

33 × 20(ext).

Inscription in at least four vertical lines. Standing man, devotional arms? Topline.

68 UM 29-16-149. **L** Nippur tablet, MB contract.

13(ext) × 42. Composite.

Inscription in six vertical lines. Man, probably with devotional arms, cross?, bird on unclear object.

69 B 9098. Seal, red jasper (with haematite inclusions?)
PBS XIV p. 293 no. 546, bought Baghdad 1890. Haynes thought, according to the old museum record, that it may have originated at Nippur.
Limet 1971, 5.4.

36 × diam. 16.

Inscription in four vertical lines, a fifth line is between the figures. Person, perhaps female, extends a hand towards a seated man holding a cup. Carrion birds perch on the inverted body of a horned animal on a groundline in the upper field above a fly. Scratchy and worn.

Inscription:

^{d}*nin-é-an-na*	Nin-Eanna,
tab-ni-i tab-bi-i	You created, you called.
[r]e-me ra-a-me	Pity and love
[ard]a pa-lí-iḫ-ki	The servant who reverences you,
GIŠ.NI/IR.**a.a**.x.x	. . . . .

The last line apparently gives the owner's name.

70   B 8973. Seal, agate.
PBS XIV p. 293 no. 547, bought Shatra 1891 (**not from Nippur**).
Limet 1971, 4.3.

28 × diam. 13.5.
Inscription in three vertical lines. Person in dress of uncertain type, perhaps female, extends an arm towards a seated man holding a cup. In field, fly, rosette and rhomb. Coarse linear engraving with drillings.

Inscription:

^{d}**mes umun gal**	Marduk, great lord,
igi.du$_8$.a.ni	Look with favour on him,
arḫuš tuku.a	Show mercy.

71   12 N 691a. Large clay lump with faceted face.
OIC 23 fig. 48:5a, fig. 92:1; Nippur area WB level III, beneath lowest floor of Kassite palace (see **10**).
Civil, OIC 23 p. 125 (n.b. not fig. 92:2 = **10**).

30(ext) × 50. Composite.
Drawn from cast shown to me by McG. Gibson. Inscription in six vertical lines. A woman (beardless with long hair) with stylised arms (probably to be understood like **69**, **70**, **72**) faces a

seated man holding something, perhaps a cup; cross and fly between them, rosette and sphinx(?) on left, rhombs on right. Above, frieze probably of animals flanking a small volute tree; below, frieze with griffin. Fine compact precise engraving, but not subtle.

Inscription:

[**ᵈutu**] x **ù**[n.na]	[Shamash], lofty lord,
[**lug**]**al an.ki.bi.**[**da**]	King of heaven and netherworld,
[x] A AN ZU x [x]	. . . . .
[**bà**]**d.gal.a.ni ḫé.**[**me.en**]	Be his great wall (i.e. protection),
[**ì**]**r ní.tuku.zu** [**ḫ**]**é.l**[**i**]	May the servant who reverences
	you rejoice,
[**me**] **tin ḫé.é**[**b**]**.s**[**i**]	May he be sated with abundance
	of life.

72   CBS 14273. Bulla fragment with two flat faces, one sealed.
PBS XIV p. 294 no. 551, Nippur.

30(ext) × 20(ext).

At least one vertical inscription line, apparently with a hatched band above, and a hatched band on the right side. A woman(?) with outstretched arm faces a vessel, perhaps held by a figure not preserved; stag's head below, locust(?) on groundline above. Frieze of birds(?) above this whole scene. The impression is folded under itself in a manner not understood by Legrain.

73   CBS 6731. L Nippur.
PBS XIV p. 224 no. 266, bulla with stringmarks.

17(ext) × 40?(ext). *

A seated figure holds a vessel. Before him a standing human in an unclear dress, perhaps a third human behind, though this could be an overrolling. A vertical (hatched?) band, probably beside an inscription, on right. Object, perhaps animal head, between the first two persons.

Legrain understood the last mentioned object as a vase with branches in the Ur III manner; however the seated figure (the only one reasonably clearly preserved) with its double lines on the dress looks Kassite to me.

Conceivably the same design as no. **72**.

74 CBS 8844. Irregular lump, sealing on curved outer surface. **L** Nippur.
PBS XIV p. 295 no. 553, bulla with stringmarks.

21(ext) × 49(ext).
This impression is very severely distorted. Inscription (inverted?) in at least two vertical lines, flanked on one side by a hatched band. It looks as though there is a very distorted standing man on the left, perhaps holding something; but I know of no parallel for the cross-hatched band running up the dress. A seated man with a hand so large that he may be grasping a vessel, but this area is damaged. Parallel lines in field beside his shoulder, object above, animal? between humans.

75 CBS 6747. Irregular bulla, surface badly cracked, sealing on outer curved surface.
L Nippur.
PBS XIV p. 295 no. 556.

40? × 52(ext).
Inscription in at least three vertical lines; it is unclear whether there is a frieze above but there may be a trace of a vase. Standing man, holding an object (perhaps a fan?) facing a seated person who holds a vessel. Two circled dots, rosette and rampant horned animal in field. Top and bottom lines.

Inscription:

^d**utu umun gal**	Shamash, great lord,
[igi].tab.a.ni	Look with favour on him,
[arḫuš] tuku.a	Show mercy.

76 A 29155. Door sealing? with leather impression?
Nippur, 2D 173 B.
Nippur I pl. 121:10; from TB 78 (stratification uncertain).
A29160A. Door sealing.
Nippur, 2D 329a.
Nippur I pl. 119:16; from TB 72 I 2, "Isin-Larsa period" (p. 54), room (pl. 62).

A29160B. Door sealing.
Nippur, 2D 329b.
Nippur I pl. 119:18; provenance as previous.

35(ext) × 46. Composite.
Standing man, holding object probably to be restored as a fan, facing seated man with cup. In field between them, monkey, rosette, small animal, five animal heads and an unclear object, perhaps a table(??). Behind them, inscription in three vertical lines beneath frieze of carrion birds perched on an inverted horned animal. Bottom line.

Inscription:

^d**mes umun bùlug** x?   Marduk, great lord,
igi.du₈.a.n[i]   Look with favour on him,
arḫuš rém tuku   Show mercy and compassion.

77   UM 29-13-775. **L** Nippur tablet, receipt for cereals.
M p. 235, Q.2.115.72, Kurigalzu 15.

20?(ext, cap) × 45.
Inscription in three vertical lines. A man in a bordered dress faces a seated man, small animal between them. Behind the seated man, perhaps a person in a flounced dress?
Cap: triangles-gran-hbone-gran.

78   N2043. **L** Tablet, MB contract?

24(ext) × 43(ext).
Inscription in at least four vertical lines. Man seated on panelled stool, faced by figure with devotional arms(?); interceding female in plain dress on right. Rhomb(s?) and disk in field. Friezes above and below, including winged creature?

79   CBS 2116. **L** MB tablet fragment, Nippur, W side of Shatt.

15(ext) × 46. Composite.
A vertical inscription in five lines is framed on either side by a hatched band, another hatched band above. Traces above this band. Main scene shows a standing human, devotional arms, facing a seated human. At least two circled dots and an animal

head between them.

80   L-29-458. Seal, Hilprecht coll.

Smooth grey material, said on the file card to be glazed frit. The surface is in such perfect condition that the material cannot be assessed from fractured edges.

28 × diam. 13.

Inscription in seven vertical lines, part of an eighth line in the figurative panel. Man in devotional posture on groundline, animal head. Topline.

Inscription:

lu né-bu	May it be called,
lu na-bu	May it be called,
lu né-bu	May his name
šu-um-šu	Be called,
lu na-me-er x-<*šu*>	May his ... shine,
ina amāt ì-lí-šu	At the command of his god,
x-*ma-at* / KA/SAG	. . . . .

The first two lines are corrupt for *lu etel pî-šu* "May his utterance be lordly."

81   L-29-451. Seal, Hilprecht coll., glass, cracked and chipped.

44 × diam. 17.

Three men, the first in plain robe, devotional posture, and round hat; the next in martial posture with curved sword, flounced dress, and pointed hat; and the last in plain robe, martial posture with curved sword, and rounded hat. Between first two men: two horned animals, the upper one inverted; between second pair: rosette and two animal heads each under a double line. Inscription in three vertical lines beneath frieze of three birds. Top and bottom lines.

Inscription:

^{d}**mes umun gal**	Marduk, great lord,
igi.du$_8$.a.ni	Look with favour on him,
arḫuš tuku.a	Show mercy.

82   CBS 8260. Irregular bulla fragment, sealing on outer curved surface. PBS XIV p. 295 no. 555, Nippur.

23(ext) × 26(ext).

Inscription in at least three vertical lines. There seems to be a line over the inscription at shoulder level which would suggest a frieze above. Two men, one with devotional arms, the other in martial posture and a flounced dress. In field, vessel(?) and unclear traces.

83   N2369. L Tablet, MB receipt, unnamed king yr. 22.

17(ext) × 38?(ext). Composite. *

Inscription in at least one vertical line. Three? standing humans, the middle one in martial posture, unclear objects between them. Corroded, salty, cracked surface.

84   CBS 11892. L Nippur envelope with tablet still inside, MB accounts.

24(ext) × 45. Composite.

Inscription in five vertical lines. Two humans face a third. The first has a plain robe with ladder-patterned strip and probably arms 11, the second a flounced dress and martial arms; the last figure is unclear.

85   CBS 10968. L Tablet and envelope, Nippur, W side of Shatt.
PBS II/2 131, p. 89 unnamed king yr. 24.
BE XIV pl. XII:33; p. 12 n. 2 ("10986" in error) the only cased tablet where the inner tablet is sealed as well as the envelope.
CBS 11593. L Nippur, W side of Shatt, MB envelope, tablet still inside.

27(ext) × 42. Composite.

Inscription in five vertical lines, bounded on the left by a double line. A standing man, arms 11, faces a set of symbols, from top: cross, locust, rosette, rhomb, dog, circled dot, and on the left vertical running spirals with a horizontal section under the cross. Sharp precise engraving.

Inscription: four lines not understood followed by the last one:

[ì]r ní.tuku.z[u]   The servant who reverences you.

86 CBS 3759. **L** Nippur, W side of Shatt, MB tablet.

21(ext) × 40(ext).
Inscription in at least two vertical lines flanked on either side by hatched bands. Standing man, dog and rhomb.

87 L-29-335. Bulla with string and reed marks.
Art Museum no. F.29-6-303. Hilprecht Bequest.

25(ext) × 21(ext).
At least one vertical inscription line. Man in martial attitude with mace at waist faces person with arms 11. Cross and two rosettes in field. Trace of face and hand (of kneeling man?) below. Topline. Exceptionally clear impression.

88 CBS 8592. Door sealing. **L** Nippur.
PBS XIV p. 296 no. 562.
UM 29-13-47. Door sealing. **L** Nippur.

30(ext) × 48(ext). Composite.
Inscription in at least five vertical lines. Two men in martial posture, dresses raised at the knee, face a third man in a plain robe, arms 11. The first man holds a mace at his waist, the second a curved sword behind him. The second man has a flounced dress and a high mitre. Two rosettes in the spaces between their heads, rhomb behind the first man, lower down three unclear objects (perhaps, following Legrain, insects) and a locust. A frieze above with a volute-tree flanked by two sphinxes. Engraving fine but not subtle.

89 CBS 14248. Fragment with smooth back, conceivably envelope as stated by Legrain.
PBS XIV p. 296 no. 561, Nippur.
CBS 14265. Irregular bulla, jar sealing?
PBS XIV p. 296 no. 561, Nippur.

34(ext) × 50. Composite.
Inscription in six vertical lines. Three men in martial posture, maces at waists, have robes raised in front to show triple tassels

between their legs. Rhombs between their heads. Frieze above with central animal and sphinx on right. Frieze of three(?) sphinxes below.

Inscription:

[ᵈni]n!-é-an-[na]   Nin-Eanna,
[tab-ni-i tab]-bi-i   [You created], you named,
   (three lines not understood)
[sa]g ní.[tu]ku.z[u]   The servant who reverences you.

90   UM 51-6-360. Shapeless clay lump with bad surface. **L** Nippur, no locality.

32(ext) × 32(ext).

Three men in dresses open in front, in martial attitude with curved swords. The central man's dress is flounced. Rhombs above between their heads, the one on the right overlapping an inscription line, perhaps due to distortion. Underneath, frieze centred on small volute-tree; the traces on the right are compatible with a winged sphinx.

91   CBS 14272. Irregular bulla. **L** Nippur.

25(ext) × 26(ext).

Inscription in at least three vertical lines. A man in a flounced dress and martial posture, behind him filling motives including a rosette, fly? and animal? Groundline.

92   12 N 81. Clay lump.
OIC 23 fig. 48:4, p. 66-7: Nippur, area WB level II, locus 6, courtyard of large Kassite palace (fig. 46).

Two men in flounced dresses and martial posture, one holding a curved sword, (unframed) cross and small animal between them, unclear object at top.

93   N1070. Door sealing. **L** Nippur.

20(ext) × 23(ext). Composite.

At least one vertical inscription line. Two men in martial attitude and flounced dresses, at least one holding an animal(?) instead of a curved sword. Baseline.

94   L-29-456. Hilprecht Coll., glass cylinder seal, originally dark blue, broken in two pieces.
Hilprecht cat. 63, gift of Sultan Abdul Hamid, Nippur.

31 × diam. 19.
Inscription in four vertical lines. Two men in martial posture with curved swords, flounced robes. Unclear objects (fish?) beneath the left figure and beyond the right figure. At top: stag's head; fly; unclear object (vase? animal head?). Top and bottom lines. Scrappy engraving.

95   CBS 14261. Roughly cylindrical bulla with smooth top, sealing on curved surface.
PBS XIV p. 294 no. 548, Nippur.
Limet 1971, 4.8.
Porada 1970, figures annexes 9.

36(ext) × 30?(ext).
Inscription in at least four vertical lines under a hatched band. Frieze above of two birds looking back at a stag's head between them. A man in a plain robe and martial posture with a curved sword stands on a groundline. Traces behind him are probably overrolled: an animal?, part of a human in a flounced robe, a volute-tree.

Inscription:

^{d}mes umun b[ùlug]	Marduk, great lord,
sag an.k[i.a]	Chief of heaven and netherworld,
igi.du$_8$.a.ni	Look with favour on him,
[ar]ḫuš tuku.a	Show mercy.

96   CBS 14280. Irregular bulla, reed impression on back.
PBS XIV p. 294 no. 549, Nippur.
CBS 14283. Irregular bulla with stringmarks.
PBS XIV p. 294 no. 549, Nippur.

35 × 34(ext). Composite.

Two men in martial posture with curved swords, one in a flounced dress with a tall hat, the other in a plain dress with a round hat. The second man impinges on the inscription which is in at least two vertical lines. In field, two rhombs, animal head, object with three projections and unclear object.

97   L-29-321. Half of a flat clay disk (end of 'visiting card'?).
Art Museum no. F.29-6-300. Hilprecht Bequest.

29 × 14(ext).
Two men in martial attitude, one with flounced dress, the other with curved sword. In field, winged monster, monkey, horned animal. Topline.

98   B 8932. Seal, blue glass, half missing.
PBS XIV p. 275 no. 467, Nippur.

26 × diam. 13.
A row of three men in martial attitude holding curved swords, the middle one with a flounced dress and possibly a tall hat. Worn.

99   UM 51-6-359. Shapeless clay lump. **L** Nippur 2ND 162, no locality.

36 × 39(ext).
Man in martial attitude holding curved sword, perhaps another behind him. Inscription in three vertical lines beneath frieze of carrion birds perched on horned animal lying on its back.

Inscription:

d!ṡà!.zu [umun]	Marduk, great lord,
x x x x	. . . . .
arḫuš tuku.a	Show mercy.

100   CBS 10167. Bulla with stringmark? **L** Nippur.

28(ext) × 39(ext).
Inscription in three vertical lines surmounted by a hatched band and a row of three rhombs. Two men in martial posture, volute-tree between them. There is a hatched band above the tree

and presumably a frieze above that. Topline, at least above the rhombs.

Inscription:

^{d}ut[u]/b[a-ba$_6$]   Shamash, (or: Baba,)
igi.du$_8$.a.[ni]   Look with favour on him,
arḫuš tuku.[a]   Show mercy.

101 14 N 52. Seal, frit.
Gibson 1983, 183 fig. 19, p. 181 Nippur, Area WC-1 level III in fill directly below NW wall of locus 31 (see **171**).

This seal, which shows two men in martial attitude, will be published by R.L. Zettler.

102 CBS 3179. **L** Nippur, W side of Shatt, MB tablet, unnamed king yr. 16.

22(ext) × 29(ext). Composite. *
The impressions are faint and their relationship is unclear. At least two men in martial posture with curved swords. A vertical hatched band behind one of them; probably a volute-tree in front of another.

103 12 N 368. Clay lump.
OIC 23 fig. 48:8, Nippur, area WB, level II, locus 12, room next to courtyard of large Kassite palace (fig. 46).
†
Two men in martial attitude, fly or animal head in field.

104 2D 588b. Clay lump.
Nippur I pl. 121:2, from Nippur, TA 117 VI, room (pl. 74A), Kassite (p. 68).
†
Trace of vertical inscription. Two men in martial attitude, one with curved sword, rosette. Topline.

105 CBS 3749. L Nippur, W side of Shatt, MB? tablet.

14(ext) × 22(ext). Composite.
Three martial men; register above with animals(?). Perhaps inscription in vertical lines. Objects between men's heads, perhaps rosette and cross. Surface very worn. Possibly same seal as **106**.

106 UM 29-15-360. L Nippur tablet, MB ledger, personal names only preserved.

15(ext) × 40(ext). Composite.
Inscription, probably in at least three vertical lines. Three martial men, rosette and cross(?) between their heads. Frieze above with animal and probably tree. Conceivably the same seal as **105**.

107 B 14363. Seal, glass, cracked, top broken off.
PBS XIV p. 298 no. 567, Nippur.

22(ext) × diam. 15.
Inscription in three vertical lines, not divided from scene on left; two men in martial posture with curved swords; ballstaff.

Inscription:

[ᵈšà].zu umun gal   Marduk, great lord,
[igi.du₈].a.a!   Look with favour on him(!),
[arḫuš] tuku.a   Show mercy.

108 L-29-457. Hilprecht coll., glass cylinder seal, greenish-blue.
Hilprecht cat. 62, gift of Sultan Abdul Hamid, Nippur.

29 × diam. 12.
Inscription in four vertical lines. Two men in ladder-patterned robes and martial attitude with curved swords; in field, two animal heads, bull, bird. The first three of these symbols were subsequently drilled out. Top and bottom lines.

Inscription:

ᵈmes umun bùlug.gá   Marduk, great lord,
dingir šà.lá.sù   Merciful god,

šá-^{d}lamassi(KAL)-damqa(sig$_5$-a)
Ša-lamassi-damqa
sag ní.tuku.bi
Is the servant who reverences him.

109 B 14347. Seal, greenish glass.
PBS XIV p. 298 no. 568, Nippur hill VIII.

29.5 × diam. 12.
Inscription in three vertical lines. Man, arms not shown but probably to be understood as martial; fly, two birds, fish. Top and bottom lines.

Inscription:

^{d}<šà>.zu umun gal Marduk, great lord,
dingir x x x ..... god,
x x x (x) . . . . .

Text apparently garbled.

110 CBS 14281. Irregular bulla with stringmarks, worn surface. **L** Nippur.

15(ext) × 10(ext).
Trace of a coarse linear design, apparently a man in a plain robe in martial posture.

111 CBS 14271. Irregular bulla. **L** Nippur.

15(ext) × 17(ext).
Inscription in at least two vertical lines. A man with a curved sword behind him which interrupts the baseline.

112 CBS 13504. **L** Nippur tablet, W side of Shatt, MB temple accounts.

19(ext) × 43? *
Inscription in two vertical lines, apparently identical. The figurative traces are not intelligible but might conceivably represent a man with a curved sword and some kind of bird, animal or monster.

113 2N 171. Impression.
Nippur I pl. 121:7, from TA 42 II, unclear context (pl. 76A), neo-Babylonian (p. 71).

†

Inscription in at least two vertical lines flanked by hatched band; man in martial attitude, birds(?).

114 UM 29-13-837. **L** Nippur tablet, MB receipt for grain.

17(ext) × 40(ext). Composite.
Inscription in at least two vertical lines, hatched band on either side, possibly frieze above. A man in martial attitude, shapes in front of him perhaps a cross and a bird?

115 CBS 3037. **L** Nippur tablet, W side of Shatt.
M p. 234, Q.2.115.44, Kurigalzu 12.
BE XIV 15, p. 62 record of a payment of grain.

14(ext) × 39. Composite.
There is a vertical hatched band beside three inscription lines. A man in martial posture faces a vessel and a bird.

116 CBS 7247. **L** Nippur tablet, temple account.
M p. 114, E.2.25.68, Burnaburiaš 25.

15(ext) × 48(ext). Composite.
Inscription in three vertical lines, hatched band on right. A man in martial posture faces a bird sitting on (??) a volute-tree. Exceptionally faint.

Inscription:

[ᵈšà].zu umun g[al]!	Marduk, great lord,
[igi].du₈.[a].n[i]?	Look with favour on him,
[arḫuš] tuku.[a]	Show mercy.

The first and third lines of no. **115** can be restored in the same way, but the middle line of that one is apparently different.

117 UM 29-15-641a. **L** Nippur tablet, contract concerning grain.
M p. 268, U.2.24.44, Nazi-Maruttaš 4.

13(ext) × 49. Composite. **

The tablet is in very poor condition and the reconstruction is conjectural. Inscription in three vertical lines, flanked on both sides by hatched bands. A man in martial attitude with a bird (above a plant?) before him.

118 CBS 6159. **L** Nippur, W side of Shatt, MB tablet, unnamed king yr. 21.

33(ext) × 46(ext).

Inscription in at least two, probably three vertical lines, flanked on either side and above by hatched bands; perhaps circled dot above. Man in martial attitude facing volute tree with three animal heads above. Bottom line.

119 CBS 12585. **L** Nippur envelope, unnamed MB king yr. 24.

21(ext) × 45. Composite.

Inscription in two vertical lines, hatched band on left and above. Frieze above that, perhaps with bird. A man in a plain robe in martial posture, probably holding a curved sword, faces an elaborate volute tree with a toothed trunk which stands on a panel. Animal head in field; perhaps rhomb in front of man's face.

120 UM 29-16-649. **L** Nippur tablet, MB business.

20(ext) × 9(ext). Composite.
Unintelligible shapes with cross-hatching (tree??).

121 CBS 14267. Irregular bulla with stringmarks.
PBS XIV p. 294 no. 550, Nippur.

22?(ext) × 20(ext).

Inscription in at least three vertical lines, bird above. Traces of a flounced dress and perhaps an arm hanging down next to a flounced dress, suggesting one or two figures in martial posture? Rosette? Overrolled.

122 CBS 14258. Irregular bulla, stringmarks on back.

PBS XIV p. 299 no. 570, Nippur.

25(ext) × 13(ext).
Inscription in at least two vertical(?) lines below a hatched band and a frieze.

123 CBS 3752. Unbroken object, probably envelope with tablet still inside.
L Nippur, W side of Shatt, MB list, unnamed king yr. 6?

29(ext) × 32?(ext). Composite. *
At least two vertical inscription lines, flanked below and on right by hatched bands. A further horizontal band may not be correctly attached. Upper border of hatched triangles.

124 CBS 14275. Irregular bulla with stringmarks.
PBS XIV p. 295 no. 558, Nippur.

22(ext) × 25(ext).
The orientation of this design is uncertain. An inscription in at least three lines with lines drawn across them. Hatched bands at right angles enclosing unidentifiable objects (tree??).

125 A29154. Clay lump with stringmarks.
Nippur, 2D 169.
Nippur I pl. 120:2, from TB 66 I1, "Isin-Larsa period" (p. 54), room or small courtyard (pl. 63).

24(ext) × 31(ext).
Band of crosses in panels flanked by hatched bands; band of rosettes; at least three inscription lines. Orientation unknown. A separate trace may show hatched triangles?

126 UM 29-15-461. L Nippur tablet, MB account of transport of 7 slaves.

15(ext) × 45(ext). Composite. **
The orientation and reconstruction of this design are uncertain. Hatched band, horned animals and circled dots, apparently in registers.

127 CBS 8074. **L** Nippur tablet, MB business document.

12(ext) × 33(ext). Composite.

The style is coarse and unusual. A sphinx behind a man in martial? posture; wedge-shaped elements, possibly including cuneiform or a tree.

128 A29179. Clay fragment with stringmarks and vessel? impression on back.

Nippur, 2D 814.

Nippur I pl. 119:2, from TB 216 IV 2 - partly paved courtyard (pl. 59), said to be Ur III (p. 43).

30(ext) × 32(ext).

Man in martial attitude in robe open in front, facing naked man subduing bull, traces of animal head? beyond and of vertical inscription line behind. Bottom line? Carefully cut, n.b. martial figure does not have curved sword.

129 12 N 691b. Impression.

OIC 23 fig. 48:5b: Nippur, area WB level III locus 25, beneath lowest floor of Kassite palace (see **10**).

Ht. 12(ext).

Drawn from a cast shown to me by McG. Gibson. There are two rollings. The lower one shows two lines of inscription next to part of the design which could be the waist of one of the two phallic bullmen shown flanking a standard in the upper impression.

130 CBS 14268. Door sealing.

PBS XIV p. 296 no. 560, Nippur.

17(ext) × 24(ext).

At least one vertical inscription line. Two sphinxes face each other, frieze with rosettes and a circled dot above. I see no sign of the 'two bulls with head turned back' mentioned by Legrain, but they may have originally appeared on the surviving fragment of the next facet of the bulla, which is now unintelligible.

131 CBS 3129. **L** Nippur envelope, W side of Shatt.

BE XIV pl. XV:48.4.
BE XV 86, p. 62 receipt, unnamed king yr. 18.

30(ext) × 48(ext). Composite. *

I do not fully understand this design and it is possible that the left hand area behind the chariot is overrolled. An archer stands in a chariot drawn by a leaping animal. The chariot has crossed quivers giving its body a triangular appearance. There are two pairs of reins which run across the animal's neck. A star beneath the animal. The baseline of the chariot body seems to continue behind, beneath an inverted horned animal with three arrows(?) in its neck. Other traces are probably of more animals. Baseline, interrupted by a chip in the original seal. Fairly coarse engraving, strongly linear.

132 CBS 3138. **L** Nippur, W side of Shatt, unnamed king yr. 16.
BE XV 49, p. 60 record of debt with promissory condition (date in error), trans. p. 17 "Seal of Sin-damaqu".

17(ext) × 42? Composite.

This seal and **133** should be understood in relation to one another. It is possible that they are impressions of the same seal, though if so the distortion is severe. The owners have different names.

A large bird and an inverted animal above an archer.

133 CBS 7237. **L** Nippur tablet, rare Sum. and Akk. contract.
M p. 161, L.2.13.109, Kadašman-Turgu 17?
PBS VIII/2 159; trans. p. 161: Siyatum buys a donkey from Hunnubu.

24(ext) × 40. Composite.

A kneeling archer aims towards two tumbling animals. Rhomb? behind his foot. Bottom line. A fan-shaped object above is, as we learn from **132**, the tail of a large bird. Faint.

134 13 N 471A and B. Clay lumps.
Nippur, area WB locus 58 floor 2 or 3.

34(ext) × 40. Composite.

Drawn from casts shown to me by McG. Gibson. A kneeling archer aims at a griffin with an arrow in its back, rhomb between them. Above, a frieze of three horned animals. Unclear traces behind the archer - could the vertical line be a crack in the original seal? Topline.

135 A29153. Irregular lump with stringmarks? Sealed on concave surface.
Nippur, 2D 157.
Nippur I pl. 121:5, from TA 49 III 2, Assyrian period (p. 69), courtyard (p. 71, pl. 75B).

19(ext) × 23(ext).
Inscription in at least two vertical lines. Four horizontal bands: respectively birds, lattice, monsters and birds. Unknown whether this is bottom of design. Heads of monsters perhaps overrolled.

136 N 7540. Fragment, probably of bulla?

13(ext) × 14(ext).
Trace of three horizontal registers, each? containing horned animals.

137 12 N 605. Clay lump.
OIC 23 fig. 21:2, p. 14: Nippur, area WA level IV B, locus 25, large room in Kassite temple (fig. 18), north corner just beyond doorway.
Gibson 1975, fig. 10.

14(caps) × 39.
Drawn from cast shown to me by McG. Gibson. Two horizontal registers, each containing two foxes or jackals. Filling symbols: above, three stars, two rhombs, stag's head, rosette; below: three rhombs, stag's head.
Cap: triangles-gran-hbone.

138 CBS 14245. Irregular bulla, stringmarks on back.
PBS XIV p. 296 no. 559, Nippur.

26(ext) × 18(ext).
Horizontal registers of rhombs, locusts and birds(?). Topline.

139 CBS 3121. **L** Envelope, Nippur, W side of Shatt.
BE XV 116, p. 63 receipt, unnamed king yr. 21.

Ht. 29(ext). **

There are substantial traces of this design but all of the rollings are badly blurred and I have been unable to form a satisfactory composite. It is most unclear which of the visible traces are parts of the design and which are irregularities on the tablet's surface.

Topline. At least one double horizontal line in the middle of the design. Horned animals. A wing, belonging to a bird or monster.

140 B7294. Cylindrical bulla, impressions on curved surface and top, cloth impression on back, stringmarks.
PBS XIV 539.

18(ext) × 43. Composite.

Inscription in six vertical lines. A fishman with water flowing over his shoulders into vessels on either side. Fish, probably above both shoulders. Traces of a fish above may be part of a frieze or conceivably of another fishman of similar size.
Cap: ??-hbone-gran.

141 CBS 9893. **L** Nippur, W side of Shatt, MB envelope.

24(ext) × 25(ext). Composite.

At least two nude kneeling men on a groundline with water flowing over their shoulders to the ground between them, where there is a vessel on at least one side. Rosette-like shapes above the junctions of the waters, connected with them by stems, are probably meant to be trees growing out of the vessels. Above, an undulating mass of blobs with a tasselled fringe, perhaps representing rain coming down from the mountains. Below, a frieze of animals. Bottom line. At top, perhaps the impression of a metal band.

142 CBS 3091. **L** MB tablet, Nippur, W side of Shatt; unnamed king yr. 22.

Small fragments. **

A finely engraved bare man's leg beside a vertical object, perhaps an inscription line. Wavy lines, perhaps overrolled.
Cap: gran-(twist?)-triangles-(twist?)-gran.
All the triangles are granulated, rather than half of them as is usual. Same cap as **143**.

143 N 869. **L** MB tablet, contract, witnesses.

**

This design is not reconstructable. There is a trace of an inscription and part of the profile of a solid object whose graceful curves look Second Kassite. The cap is the same as **142** but combining the traces does not make either of them more intelligible.
Cap: twist-triangles-twist-gran. The triangles are all granulated as in **142**.

144 N1903. Irregular bulla, stringmarks, cuneiform sign beside a small hole.

Ht. 15(ext). *

The impression is very faint and seems to be overrolled. There is a being, perhaps a mountain god, with hands together at the waist; the trace to the left could be an overrolling of the same thing. Conceivably trace of flowing waters?
Cap: triangles-hbone-twist-hbone-gran-plate?

145 15 N 79. Seal, composition.
IM 87846.
Nippur, WC-2 173, below floor 1 in mud brick packing.

44 × diam. 14. * (†)

Drawn from an impression and enlarged photographs shown to me by McG. Gibson: as the surface of the seal is soft and damaged it was not possible for the impression to be made deeply but the details could be added from the photographs. These show colour differences more clearly than relief.

Inscription in three vertical lines. A god in a hatched headdress whose body flows down to the ground grasps a vessel(?) against his chest with both hands; water flows from it over his shoulders on each side up to an eagle and down to a fishman with a vessel. Cross and rhomb. At top, plant flanked by sphinxes. Topline.

146 CBS 7380. **L** Nippur tablet, business document.
Jena, HS 153.
TuM NF V, pls. CXXIX-CXXX, seal VIII; p. 11: Šagarakti-Šuriaš yrs. 9-12, large *aklu* text.

c. 20(ext, cap) × c. 38. Composite. * (†)
Almost all of the detail comes from the Jena photographs which I have scaled from the very fragmentary Nippur impression. W.G. Lambert lent me clear prints and assisted me here in drawing the cuneiform.
At top, horizontal inscription in one line with some signs below. A being with hands held together at the waist and a very rectangular head has streams of water flowing down on either side from two eagles. Terminal volute-tree.
Cap: triangles-hbone-twist-hbone-gran-plate?

Inscription:

ina amāt ^d*marduk be-lí-šu šá-kin-šu lí-bur liš-lim*

At the command of Marduk, his lord, may the one equipped with it (the seal) be established and prosper.

147 UM 29-16-340. **L** Nippur tablet; decree (*rikiltu*) of governor of Nippur regarding activities of persons should they leave Nippur.
M p. 297, V.2.10.147, Šagarakti-Šuriaš 10; p. 391-3, text no. 24; seal of Esagil-lidiš, *nagir*-herald of Nippur.

28?(ext) × 54? Composite. **
Although the tablet is essentially complete and is rolled on all surfaces with at least 9 impressions I have been unable to find a satisfactory reconstruction. The upper edge is from a continuous impression but the rest is combined from fragments and is presented only to give an idea of what may be there.
Two undulating edges may be the body of a mountain god. This god is never winged so the wings at the top probably belong to a large bird, perhaps with streams of water running down on both sides. The god normally either holds his hands out to dominate animals or holds them together to grasp a flowing vase. Here the traces suggest both that the arms are held out and that

there are flowing waters, but this does occur in Thebes 26. If this is so, then the objects on either side should be fishmen, and the general layout may have resembled Thebes 27. There are probably at least two rhombs in the field and lines texturing the god's body, but I can make no sense of the area where the god's head and the bird's tail should be.

148 CBS 3337. **L** Nippur tablet, W side of Shatt.
    M p. 280, U.2.24.358, Nazi-Maruttaš.
    BE XIV 87, p. 68 payment of an official's salary, index mentions Rimutu.
    CBS 3349. **L** Nippur tablet, W side of Shatt.
    M p. 279, U.2.24.333, Nazi-Maruttaš 23.
    BE XIV 81, p. 67 payment of salaries, Rimutu mentioned in index.
    CBS 6079. **L** Nippur tablet, W side of Shatt.
    M p. 279, U.2.24.334, Nazi-Maruttaš 23.
    BE XIV 82, p. 67 payment of official's salary, index mentions Rimutu.
    CBS 6080. **L** Nippur tablet, W side of Shatt.
    M p. 276, U.2.24.233, Nazi-Maruttaš 16.
    BE XIV 71, p. 66 payment of an official's salary, index mentions Rimutu.
    CBS 6081? **L** Nippur tablet, W side of Shatt.
    M p. 276, U.2.24.234, Nazi-Maruttaš 16.
    BE XIV 70, p. 66 payment of an official's salary, trans. p. 29: 'Seal of Rimutum'.
        The design on this tablet is unintelligible but it has the same cap as the others and the date and owner leave no doubt that it was the same seal.
    CBS 6090. **L** Nippur tablet, W side of Shatt.
    M p. 279, U.2.24.331, Nazi-Maruttaš 22.
    BE XIV 80, p. 67 payment of an official's salary, index mentions Rimutu.
    CBS 6635. **L** Nippur tablet.
    M p. 281, U.2.24.369, Nazi-Maruttaš.
    BE XIV 87a, p. 68 payment of an official's salary, p. 14 Rimutu *rab riqqu* (i.e. *sirāšu*). Seal of Ninurta-KI-pišu (S. Dalley).
    CBS 6649. **L** Nippur tablet.
    M p. 280, U.2.24.339, Nazi-Maruttaš 24.
    'Seal of Rimutu' (Brinkman).
    CBS 7261. **L** Nippur tablet, temple account.

M p. 157, L.2.13.34, Kadašman-Turgu 6.

Note that this tablet, CBS 8657 and Ni 2253 are the only ones not dated to Nazi-Maruttaš.

CBS 7788. **L** Nippur tablet, Kassite temple account.

CBS 8559. **L** Nippur tablet, contract.

M p. 277, U.2.24.264, Nazi-Maruttaš 18.

CBS 8657? **L** Nippur tablet, contract.

M p. 161, L.2.13.95, Kadašman-Turgu 15.

CBS 9514 = Istanbul, Ni. 7968. Cast of tablet.

M p. 275, U.2.24.222, Nazi-Maruttaš 16.

CBS 9517? = Istanbul, Ni 844. Cast of tablet.

M p. 276, U.2.24.238, Nazi-Maruttaš 16.

'Seal of Rimutu' (Brinkman).

The design is almost unintelligible on the cast but can be understood as part of our design, and the cap, date and owner make this almost certain.

CBS 9898. **L** Nippur tablet, W side of Shatt.

M p. 280, U.2.24.353, Nazi-Maruttaš 24.

CBS 10250. **L** Nippur, MB tablet.

CBS 10254. **L** Nippur tablet.

M p. 269, U.2.24.77, Nazi-Maruttaš 6.

BE XIV 48a, p. 65 salary payments.

CBS 10981? **L** Nippur tablet, MB accounts, W side of Shatt.

Design with birds probably the same as the others.

CBS 11467. **L** Nippur tablet.

M p. 275, U.2.24.224, Nazi-Maruttaš 16(+).

CBS 13352. **L** Nippur tablet, temple record.

M p. 269, U.2.24.70, Nazi-Maruttaš 5.

CBS 13370. **L** Nippur tablet, temple record.

UM 29-13-251. **L** Nippur tablet, account of beer and pots, Nazi-Maruttaš.

UM 29-13-946. **L** Nippur tablet, ledger, personal names and numbers in *sutu* and *qa*; unnamed MB king yr. 15.

UM 29-15-38a. **L** Nippur tablet, receipt.

M p. 278, U.2.24.294, Nazi-Maruttaš 19.

UM 29-15-54. **L** Nippur tablet, business.

M p. 281, U.2.24.367, Nazi-Maruttaš.

UM 29-15-154 + 29-16-178 (join). **L** Nippur tablet.

MB contract (E. Leichty).

UM 29-15-685. **L** Nippur tablet, ledger.

M p. 270, U.2.24.88, Nazi-Maruttaš 8.

UM 29-15-713. **L** Nippur tablet; ledger, expenditures of cereals and spices.

UM 29-16-378. **L** Nippur tablet, MB ledger, cereals, rations for sheep.

UM 29-16-593. **L** Nippur tablet, MB ledger, cereals.
Especially good impression of the centre of the design.

UM 29-16-698. **L** Nippur tablet; MB ledger, various commodities; unnamed king yr. 24.

N 2432? **L** MB Tablet, account of rations, unnamed king yr. 4.
Very faint and overwritten, similar cap, possibly same design.

N 2872. **L** Tablet, MB ledger.

N 2907. **L** Tablet, MB account.

N 3410? **L** Tablet, MB account, personal names?

Istanbul: the following tablets are listed by Porada 1952, 188 no. 5, and should be assigned here because they have the right date or name (the names were kindly supplied to me by J.A. Brinkman from his notes) :

Ni 158, 'Seal of Rimutu', Nazi-Maruttaš 23.
Ni 295, 'Seal of Rimutu', Nazi-Maruttaš 24.
Ni 6052, Nazi-Maruttaš 5.
Ni 7948, 'Seal of Rim[', Nazi-Maruttaš 19.

The following tablets in Istanbul probably also have this impression:

Ni 2253, 'Seal of Rimutu', Kadašman-Turgu 13.
Ni 7835, 'Seal of Rimutu', Nazi-Maruttaš 15.
Ni 8847, 'Seal of Rimutu', Nazi-Maruttaš?
Ni 12216, 'Seal of Rimutu', Nazi-Maruttaš 15.

Porada 1952, no. 5. It is apparent from the dates and the owners' names given to me by J.A. Brinkman that the list of Istanbul tablets given by Porada includes impressions both of this seal of Rimutu and of the seal of Amil-Marduk, no. **149**. This confusion is not surprising considering the remarkable similarity between the two designs and the fact that most of the known cases are fragments of impressions on small tablets: the easiest way of distinguishing the two is usually the cap, as Amil-Marduk has a large and elaborate cap while Rimutu's is small and unusually plain. No errors seem to have appeared in Porada's drawing because of this, and it should be consulted for some details that are not preserved in Philadelphia.
PC no. 131; Collon 1987, no. 842

33(caps) × 39. Composite.

A small man kneels with water pouring over his shoulders. Triangles round about probably represent mountains and the whole figure is enclosed in a large mountain which develops into a Janus-headed god in a tall headdress who grasps a rampant winged griffin on either side. A flock of nine birds flies overhead, with a small animal among them. At least 12 cuneiform signs in the field. A tall terminal volute-tree, with a bird perched on either side.

Cap: triangles-gran. CBS 7261 shows a narrow wire twist above the triangles which might be a reworking as it is a late tablet, though this was not observed on CBS 8657. There may be the same cap on CBS 3366.

Inscription: the present writer has not succeeded in making sense from the inscription, which is scattered about in the design. The signs on the right of the mountain deity (AN É? x x LÍL) seem to make no sense, and those on the left can be read: **ìr dingir.mu** ^d**nin.líl** "servant of my god, Ninlil", but this is not fully convincing.

149 CBS 6616. **L** Nippur tablet, list of accounts.
M p. 302, V.2.10.261, Šagarakti-Šuriaš, year unknown.
CBS 10623. **L** Nippur tablet, MB or later.
This is the only impression showing the inscription.
CBS 10738. **L** Tablet, account list; from third Nippur expedition.
CBS 10772. **L** Tablet, account list; Nippur, Tablet Hill.
M p. 299, V.2.10.185, Šagarakti-Šuriaš 11(+).
CBS 11060. **L** Nippur, W side of Shatt, MB? tablet.
CBS 11105. **L** Nippur tablet, W side of Shatt.
M p. 299, V.2.10.186, Šagarakti-Šuriaš 11.
'Seal of Amil-Marduk, *šandabakku*'; Cattle account (Brinkman).
CBS 11107. **L** Nippur tablet, W side of Shatt, account list.
M p. 300, V.2.10.224, Šagarakti-Šuriaš 12?
'Seal of Amil-Marduk' (Brinkman).
CBS 12910. **L** Nippur tablet, W side of Shatt.
M p. 297, V.2.10.153, Šagarakti-Šuriaš 10.
BE XIV 137, pl. XIV:39 (cap).
UM 29-13-642. **L** Nippur tablet, MB contract?
This is the only impression with the lower part of the design.
UM 29-15-112. **L** Nippur tablet, ledger: cattle, listed by age.
M p. 299, V.2.10.191, Šagarakti-Šuriaš 11.
Particularly good impression of the tree.

UM 29-15-312. **L** Nippur tablet, ledger, oxen and cattle; 'Awel-Marduk'.
M p. 297, V.2.10.152, Šagarakti-Šuriaš 10.

Istanbul: the following tablets are listed in Porada 1952, 188, no. 5, and should be assigned here because they have the right date or owner (the owners were kindly supplied to me by J.A. Brinkman from his notes):

Ni 2243, Kaštiliaš yr. 1 (rations to gate guardian).
Ni 6272, 'Seal of Amil-Marduk', Šagarakti-Šuriaš 11.
Ni 8586, 'Seal of Amil-Marduk', Šagarakti-Šuriaš 11.
Ni 8721, Šagarakti-Šuriaš.

The following tablets in Istanbul probably also have this impression:

Ni 7972, 'Seal of Amil-Marduk', Kaštiliaš yr. 1.
Ni 8492, probably 'Seal of Amil-Marduk'.
Ni 8736, 'Amil-Marduk', Šagarakti-Šuriaš.

46(ext, cap) × 54. Composite.
Two rampant griffins with lions' tails are grasped by a being with a human torso, perhaps Janus-headed like **148**. Its lower body has an undulating profile like a 'mountain'; traces of lines within might be streams of water, cf. **148**. At least ten birds fly overhead, and above them at least two horizontal lines of inscription. A wing(?) to the left of the being's head may be overrolled. Unclear traces between the inscription and the birds. An object among the birds might be overrolled or conceivably an animal as in **148**. A DINGIR(?) sign behind the griffin on the left. Elaborate terminal volute-tree, with birds sitting on either side; an uncertain solid object on the right. The tree seems to grow out of a vessel with streams of water, cf. Thebes 27.
The cap is normally impressed only on the sides of the tablets and its relationship with the design is uncertain: triangles-hbone-twist-hbone-gran.

Inscription: the horizontal inscription has not been read, but the three signs scattered in the design read ^{d}**nin.líl** "Ninlil".

150 CBS 8600A. **L** Nippur tablet.
Legal text dealing with runaway slave, date not preserved (Brinkman).

16??(ext) × 40???. Composite. **

Although substantial traces of at least seven impressions survive, their fragmentary nature and heavy overrolling makes reliable reconstruction impossible: the drawing is no more than a suggestion. A figure stands with arms held out in the attitude for mastering animals on either side. The figure's head is not preserved. Large rosettes (or trees??), probably on either side of his legs. A bird, probably with head and tail below the wings, beneath a topline. Further very doubtful traces might suggest that a griffin and a lion are attacking the animals dominated by the central figure. Scenes of the mastery of animals usually have either a tree or an inscription as a terminal. Neither of these is likely here as they are both distinctive even in small fragments. If they are absent, then there would be room for the extra figures, though they would be most unusual.

151 13 N 519. Clay lump.
Nippur, Area WB locus 18, fill above floor 3.

* †

Drawing made from a photograph given to me by R.L. Zettler. There are at least two rollings and it looks likely that a disentangled composite could be made from the original object. An elaborate volute tree, its top visible on the right, and the middle, with a bird perched on a branch, at the top. A large wing beside the top of the tree probably belongs to a demon, and there may be a trace of the other wing on the other side of the tree, to give an effect like **152**. The size of the wing makes a pair of birds, as in **146**, less likely. The demon holds an animal, no doubt one of a pair, by a hindleg. Traces beside the animal body might be an overrolling of a different part of the animal, perhaps including curving horns or forelegs, or some quite different figure.

152 A29349. Cylinder seal in dark red jasper, pronounced concave profile. **Not from Nippur.**
Acquired from coll. E.S. David of Long Island.

41 × diam. 15.

Winged human-headed demon with bird feet holds two horned animals upside down; terminal volute tree. Horizontal inscription line above the demon. Top and bottom lines; ground lines beneath the animals, or rather, following W.G. Lambert (below), guide-lines for the unfinished part of the text. Perhaps unfinished, to judge from the irregular application of the fine detail.

Inscription: the inscription in the top horizontal line is incomplete, and the remainder was no doubt planned for the bottom spaces either side of the feet of the monster. Since it was a standard type of inscription it can easily be restored:

^dmes umun gal ìr ní.<tuku.zu arḫuš tuku(.a)>

Marduk, great lord, on the servant who reverences you show mercy.

This confirms the conclusion of D.M. Matthews that the seal is unfinished, and most interestingly proves that in this case one craftsman cut both the art work and the inscription.

153 N 4185. **L** MB tablet, letter?

37 × 43. Composite.
A winged demon, with non-human head and legs, holds two animals upside down, and stands on or beside two animals, probably above a horizontal inscription line (there is room for another at top). Terminal volute tree; top and bottom lines. Fine workmanship, unfortunately preserved only in traces.

154 CBS 9838. **L** Nippur tablet, W side of Shatt.
M p. 178, O.2.27.24, Kaštiliaš, accession year.
UM 29-15-982. Tablet, apparently formed around a string. **L** Nippur, account.
M p. 300, V.2.10.213, Šagarakti-Šuriaš 12.

34 × 30(ext). Composite. *
The design is unclear and the three fragments cannot be joined (two have a lion each and the third has the rear half of the bird). The drawing brings them as close together as possible. Two rampant lions each apparently place a foot on an object, presumably an animal. It is impossible to say whether they face one another or a central figure. Two rhombs and a vertical line behind the lion on the left, the same probably on the right. The vertical lines presumably demarcate an inscription. At the top,

traces of a large bird. Top and bottom lines.

155   CBS 3053. **L** Nippur tablet, W side of Shatt.
     M p. 272, U.2.24.136, Nazi-Maruttaš 11.
     BE XIV 53, pl. XIV:42 (cap), p. 65 record of a debt of three fat young oxen.
   CBS 3339. **L** Nippur tablet, W side of Shatt.
     M p. 279, U.2.24.319, Nazi-Maruttaš 22.
     BE XIV 78, pl. XIV:41, p. 67 payment of an official's salary; index mentions Ninib-kin-pishu.
   CBS 3351. **L** Nippur tablet, W side of Shatt.
     M p. 280, U.2.24.347, Nazi-Maruttaš 24.
     BE XIV 85, pl. XIV:40, p. 67 payment of an official's salary, trans. p. 30 'Seal of Ninib-kin-pishu'.
   CBS 3361. **L** Nippur tablet, W side of Shatt.
     M p. 280, U.2.24.343, Nazi-Maruttaš 24.
     BE XIV 83, pl. XIV:43, 45; p. 67 payment of an official's salary.
   CBS 6643. **L** Nippur tablet.
     M p. 280, U.2.24.341, Nazi-Maruttaš 24?
     BE XIV 80a, p. 67 payment of an official's salary, index mentions Ninib-kin-pishu.
   CBS 9511? = Ni 1508. Cast of tablet.
     M p. 279, U.2.24.328, Nazi-Maruttaš 22.
     The cap and date are similar to the others but no part of the design can be seen on the cast.
   CBS 9528? Cast of a tablet presumably in Istanbul.
     The old Museum records give Nazi-Maruttaš yr. 24 but this is unknown to J.A. Brinkman ('only a partial date'). The cap is similar to the others and there seems to be a trace of the row of small animals and monsters.
   CBS 9543 = 9770; = Ni 329. Cast of tablet.
     M p. 279, U.2.24.322, Nazi-Maruttaš 22.
   CBS 9781. Cast of a tablet, presumably in Istanbul; J.A. Brinkman thinks it may be Ni 318. The old Museum record says it is Peters no. 702 and is dated Nazi-Maruttaš 22.
   CBS 9896? **L** Nippur tablet, W side of Shatt, administrative text.
     M p. 279, U.2.24.315, Nazi-Maruttaš 21.
     The cap is like the others and the traces could be of the same design.
   CBS 11460. **L** Nippur tablet, receipt.
     M p. 157, L.2.13.25, Kadašman-Turgu 4.

Much of surface flaked off.

UM 29-15-784? **L** Nippur tablet, account of rations expended; Dur-Enlil.

M p. 279, U.2.24.327, Nazi-Maruttaš 22.

Very faint impression, possibly the same cap and demon torso.

N 2683. **L** Tablet, account; Nazi-Maruttaš 2?

N 2982. **L** MB tablet, administrative.

J.A. Brinkman tells me that Ni 329 in Istanbul has the impression of a seal of Ninurta-ken-pišu which he noted as a 'large bird' - this would be a reasonable description of a fragment showing only the wings of the demon.

41(caps) × 40. Composite.

Inscription in horizontal lines, two above the scene and two below. A winged human headed demon raises a club in smiting posture and probably grasps the tail of a winged bull in front. The demon has a curly tail and animal legs: a claw is preserved on one foot but it is not certain whether it is an eagle or a lion foot - more probably the latter. The exact form of the demon's body is not well preserved on any of the tablets. The demon stands on two small animals and the winged bull stands on two small winged sphinxes: these four creatures form a frieze along the bottom. A horizontal line behind each sphinx's head is probably a baseline for the winged bull: this effect is given for the demon by the animals' horizontal backs, but this is impossible for the sphinxes because of their wings. The demon's wings are outstretched towards a tiny terminal volute tree which stands on a baseline. This baseline runs over the bull to form the topline of a three line vertical inscription in front of the bull, behind the demon and above the frieze of animals and sphinxes. Topline.

Cap: hbone-diamonds-hbone-twist-hbone-gran.

Inscription: only the vertical inscription has been read:

at-kal-ku	I trust in you,
a-a-ba-aš	May I not be put to shame,
arḫuš tuku.a	Show mercy.

156 CBS 13101. **L** Nippur tablet, W side of Shatt, Mound X.
M p. 270, U.2.24.96, Nazi-Maruttaš 8.
PBS II/2 24.

22(ext, cap) × 38.

A winged demon with a curly tail, in smiting attitude, grasps the tail of a winged bull. There is a two-line vertical inscription behind the demon and a small volute tree above the bull. The design is apparently an imitation of **155** but the style is coarser.

Cap: band with at least 3 rows of granulation - hbone with 3 rows - gran - plate.

157   CBS 13377. Tablet. **L** Nippur temple record.
M p. 196, P.2.6.124, Kudur-Enlil 3.

24?(ext) × 41? Composite. *

This design, which is exquisitely engraved, cannot unfortunately be reconstructed with assurance - the tablet is very small. Archer; a very faint and uncertain line running across the lower end of his bow, if real, would suggest a chariot scene. A beautifully modelled horse(?) with its legs in disarray is apparently in the upper field and transfixed by an arrow. In another rolling there is a trace of what could be this animal's head above the archer, and the width of the design is reconstructed on that basis. If a projection from the head is an ear, then the head is upside down, again suggesting death. Above the horse is the outline of an outstretched animal, apparently with the forepaws of a lion, with its hindlegs running into traces which I am unable to understand. Another rolling shows a horizontal line of inscription with a bird beneath it, and these traces might be a part of this bird; but a rolling which clearly shows a voluted projection just above the archer's outstretched hand is not easily compatible either with the lion or with the bird. It seems most probable that one of these relationships is due to an overrolling, but I cannot guess which one. The beauty and importance of this design is such that we may earnestly hope that a better impression will one day come to light in Jena or Istanbul.

158   CBS 3176. Apparently an unopened envelope.
L Nippur, W side of Shatt.
BE XIV p. 15 and pl. XV:48.6.
BE XV 48c, p. 60 official's salary; unnamed king yr. 15.
Porada 1952, no. 2.

26(ext, cap) × 48. Composite.

A centaur leaps over three small twisted trees towards an elaborate volute tree which rises from 'mountains'. A horned animal between centaur and tree. The centaur has the body and legs of a stallion and the tail of a scorpion. A scaled fish(?)-skin covers the upper animal body, and two short wings at the shoulder and four volutes at the tail may be intended to represent fins. A large wing projects horizontally from the rump. The human torso is aiming an arrow. There is a crook(?) across the waist and a row of small tassels hanging from each arm. A quiver containing tasselled(?) objects is hung across the shoulders. A crooked line hangs down to the animal body behind the waist; the bearded head is looking backwards. The minute engraving is of a quality that remains unsurpassed in Second Kassite.

Cap: Diamonds-hbone-twist-hbone-gran.

159 Jena, HS 132.
TuM NF V seal VI, pp. 11-14 legal document, receipt of sale price of a slave woman, Nazi-Maruttaš 23.

†

Winged griffin facing rosette and framed cross, trace of horn(?) below might belong to the monster's victim. It is uncertain whether the head and body of the monster visible on either side of the symbols belong to the same monster.

160 CBS 3187. **L** Nippur envelope, W side of Shatt.
BE XIV pl. XV:48.5.
BE XV 114, p. 63 receipt, unnamed king yr. 21.

39 × 31(ext). Composite. *

The impressions are overrolled in a complicated way and I have not been able to understand much more than can be seen in the BE XIV photograph. A large winged lion(?) is surrounded by various objects, perhaps a bird above and a horned animal in front. The objects underneath are especially enigmatic. Top and bottom lines. Overrolled traces of straight lines might be from an inscription?

161 CBS 3135. **L** Nippur envelope, W side of Shatt.
BE XIV pl. XV:48.8.

BE XV 65, p. 61 official's salary; unnamed king yr. 17.
Porada 1952, no. 3; *PC* no. 163.

18(ext, cap) × 47. Composite.
A winged bull(?) faces an elaborate volute tree. A bird sits on the tree and another flies towards it. At the top, an undulating tasselled object, with an infilling like 'mountain-scales', possibly representing rain coming from the mountains. Best minute engraving, like **158**.
Cap: ??-diamond-hbone?-twist-hbone-gran.

162 CBS 3009. **L** Nippur envelope, W side of Shatt.
  M p. 272, U.2.24.152, Nazi-Maruttaš 12.
  BE XIV 55, pl. XII:31, p. 65 official's salary.
  This is the only impression in which the baseline is visible: possibly the lower cap had been reattached slightly lower down.
  CBS 3273. **L** Nippur envelope, W side of Shatt.
  BE XIV pl. XV:48.10a.
  BE XV 8, p. 57-8 payment of an official's salary, unnamed king yr. 2.
  CBS 3275. **L** Nippur envelope, W side of Shatt, year 4.
  CBS 3453. **L** Nippur envelope, W side of Shatt.
  BE XIV pl. XV:48:10b.
  BE XV 14, p. 58 official's salary; unnamed king yr. 4.

  25(caps) × 34. Composite.
  Top and bottom lines. A winged lion, probably human-headed (it is uncertain whether the head is frontal or in profile), faces a volute tree, which interrupts a single horizontal inscription line above. Most details unclear.
  Cap: gran-hbone-diamond-hbone-gran-plate.

163 CBS 6636. **L** Nippur tablet.
  M p. 276, U.2.24.235, Nazi-Maruttaš 16.
  BE XIV 72 (not described p. 66).

  17(ext) × 35(ext).
  At least two horizontal inscription lines, the lower one interrupted by a rhomb. There is probably a cross beneath the rhomb. A large wing under the inscription.

164 CBS 3657. **L** Nippur tablet, W side of Shatt, temple archive.

M p. 268, U.2.24.41, Nazi-Maruttaš 4.

PBS II/2 20, pp. 65-68 with drawing and textual evidence for ploughing in a group of three.

PBS XIV pp. 298-9, no. 569.

CBS 4903. **L** Nippur, MB? tablet, list of grain assignments.

CBS 6886. **L** Nippur tablet.

M p. 267, U.2.24.28, Nazi-Maruttaš 3.

CBS 10238. **L** Nippur tablet.

M p. 270, U.2.24.89, Nazi-Maruttaš 8.

CBS 12901. **L** Nippur tablet, W side of Shatt.

M p. 269, U.2.24.62, Nazi-Maruttaš 5.

PBS II/2 22.

Good impression of the feet.

UM 29-15-548. **L** Nippur tablet, receipt for grain delivered; unnamed MB king yr. 9.

Clear impression of cap rosettes.

UM 29-16-156. **L** Nippur tablet, MB ledger, cereals.

N6310. MB tablet.

Jena, HS 134.

TuM NF V, seal VII, pp. 11-14 list of barley for workers, animals, etc., Nazi-Maruttaš 8.

Jena, HS 155.

TuM NF V, seal IX, pp. 11-14 list of persons, surely slaves; undated, surely Burnaburiaš II. On this, J.A. Brinkman tells me that the prosopography links up with HS 151 and HS 2068 (TuM NF V, nos. 65 and 66), both dated Burnaburiaš yr. 18, so the date, though surprising, seems good.

33(caps) × 40. Composite. (†)

The design is framed by four horizontal inscription lines, two above and two below (the top line is only visible on the Jena photographs). Two humped oxen draw an elaborate seeder plough, attended by three men, one behind the oxen grasping a stick, one behind the seeder, presumably feeding it, the third holding the plough handles. Cross and rhomb in upper field.

Cap: rosettes - hbone. It is not certain that the rosettes were metallic but it is unknown for the stone to be visible on both sides of a metal band (though cf. on Cyprus, Kenna 1971, no. 42). Owing to overrolling the cap is misunderstood in Clay 1912, p. 66.

Inscription:

. . . .	(So-and-so, son of So-and-so)
dumu.dumu ^{d}*nin-urta-na-di-in-aḫ-ḫe-e*	Grandson of Ninurta-nadin-aḫḫe,
ìr ^{d}**nin.šar**	Servant of Ninshar
ù ^{d}**un.gal.nibru**^{ki}	And Sharrat-Nippuri.

165 CBS 7738. **L** Nippur tablet, Kassite temple account.

16(ext) × 40(ext). Composite. *

There is a separation of 37 mm between two cap impressions, as shown in the drawing, but this could be due to overrolling. Exceptionally faint: traces cannot all be combined. If the larger height is true then the design was in two registers but there are no intelligible traces of the lower one.

Horizontal inscription, probably in two lines round the seal and another two short ones in the scene. Three(?) men guide a plough on a groundline in a manner similar to **164**, though in the opposite direction: the plough itself is not preserved. There seem to be two oxen with the head of one rising above that of the other. Object behind the ploughmen, possibly a rhomb. Bird(?) above the inscription, probably overrolled.

Cap: gran-diamonds-gran-plate.

166 Jena, HS 124.

TuM NF V, seal IIIb, pp. 11-14 small animal list, Kudur-Enlil 7. Same tablet as **208**.

†

Trace of two humans, one in a 'smiting' attitude. Comparison with **165** gives reason tentatively to reconstruct a ploughing scene.

167 CBS 19793. **L** Envelope fragment, Nippur, Mound X, temple library.

Radau, BE XVII/1 pp. 43-51, 68-9, 101-4, pls. I-II.

Oppenheim 1967, 116-7, no. 60.

Letter from Kalbu to the **guenna** (governor) of Nippur: he complains of his responsibilities in Mannu-gir-Adad in the face of encroachments by his enemies and a disastrous lack of water.

Note that 'the **guenna** of your father Nazi-Enlil' in Oppenheim's translation should be corrected to 'the **guenna**, your father Nazi-Enlil', thus avoiding the chronological difficulties involved in having a 'King Nazi-Enlil', otherwise unknown. I am indebted to J.A. Brinkman for explaining this to me.

27(ext) × 48. Composite.
The field is divided into two registers with a volute-tree spanning both. In the upper register it is flanked by rosettes and rampant animals and there is an inscription in four vertical lines. Unclear objects between tree and rosettes; rhomb(?) above one animal. In the lower register a small sphinx(?) and monkey(??) flank the tree; two large bulls rear over another tree, probably to be restored as the 'twisted' type.

168 CBS 11657. **L** Nippur tablet, contract.
M p. 292, V.2.10.52, Šagarakti-Šuriaš 3.
PBS II/2 50.

22(ext) × 37(ext).
Inscription in at least four vertical lines. Two rampant antithetic caprids with folded forelegs.

169 CBS 4906. **L** Nippur tablet, MB list of names.

15(ext) × 47(ext). Composite.
A pair of rampant animals with forelegs folded together, heads missing, rear over a small round tree; terminal palm tree with three large stems.

170 CBS 8706. **L** Nippur tablet, MB contract.

13(ext) × 53. Composite.
Inscription in five vertical lines. Two animals with missing heads rampant over a small tree with twisted trunk, flowers or rosettes on either side.

171 14 N 81. Sealing.
Gibson 1983, fig. 20; p. 181 Nippur, Area WC-1, level III, locus 31, small room in large building - room also contained tablet of Šagarakti-Šuriaš.

†

A rampant bull with folded forelegs faces a bird on top of a round tree. This impression will be fully published by R.L. Zettler, who explained to me the nature of the scene (*PC* pp. 65, 90 n. 13 (no. 169) in error).

172 14 N 117. Sealing.
Gibson 1983, fig. 21; p. 181 same provenance as **171**.

†

Two rampant animals flank a round tree with a human on the right. This impression will be fully published by R.L. Zettler.

173 CBS 3058. **L** Nippur tablet, W side of Shatt.
M p. 260, L.2.13.87, Kadašman-Turgu yr. 14.
BE XIV 108, trans. p. 14 Seal of Shigu-Gula, p. 69 receipt given for wool received from another.

40(ext) × 43(ext). Composite. *

An inscription in four or more vertical lines. A standing man with arms 11 faces a twisted tree with a bird perched on top; cross and flying bird above. Rosette beside the trunk. Topline, at least over inscription. The attachment of the signs at top right of inscription is uncertain.

Inscription:

^{d}[. . . . .] x **gal?** [(..   God[. . . . .] great [lord(?)],
s[a]g an.ki.a dingir š[à.lá.s]ù Chief of heaven and netherworld,
                                merciful god,
a.ra.zu.zu giš.tuku x x x x   Who hears prayer, ...,
x x (x) ì[r] ní.[tuku].zu   . . ., on the servant who reverences
                                       you

[arḫuš] tuku.a.a[b]   Show mercy.

174 UM 29-13-971. **L** Nippur tablet, receipt for 40 mana?
M p. 271, U.2.24.128, Nazi-Maruttaš 11.

27(ext) × 39(ext). Composite.

Inscription in at least four vertical lines. Standing man, bird on twisted tree before him, unintelligible traces between them.

Inscription: the second line gives epithets of a god: [...] **an.ki.a** "[...] of heaven and netherworld."

175 UM 29-16-129. **L** Nippur tablet, MB list of garments and descriptions, unnamed king yr. 4.
Seal of Luṣi-ana-nūr-Enlil (Brinkman).

29(ext) × 43. Composite.
Inscription in five vertical lines. A standing man with arms 11 faces an elaborate volute tree with birds perched on the branches; two rhombs behind him. Groundline. Perhaps same seal as **176**.

176 N 2727. **L** Tablet, account, garments.

24(ext) × 27(ext). Composite. *
I drew this impression in Philadelphia without knowledge of **175**, which has been lent to J.A. Brinkman in Chicago. It apparently shows a palm tree with volutes, which is otherwise unknown. It seems to me likely that it is in fact the same design as **175**, and that I misunderstood the birds' tails as palm branches. UM 29-16-129 is a tablet with one corner missing; N 2727 is a tablet corner. I predict, therefore, that they will be found to join when they are reunited. N 2727 adds to the description given for **175** some cuneiform signs below the last inscription line above the rhombs behind the man.

177 CBS 12933. **L** Nippur tablet, W side of Shatt.
M p. 271, U.2.24.107, Nazi-Maruttaš 10.
PBS II/2 25.

27(ext) × 40. Composite. *
Inscription in four vertical lines; the last two are truncated to make room for the branches of a large palm tree with a bird sitting on it. Rhomb(?) and locust(?) on either side of the branch ends. A man, seated(?) on a chair with a back(?) holds a flower(?); mace(?) at his waist. Reconstruction uncertain.

178 CBS 3341. Tablet.
M p. 290, V.2.10.8, Šagarakti-Šuriaš, accession year.
BE XIV 127, p. 71 hire of slaves.

15(ext) × 45(ext). Composite.

Inscription in at least three vertical lines. Person with long hair down back raises one hand and grasps a staff with the other. Winged(?) object in front, perhaps bird. Uncertain traces above, perhaps rhomb and cross. Excessively faint.

179 UM 29-16-362. **L** Nippur tablet, MB business.

17(ext, cap) × 40.

Inscription in five vertical lines. A large bird, with wings below its body; unidentifiable traces.

Cap: triangles - hbone (in three rows?) - gran - plate.

180 UM 29-13-915. **L** Nippur tablet, contract for metal.
M p. 199, P.2.6.181, Kudur-Enlil 8.

Unintelligible fragments of design; may have included inscription.

Cap: triangles-hbone-hbone. The herringbones seem to have been formed from short incisions into the backing plate rather than the normal filigree. Perhaps this was a cheaper equivalent - one might speculate that a less precious metal was used.

181 UM 29-13-477. **L** Nippur envelope, MB contract or letter.

Trace of cap only: triangles-hbone-hbone-gran.

182 CBS 8503. **L** Nippur.

Bulla in the form of a half cylinder. Three stringholes enter at one end (and perhaps a fourth from the flat side) and join to form one large hole at the other. There is a short text and at least four impressions of the seal on the curved surface, and an impression on each of the ends.

c. 14 × width 14(ext). Composite.

It seems most probable that this is a Kassite ring-stamp. I am indebted to Professor Porada and Professor Zettler for their opinions on it. Two rampant animals, at least one winged, flank a small twisted tree.

183 14 N 244.

This Second Kassite ring-stamp will be published by R.L. Zettler.

184 14 N 248.

This Second Kassite ring-stamp(?) will be published by R.L. Zettler.

185 B4579. Bulla with stringmarks.
PBS XIV p. 325, no. 744, calls it CBS 4519, and so does the old Museum record.

15 × width 18(ext). Composite.
Impression of ring stamp. Two small horned animals stand on the upper branches of a tree which is beneath unclear traces (rosette??); on either side a rosette and a smaller tree, bird on top of the one on the left at least.

186 13 N 518. About 17 impressions on a round plano-convex object: a circular mark on the flat side suggests that it was attached to the rim of a vessel, but the impressions were made both inside and outside this.
Nippur, Area WB locus 18.

15 × (width of oval engraved area) 22. Composite.
Drawn from cast kindly shown to me by McG. Gibson. Ring-stamp, eagle with spread wings above lamb; rosette. There is a thin border line below and probably also above.

187 CBS 9769. Cast of HS 738, tablet, still inside HS 2887, envelope.
M p. 158, L.2.13.57, Kadašman-Turgu 10.
Petschow 1974, no. 25.

24?(caps) × 15(ext). Composite.
It is unclear on the cast whether one or both caps are visible. Inscription, apparently in only one vertical line. Elaborate tree, coarsely drawn.
Cap: ??-twist-hbone-gran-plate.

188 CBS 3033. **L** Nippur tablet, W side of Shatt.
 M p. 237, Q.2.115.104, Kurigalzu 18.
 BE XIV 27, pl. XIV:44, pl. XV:3, p. 15 drawing, p. 63 record of
 an official's salary.
 CBS 3331. Nippur envelope, W side of Shatt.
 BE XIV pl. XV:11.
 BE XV 70, pl. III:6, p. 61 official's salary; unnamed king yr. 17.
 Weber 12; Beran 1957-8, no. 11; *PC* no. 195.

 31(caps) × 39. Composite.
 This design was presumably misunderstood by Clay to be two
 separate impressions, one, which he drew, with the tree, and the
 other, which he omitted, with the human and inscription. It is
 clear, however, that they do go together because the relative
 spacing is exactly the same on the two tablets.
 Seated figure with horned crown beneath an inscription in six
 vertical lines: the first line is longer than the others and two of
 them are wider to contain two rows of signs. Elaborate volute
 tree, running the whole height of the seal, faced by an animal on
 one side. Traces of a second animal could be the result of
 overrolling.

 Inscription:

^{d}šamaš(? ALAM?)-x x x (x)	Shamash(?)-........., (owner of seal)
gudu$_4$ ^{d}nuska	Gudu-priest of Nuska,
x x x	(priest/official)
[^{d}un].gal.nibru^{ki}	Of Sharrat-Nippuri,
ìr ^{d}ku-ri-gal-zu	Servant of Kurigalzu,
lugal kiši	King of the world.

189 CBS 3818? **L** Nippur, W side of Shatt, MB bulla.
 Bulla has curved outer surface bearing a short text and the
 impression; trace of a flat top; stringmarks within. This is the
 only bulla with this seal.
 CBS 7160. **L** Nippur tablet, names and assignments.
 CBS 7188. **L** Nippur tablet, business *aklu* document.
 M p. 196, P.2.6.128, Kudur-Enlil 3.
 PBS XIII 71, trans. p. 99 food receipt under the seal of Ninib-
 nadin-..., 'food for the expedition of Larsa'. J.A. Brinkman finds
 parts of the translation 'not very likely' and gives the name of
 the recipient as Lūṣi-an(a)-nūr-Adad.
 CBS 7243. **L** Nippur tablet, temple account.

M p. 195, P.2.6.101, Kudur-Enlil 3.

CBS 7255. **L** Nippur tablet, temple account.

M p. 194, P.2.6.60, Kudur-Enlil 2.

CBS 7257. **L** Nippur tablet, temple account.

M p. 194, P.2.6.73, Kudur-Enlil 2.

CBS 7260. **L** Nippur tablet, temple account.

M p. 196, P.2.6.126, Kudur-Enlil 3.

CBS 7262. **L** Nippur tablet.

Account dealing with flour and grain; Kudur-Enlil(?) yr. 3 - very tentative. (Brinkman).

CBS 7694. **L** Nippur tablet, business document.

CBS 7698. **L** Nippur tablet, Kassite business document.

The only tablet bearing this seal to have a trace of an envelope.

CBS 7700. **L** Nippur tablet, contract.

M p. 197, P.2.6.142, Kudur-Enlil 4.

CBS 7705. **L** Nippur tablet, business document.

M p. 137, J.2.22.17, Kadašman-Enlil 6.

CBS 7707. **L** Nippur tablet, business document.

M p. 195, P.2.6.80, Kudur-Enlil 2.

CBS 7712. **L** Nippur tablet, temple account.

M p. 194, P.2.6.61, Kudur-Enlil 2.

CBS 7714. **L** Nippur tablet, temple account.

M p. 196, P.2.6.129, Kudur-Enlil 3.

CBS 7721. **L** Nippur tablet, temple account.

N.B. *not* the same tablet as **M** p. 239, Q.2.115.151 (Kurigalzu).

CBS 7731. **L** Nippur tablet, business document.

M p. 199, P.2.6.193, Kudur-Enlil, possibly yr. 1.

CBS 7736. **L** Nippur tablet, temple account.

M p. 137, J.2.22.15, Kadašman-Enlil 6(+).

CBS 7740. **L** Nippur tablet, temple account.

M p. 138, J.2.22.28, Kadašman-Enlil 7.

CBS 7810. **L** Nippur tablet, list of food supplies.

M p. 195, P.2.6.87, Kudur-Enlil 2.

CBS 7868. **L** Nippur tablet, Kassite account.

CBS 8091. **L** Tablet, Abu Hatab, contract.

There is an old note with Arabic writing and a blob of sealing wax with string. Written on this note is '3 tablets said to be from Abu Hatab purchased 27th. Dec. 1895.' In a *different* hand is added '8089-91': in view of the seal impression on this tablet it seems likely that the second addition is in error.

M p. 136, J.2.22.2, Kadašman-Enlil yr. 1.

CBS 8112. **L** Nippur tablet, record of kinds of beer.

M p. 197, P.2.6.147, Kudur-Enlil 4.

CBS 8573. **L** Nippur tablet, MB business document.

CBS 8583. **L** Nippur tablet, contract.
M p. 195, P.2.6.94, Kudur-Enlil 3.

CBS 8587. **L** Nippur tablet, conveyance.
M p. 193, P.2.6.43, Kudur-Enlil yr. 1.

CBS 8594. **L** Nippur tablet, contract.
M p. 196, P.2.6.117, Kudur-Enlil 3.

CBS 8671. **L** Nippur tablet, security document.
M p. 196, P.2.6.130, Kudur-Enlil 3.

CBS 8674. **L** Nippur tablet, business document.
M p. 193, P.2.6.38, Kudur-Enlil yr. 1.
N.B. this is not the agate cameo, **M** p. 133.

CBS 8676. **L** Nippur tablet, business record.
M p. 194, P.2.6.54, Kudur-Enlil 2.

CBS 8682. **L** Nippur tablet, business record.
M p. 194, P.2.6.76, Kudur-Enlil 2.

CBS 8683. **L** Nippur tablet, business record.
M p. 139, J.2.22.47, Kadašman-Enlil.

CBS 8688. **L** Nippur tablet, contract.
M p. 138, J.2.22.23, Kadašman-Enlil 6.

CBS 8689. **L** Nippur tablet, temple record.
M p. 195, P.2.6.105, Kudur-Enlil 3.

CBS 8690. **L** Nippur tablet, temple record.
M p. 196, P.2.6.118, Kudur-Enlil 3.

CBS 8716. **L** Nippur tablet, temple record? contract?
M p. 195, P.2.6.82, Kudur-Enlil 2.

CBS 8717. **L** Nippur tablet, temple record.
M p. 192, P.2.6.9, Kudur-Enlil yr. 1.

CBS 8718. **L** Nippur tablet, temple record.
M p. 196, P.2.6.127, Kudur-Enlil 3.

CBS 8719. **L** Nippur tablet, temple record.
M p. 192, P.2.6.13, Kudur-Enlil yr. 1.

CBS 8721. **L** Nippur tablet, temple record.
M p. 194, P.2.6.68, Kudur-Enlil 2.

CBS 8735. **L** Nippur tablet, temple record.
M p. 196, P.2.6.109, Kudur-Enlil 3.

CBS 8741. **L** Nippur tablet, temple record.
M p. 193, P.2.6.27, Kudur-Enlil yr. 1.

CBS 8806. **L** Nippur tablet, temple record.
M p. 196, P.2.6.111, Kudur-Enlil 3.

CBS 8810. **L** Nippur tablet, temple record.
M p. 138, J.2.22.37, Kadašman-Enlil 7.

CBS 9960. **L** Nippur tablet, W side of Shatt.

M p. 192, P.2.6.18, Kudur-Enlil yr. 1.

CBS 12919. **L** Nippur tablet, W side of Shatt.

M p. 193, P.2.6.39, Kudur-Enlil yr. 1.

PBS II/2 45.

CBS 12921. **L** Nippur tablet, W side of Shatt.

M p. 138, J.2.22.30, Kadašman-Enlil 7.

PBS II/2 45.

CBS 13354. **L** Nippur tablet, contract.

M p. 138, J.2.22.32, Kadašman-Enlil 7.

CBS 13357. **L** Nippur tablet, temple record.

M p. 193, P.2.6.33, Kudur-Enlil yr. 1.

CBS 13359. **L** Nippur tablet, temple record.

M p. 194, P.2.6.66, Kudur-Enlil 2.

CBS 13360. **L** Nippur tablet, contract.

M p. 193, P.2.6.40, Kudur-Enlil yr. 1.

CBS 13362. **L** Nippur tablet, temple record.

CBS 13364. **L** Nippur tablet, temple record.

M p. 195, P.2.6.104, Kudur-Enlil 3.

CBS 13365. **L** Nippur tablet, temple contract.

M p. 196, P.2.6.120, Kudur-Enlil 3.

CBS 13367? **L** Nippur tablet, temple record.

M p. 196, P.2.6.124, Kudur-Enlil 3.

CBS 13371. **L** Nippur tablet, temple record.

M p. 196, P.2.6.113, Kudur-Enlil 3.

CBS 13373. **L** Nippur tablet, temple record.

M p. 193, P.2.6.44, Kudur-Enlil yr. 1.

CBS 13375. **L** Nippur tablet, temple record.

CBS 14197. **L** Nippur tablet, *aklu* food expenses.

M p. 197, P.2.6.134, Kudur-Enlil 3.

PBS XIII 74, p. 100 food expense by the hands of Uzipu.

CBS 15015. Tablet.

M p. 194, P.2.6.57, Kudur-Enlil 2.

CBS 15016. Tablet.

M p. 194, P.2.6.70, Kudur-Enlil 2.

CBS 15017. Tablet.

M p. 195, P.2.6.102, Kudur-Enlil 3.

CBS 15018. Tablet.

M p. 194, P.2.6.58, Kudur-Enlil 2.

CBS 15019. Tablet.

M p. 194, P.2.6.69, Kudur-Enlil 2.

CBS 15020. Tablet.

M p. 194, P.2.6.74, Kudur-Enlil 2.

CBS 15026. Tablet.

M p. 194, P.2.6.64, Kudur-Enlil 2.
CBS 15027. Tablet.
M p. 192, P.2.6.23, Kudur-Enlil yr. 1.
CBS 15028. Tablet.
M p. 194, P.2.6.75, Kudur-Enlil 2.
CBS 15029. Tablet.
M p. 194, P.2.6.49, Kudur-Enlil yr. 1.
CBS 15030. Tablet.
M p. 137, J.2.22.16, Kadašman-Enlil 6.
CBS 15038. Tablet.
M p. 193, P.2.6.29, Kudur-Enlil yr. 1.
CBS 15039. Tablet.
M p. 197, P.2.6.136, Kudur-Enlil 3.
UM 29-13-276? **L** Nippur tablet, ledger.
M p. 196, P.2.6.121, Kudur-Enlil 3.
UM 29-13-490. **L** Nippur tablet, account of grain and flour.
M p. 196, P.2.6.115, Kudur-Enlil 3.
UM 29-13-907. **L** Nippur tablet, MB economic.
UM 29-13-917. **L** Nippur tablet, account of expenditures.
M p. 196, P.2.6.108, Kudur-Enlil 3.
UM 29-15-726. **L** Nippur tablet, ledger; expenditures of barley for a man.
M p. 196, P.2.6.116, Kudur-Enlil 3.
UM 29-15-778. **L** Nippur tablet, receipt.
M p. 192, P.2.6.22, Kudur-Enlil yr. 1.
The computer printout gives 'seal of Enlil-nadin-ahe' for this tablet and for UM 29-15- 780, 947, 983; but in view of the known owner Ninurta-nadin-ahhe (CBS 7188, UM 29-16-83) I am inclined to regard this as a slip. I have not been able to check it.
UM 29-15-780. **L** Nippur tablet, account of expenditure; Babili.
M p. 192, P.2.6.5, Kudur-Enlil yr. 1.
UM 29-15-947. **L** Nippur tablet, ledger, expenditures.
M p. 193, P.2.6.34, Kudur-Enlil yr. 1.
UM 29-15-967. **L** Nippur tablet, ledger, rations.
M p. 195, P.2.6.93, Kudur-Enlil 2.
UM 29-15-968. **L** Nippur tablet, account of flour rations.
M p. 138, J.2.22.31, Kadašman-Enlil 7.
UM 29-15-980. **L** Nippur tablet, ledger, rations of flour and barley for Taribu.
M p. 197, P.2.6.145, Kudur-Enlil 4.
UM 29-15-983. **L** Nippur tablet, ledger, expenditures.
M p. 192, P.2.6.6, Kudur-Enlil yr. 1?

UM 29-15-984? **L** Nippur tablet, ledger.
M p. 197, P.2.6.140, yr. 3, perhaps of Kudur-Enlil.
UM 29-15-989. **L** Nippur tablet, ledger, expenditures.
M p. 193, P.2.6.32, Kudur-Enlil yr. 1.
UM 29-16-83? **L** Nippur tablet, ledger, rations.
M p. 192, P.2.6.16, Kudur-Enlil yr. 1.
Seal of Ninurta-nādin-aḫḫē (Brinkman).
UM 29-16-127. **L** Nippur tablet, receipt for rations in the 'hand of' Nahiranu.
M p. 193, P.2.6.48, Kudur-Enlil yr. 1.
UM 29-16-134. **L** Nippur tablet, receipt for rations.
M p. 194, P.2.6.65, Kudur-Enlil 2.
UM 29-16-154. **L** Nippur tablet, MB ledger; garments with description.
UM 29-16-158. **L** Nippur tablet, MB ledger, personal and month names and numbers preserved.
UM 29-16-305. **L** Nippur tablet, receipt for liquids.
M p. 195, P.2.6.85, Kudur-Enlil 2.
N 2023. **L** MB ledger.
N 2036. **L** MB ledger, cereal rations?
N 2208. **L** Tablet, expenditure of male sheep.
M p. 138, J.2.22.25, Kadašman-Enlil 6.
N 2240. **L** Tablet, ledger, expenditures.
M p. 193, P.2.6.46, Kudur-Enlil yr. 1.
N 2645. **L** Tablet, MB ledger, cereals (*qa*).
N 2889. **L** Tablet, ledger.
M p. 200, P.2.6.196, Kudur-Enlil.
N 6307. **L** Tablet, frag.
N 6308. **L** Tablet, adm.
M p. 194, P.2.6.50, Kudur-Enlil yr. 1.
Jena, HS 118.
TuM NF V, seal I, pp. 11-14 *aklu* text, Kudur-Enlil yr. 1.
Jena, HS 120.
TuM NF V, seal II, pp. 11-14 *aklu* text, Kudur-Enlil yr. 1.
Jena, HS 126.
TuM NF V, seal IV, pp. 11-14 large *aklu* text, distribution of flour and barley for offering, as animal feed and to persons, Kudur-Enlil yr. 2.
Jena, HS 127.
TuM NF V, seal I, pp. 11-14 *aklu* text, distribution of flour and barley, Kudur-Enlil yr. 1.

J.A. Brinkman tells me that Ni 7947, 7959, 8013, 8027 and 8375 in Istanbul all bear the 'seal of Ninurta-nadin-ahhe'.

34 × 39. Composite.

The design is laid out in two registers, staggered so that the lower figurative scene leads up to the upper one. There are six-line vertical inscriptions above and below, staggered by four lines with respect to each other. In the lower scene, a leading goddess in a flounced dress leads a bald man in a fringed robe with a smaller goddess in a flounced dress behind. A god in a flounced dress sits above on a panelled throne receiving the presentation. His head and hand are unclear, the best impression being TuM NF V pl. CXXII:2 which may conceivably show something above the hand. Despite the multiplicity of impressions no good evidence for the topmost part of the seal exists. Top and bottom lines.

Inscription:

^{d}en.líl. / al.ša$_6$	Enlil-alsha,
[n]u!-èš / [^{d}]en.líl	Prelate of Enlil,
gudu$_4$ / [^{d}]nin.líl$_{ki}$	Gudu-priest of Ninlil,
gá.dub.ba / nibru^{ki}	Governor of Nippur,
dumu ^{d}en-líl- / ki-di-ni	Son of Enlil-kidinni,
[l]ú?.mug? / ^{d}[n]in?.[tin].lu.ba	(Official) of Nintinluba(?).

190 CBS 6653. L Nippur envelope, unknown MB king yr. 7.
BE XIV pl. XII:34.

19(ext) × 50.

Rough surface, poorly preserved. Inscription in five vertical lines. The scene is in two registers, each showing an unusual volute tree flanked by rampant animals.

191 CBS 14407. Bulla fragment with stringmarks. L Nippur, Hill VIII.

10(ext) × 12(ext).

Two winged monsters with lion tails back to back, at least one of them human-headed.

192 12 N 353. Bulla with two facets and stringmark.
OIC 23 fig. 19:4a-b, p. 13 from Nippur, Area WA ash pit (level

IV C) under Kassite temple.

c. 13?(ext) × 23?(ext). Composite. †
The drawing is a simplification of the one given in OIC 23, based on my understanding of the photograph. From left, man? fighting lion, two dots; man with bent body (probably not sitting as he is facing the other way) under animal head?; two dots and linear object (fish??); horned animal menaced by griffin; scorpion(??).

193 12 N 790. Clay tag, stringmark?
OIC 23 fig. 21:3a-b, p. 14 from Area WA level IV B, locus 4 floor 14, outside Kassite temple (fig. 18).

14(ext) × 16?(ext). †
The drawing is a simplification of the one given in OIC 23 based on my understanding of the photograph. Interceding figure, perhaps facing a standard such as a winged disk on a pole; spear or tree behind; traces (of star?); topline.

194 CBS 7272. Tablet.
M p. 239, Q.2.115.157, Kurigalzu.
PBS VIII/2 no. 158, p. 216 contents destroyed.

24(ext) × 37?(ext). Composite.
The design is in two registers with a row of nude females above and of monkeys (or, conceivably, lions) below. The period of rotation is unknown. Crudely engraved.

195 B 14342. Seal, grey composition, broken.
PBS XIV p. 312 no. 634, Nippur 1894.

25(ext) × diam. 11.
Row of five men facing a sixth, topline; bottom missing.

196 B8919. Seal, grey composition.
PBS XIV p. 312 no. 633, Nippur.

28 × diam. 12.5.
Four human heads in panels, "grill-pattern" above.

197 UM 51-6-357. Cylindrical bulla fragment with stringmarks, sealed on curved surface and ends.
Nippur, 2D 168 from TB 75D.
Nippur I pl. 120:6, p. 62 'OB' context, room near street corner (pl. 64).

25 × 37?
Crossed stags, three human heads at right angles, hatched panel, top and bottom lines. Not a stamp seal impression!

198 14 N 6. Seal.
Gibson 1983, fig. 14; Nippur, Area WC-1 level III locus 7, clay fill.

†
Two bulls with their bodies crossed at the shoulder; double grill pattern, resembling two-line inscription. This seal will be fully published by R.L. Zettler.

199 CBS 14279. Irregular bulla with cloth(?) impression.
PBS XIV p. 282 no. 498, Nippur.

26(ext) × 20(ext).
Two registers separated by a double line. Above, an animal at right angles. Below, schematised running spirals. Traces of a 'bouquet-tree' in upper register, uncertain whether it runs further down. Top and bottom lines. Completely misunderstood by Legrain.

200 3 N 144. Seal, white composition with blue surface.
Nippur I pl. 113:3, from TA X 1, p. 62 'Old Babylonian'.

21 × diam. 9. †
Two stags with their bodies at right angles; top and bottom lines.

201 13 N 488. Seal.
Gibson 1978, pp. 119-120, fig. 24: from Nippur, Area WC-1, on low floors in large Kassite house. The seal will be fully published by R.L. Zettler. Gibson 1983, 180 n. 16: in the blocking of the door between loci 6 and 12 connected with deliberate fill preparatory to laying Floor 2.

30 × diam. 12.

Drawn from impression shown to me by McG. Gibson. Stag with its body at right angles; three 'winged disks'. Top and bottom lines.

202 B6191. Seal, light brown composition. **L** Nippur.
PBS XIV p. 312 no. 636.

30 × diam. 14.

Three fish, three 'winged disks'(?). Top and bottom lines.

203 UM 51-6-354. Jar? sealing with stringmarks. **L** Nippur, no locality.

20(ext) × 22 (ext).

Horizontal row of fish, lattices above and below.

204 B 14321. Seal, green glazed composition.
PBS XIV p. 312 no. 632, Nippur 1894, hill X, grave 53.

46 × diam. 13.5.

Two men with extended arms, three birds. Top and bottom lines.

205 UM 53-11-366. Jar sealing?, stringmarks.
Nippur, 3D 52 from TA VII.
Nippur I, pl. 120:17, p. 68 Kassite level.

19(ext) × 32(ext).

I do not understand this crude, fragmentary and schematic design - perhaps an animal at right angles in the middle? Possibly overrolled.

206 B 3793. Seal, grey composition. **L** Nippur, "place of discovery [i.e. within Nippur] not reported to H.V.H[ilprecht]".
PBS XIV p. 311 no. 631.

24.5 × diam. 12.

Man facing seated man, tree, two circled dots. Top and bottom lines. Distinctive stylisation.

207 N 2101. Irregular bulla.

19(ext) × 26(ext).
A twisted tree on a hill, flanked by a rampant horned animal and a lion(?).

208 Jena, HS 124.
TuM NF V, seal IIIa, pp. 11-14 small animal list, Kudur-Enlil 7.
Same tablet as **166**.

†

Only the lower edge of the scene is preserved. The style is simple utilising large drillings. A squatting person or monkey on a low platform faces a seated person. Two hatched strips flank a large round object.

209 UM 29-13-984. **L** Nippur tablet, MB contract.

24(ext) × 38(ext). Composite. *
At top, a herringbone band beneath perhaps a horizontal line of inscription. Below, two men, kneeling or sitting, raise their hands over something unintelligible between them, two or more small men behind them.

210 N 2644. Tablet, sale, unnamed king yr. 4.
Dr. Ran Zadok kindly drew this impression to my attention; he said the tablet is early first millennium.

19(ext) × 41(ext). Composite.
A bird-footed demon with a tail stands on two animals and probably holds two other animals upside down. Two animals or monkeys flank an upright object, perhaps a palm tree.

BIBLIOGRAPHY

List of Abbreviations used in the text

Adana	Tunca 1977
Aleppo	Hammade 1987
Ash	Buchanan 1966
Ash.supp.	Moorey-Gurney 1978
BE XIV	Clay 1906
BE XV	Clay 1906
BE XVII/1	Radau 1908
Birmingham	Lambert 1966
BM	(British Museum)
BM II	Collon 1982b
BM III	Collon 1986a
BN	Delaporte 1910
Brett	von der Osten 1936
Brussels	Speleers 1917, 1943
CANES	Porada 1948
CCT VI	Garelli and Collon 1975
Choga Zanbil	Porada 1970
Collon AOAT	Collon 1975
Collon BAR	Collon 1982a
Copenhagen	Ravn 1960
de Clercq	de Clercq 1888
Enkomi	Porada 1971a
Failaka	Kjaerum 1983
Fakhariyah	Kantor 1958
FI	Collon 1987
Geneva	Vollenweider 1967
12 Glyptik	Moorgat 1944
13 Glyptik	Moortgat 1942
14 Glyptik	Beran 1957
Guimet	Delaporte 1909
HSS XIV	Lacheman 1950
IM	(Iraq Museum)
Louvre A	Delaporte 1923
Louvre D	Delaporte 1920
Louvre S	Delaporte 1920
M	Brinkman 1976
Marcopoli	Teissier 1984
Marlik	Negahban 1977

BIBLIOGRAPHY

Mohammed Arab	Collon 1988
Moore	Eisen 1940
Newell	von der Osten 1934
Nippur I	McCown and Haines 1967
Nuzi	Porada 1947
OIC 23	Gibson 1978
Palestine	Parker 1949
PBS II/2	Clay 1912
PBS VIII/2	Chiera 1922
PBS XIII	Legrain 1922
PBS XIV	Legrain 1925
PC	Matthews 1990
Peiser	Peiser 1905
Rimah	Parker 1977
RS	Schaeffer-Forrer 1983
Southesk	Carnegie 1908
Subeidi	Boehmer 1981
Surkh Dum	Williams-Forte 1981
Susa	Amiet 1972
Thebes	Porada 1981/2
TuM NF V	Bernhardt 1976
Turin	Bergamini 1987
UET VII	Gurney 1974, pl. 79
UEX	Legrain 1951
VR	Moortgat 1940
Ward	Ward 1910
Weber	Weber 1920
Wien-Graz	Bleibtreu 1981

List of Abbreviations used in the Bibliography.

AfO	Archiv für Orientforschung.
BaM	Baghdader Mitteilungen.
Bib.Mes.21	Kelly-Buccelati, M. (ed) 1986. Insight through images, Studies in honor of Edith Porada. *Bibliotheca Mesopotamica* 21. Malibu, Undena.
JNES	Journal of Near Eastern Studies.
MDAI	Mémoires de la Délégation Archéologique en Iran.
Moortgat Festschrift.	Bittel, K. et al. (ed) 1964. *Vorderasiatische Archäologie ... Anton Moortgat.* Berlin, Mann.
NABU	Nouvelles Assyriologiques Brèves et Utilitaires.
OIP	Oriental Institute Publications, Chicago.
RA	Revue d'Assyriologie et d'archéologie orientale.

List of Abbreviations used in the Bibliography.

UF	Ugarit Forschungen.
WO	Die Welt des Orients.
ZA	Zeitschrift für Assyriologie und vorderasiatische Archäologie.

Mohammed Zeki Abdul Kerim 1987. Excavations at Tell Sa'ud, **in** *Researches on the Antiquities of Saddam Dam basin salvage and other researches*, Baghdad, State Organisation of Antiquities and Heritage, pp. 125-128 (Arabic section).

Amiet, P.   1972. Glyptique Susienne. *MDAI* 43. 2 vols.
                 1973. Bas-reliefs imaginaires de l'ancien orient d'après les cachets et les sceaux-cylindres, Hotel de la Monnaie, Juin-Octobre 1973. Paris, Imprimerie Nationale.
                 1980 Les Sceaux. *Assur* 3/1, 55-63.
                 1986. Kassites ou Elamites? *Bib.Mes. 21*, 1-6.

Baqir, T.   1945. Iraq Government excavations at 'Aqar Quf, second interim report 1943-1944. *Iraq*, supplement.
                 1946. Iraq Government excavations at 'Aqar Quf, third interim report 1944-1945. *Iraq* 8, 73-93.

Basmachi, F.   1976. Treasures of the Iraq Museum. Baghdad, Ministry of Information, Directorate General of Antiquities.

Beck, P.   1967 (May). Problems in the glyptic art of Palestine. PhD Columbia University (*Dissertations Abstracts International* 31/06-A p. 2823; order no. 70-23424).

Beran, T.   1957. Assyrische Glyptik des 14. Jahrhunderts. *ZA* 52 (NF 18), 141-215.
                 1957-8. Die babylonische Glyptik der Kassitenzeit. *AfO* 18, 255-278.

Bergamini, G.   1987. Sigilli a cilindro. *Catalogo del Museo Egizio di*

143

Torino, Serie Seconda - collezione V. Torino, Istituto Editoriale Cisalpino - La Goliardica.

Bernhardt, T.   1976.   Sozialökonomische Texte und Rechtsurkunden aus Nippur zur Kassitenzeit. *Texte und Materialen der Frau Professor Hilprecht-Sammlung vorderasiatischer Altertümer im Eigentum der Friedrich-Schiller-Universität Jena*, NF V. Berlin, Akademie Verlag.

Beyer, D.   1980.   Notes préliminaires de sceaux de Meskéné, **in** J.C. Margueron (ed), *Le Moyen Euphrate*, Leiden, E.H.Brill, pp. 265-283.

1982.   Du moyen-Euphrate au Luristan: bagues-cachets de la fin du deuxième millénaire. *Mari, Annales de Recherches Interdisciplinaires* 1, Paris, Editions Recherche sur les Civilisations, pp. 169-189, pls. 7,8.

Bleibtreu, E.   1981.   Rollsiegel aus dem vorderen Orient (Wien und Graz). Sonderausstellung der Ägyptisch-Orientalischen Sammlung im Münzkabinett des Kunsthistorischen Museums in Wien. Wien, Verlag für vorderasiatische Archäologie.

Boehmer, R.M.   1981.   Glyptik der späten Kassiten-Zeit aus dem nordöstlichen Babylonien. *BaM* 12, 71-81.

Brinkman, J.A.   1976.   Materials and Studies for Kassite History, I. Chicago, Oriental Institute.

Buchanan, B.   1966.   *Catalogue of ancient Near Eastern seals in the Ashmolean Museum*, I: Cylinder seals. Oxford, University Press.

Carnegie, Lady Helena   1908.   Catalogue of the collection of antique gems formed by James, Ninth earl of Southesk. London.

Chiera, E.   1922.   Old Babylonian contracts. *University of Pennsylvania, the University Museum, Publications of the Babylonian Section* VIII/2.

Clay, A.T. 1906. Documents from the temple archives of Nippur, dated in the reigns of Cassite rulers. *The Babylonian Expedition of the University of Pennsylvania, series A: cuneiform texts* XIV (complete dates) and XV (incomplete dates). Philadelphia, Department of Archaeology, University of Pennsylvania.

1912. Documents from the temple archives of Nippur dated in the reigns of Cassite rulers. *University of Pennsylvania, University Museum, Publications of the Babylonian Section* II part 2.

Collon, D. 1975. The seal impressions of Tell Atchana/Alalakh. *Alter Orient und Altes Testament* 27.

1982a. The Alalakh cylinder seals. (*BAR International Series* 132). Oxford, British Archaeological Reports.

1982b. *Catalogue of the Western Asiatic seals in the British Museum*: Cylinder seals II. Akkadian - post Akkadian - Ur III periods. London, British Museum Publications.

1986. *Catalogue of the western Asiatic seals in the British Museum*: Cylinder seals III. Isin-Larsa and Old Babylonian periods. London, British Museum Publications.

1987. First Impressions: cylinder seals in the ancient Near East. London, British Museum Publications.

1988. Some cylinder seals from Tell Mohammed Arab. *Iraq* 50, 59-77.

Contenau, G. 1926. Les tablettes de Kerkouk et les origines de la civilisation assyrienne. *Babyloniaca* IX, fasc. 2-4. Paris, Geuthner.

de Clercq, L. 1888. *Collection de Clercq, catalogue méthodique et raisonné. Antiquités Assyriennes.* Vol. I. Cylindres Orientaux. Paris, Leroux.

Delaporte, L. 1909. Catalogue du musée Guimet, cylindres orientaux. *Annales du musée Guimet* 33.

1910. Catalogue des cylindres orientaux et des cachets assyro-babyloniens, perses et syro-cappadociens de la Bibliothèque Nationale. 2 vols. Paris, Leroux.

1920,1923. *Musée du Louvre, catalogue des cylindres orientaux, cachets et pierres gravées du style oriental.*
Vol. I. Fouilles et Missions (1920).
Vol. II. Acquisitions (1923).
Paris, Librairie Hachette.

Paris, Nouveau Drouot, 30 Mars 1981. Bronzes et terres cuites du Luristan et de la Caspienne, Glyptique.

Eisen, G.A. 1940. Ancient oriental cylinder and other seals with a description of the collection of Mrs. William H. Moore (*OIP* 47). Chicago, University Press.

Frankfort, H. 1939. Cylinder Seals. London, Methuen.

Garelli, P. and Collon, D. 1975. *Cuneiform texts from Cappadocian Tablets in the British Museum* VI. London, British Museum Publications.

Gerardi, P. 1984. A bibliography of the tablet collections of the University Museum. *Occasional Publications of the Babylonian Fund* 8. Philadelphia, University Museum.

Gibson, McG. 1975. The eleventh and twelfth seasons at Nippur. *Sumer* 31, 33-39.
1978. Excavations at Nippur, Twelfth Season. *Oriental Institute Communications* 23. Chicago, Oriental Institute.
1983. The southern corner of Nippur: excavations during the 14th. and 15th. seasons. *Sumer* 39, 170-190.

Gurney, O.R. 1974. Middle Babylonian legal documents and other texts. *Ur Excavations Texts* VII. London, British Museum Publications.
1983. The Middle Babylonian legal and economic texts from Ur. British School of Archaeology in Iraq.

Hammade, H. 1987. Cylinder seals from the collections of the

Aleppo Museum, Syrian Arab Republic. *BAR International Series* 335. Oxford, British Archaeological Reports.

Kantor, H.J. 1958. The glyptic, in C.W. McEwan et al. *Soundings at Tell Fakhariyah* (*OIP* 79), Chicago, University Press, pp. 69-85.

Kenna, V.E.G. 1971. Catalogue of the Cypriote seals of the Bronze Age in the British Museum. *Corpus of Cypriote Antiquities* 3. *Studies in Mediterranean Archaeology* XX:3. Gothenburg, Paul Åström.

King, L.W. 1912. Babylonian boundary-stones and memorial-tablets in the British Museum. 2 vols. London, Trustees of the British Museum.

Kjaerum, P. 1983. *Failaka/Dilmun, the second millennium settlements*, 1:1. The stamp and cylinder seals. *Jutland Archaeological Society Publications* XVII:1.

Lacheman, E.R. 1950. *Excavations at Nuzi, V: Miscellaneous texts from Nuzi II*. The palace and temple archives. *Harvard Semitic Series* XIV. Cambridge, Mass., Harvard University Press.

Lambert, W.G. 1966. Ancient Near Eastern Seals in Birmingham collections. *Iraq* 28, 64-83.

1970. Objects inscribed and uninscribed. *AfO* 23, 46-51.

1975. Review of Limet 1971. *Bibliotheca Orientalis* 32, 219-223.

1987. Gilgamesh in literature and art: the second and first millennia, in A.E. Farkas et al. (eds) *Monsters and Demons in the ancient and mediaevel worlds, papers presented in honor of Edith Porada*, Mainz, Philipp von Zabern, pp. 37-52.

Legrain, L. 1922. Historical fragments. *University of Pennsylvania, the University Museum, Publications of the Babylonian Section* XIII.

147

1925. The culture of the Babylonians from their seals in the collections of the museum. *University of Pennsylvania, the University Museum, Publications of the Babylonian Section* XIV. 2 vols. Philadelphia, University Museum.

1951. *Ur Excavations* X. Seal Cylinders. Publications of the joint expedition of the British Museum and of the University Museum, University of Pennsylvania, Philadelphia to Mesopotamia.

Limet, H. 1971. Les légendes des sceaux cassites. *Académie royale de Belgique, classe des lettres et des sciences morales at politiques, Mémoires, collection in-8o*, LX fasc. 2. Bruxelles.

McCown, D.E. and Haines, R.C. 1967. *Nippur* I. Temple of Enlil, Scribal Quarter, and Soundings (*OIP* 78). Chicago, University Press.

Mallowan, M.E.L. 1966. Nimrud and its Remains (2 vols and plans). London, Collins.

Matthews, D.M. 1988. Principles of composition in Near Eastern glyptic of the later second millennium B.C. University of Cambridge, unpublished PhD thesis.

1990. Principles of composition in Near Eastern glyptic of the later second millennium B.C. *Orbis Biblicus et Orientalis, series archaeologica* 8, Freiburg Schweiz und Göttingen.

forthcoming. Middle Assyrian glyptic from Tell Billa.

Matthews, D.M. and Brinkman, J.A. forthcoming. A Grandson of Kurigalzu. *NABU.*

Mayer-Opificius, R. 1985. Review of Schaeffer-Forrer 1983. *UF* 17, 415-420.

Maxwell-Hyslop, K.R. 1971. Western Asiatic Jewellery, c. 3000-612 B.C. London, Methuen.

Mazzoni, S. 1986. Continuity and development in the Syrian and Cypriote Common glyptic styles. *Bib.Mes. 21,*

171-182.

Meissner, B.   1934.   Die Babylonischen Kleinplastiken. *Texte und Materialen der Frau Professor Hilprecht Collection of Babylonian Antiquities im Eigentum der Universität Jena* IV. Leipzig, J.C. Hinrichs.

Ménant, J.   1883.   Les pierres gravées de la Haute-Asie. Recherches sur la glyptique orientale I: cylindres de la Chaldée. Paris, Maisonneuve.

Moorey, P.R.S.   1985.   Materials and manufacture in ancient Mesopotamia: the evidence of archaeology and art. Metals and metalwork, glazed materials and glass. *BAR International series* 237. Oxford, British Archaeological Reports.

Moorey, P.R.S. and Gurney, O.R. 1978. Ancient Near Eastern Seals acquired by the Ashmolean Museum, 1963-1973. *Iraq* 40, 41-60.

Moortgat, A.   1940.   Vorderasiatische Rollsiegel. Berlin, Mann.
                   1942.   Assyrische Glyptik des 13 Jahrhunderts. *ZA* 47 (NF 13), 50-88.
                   1944.   Assyrische Glyptik des 12 Jahrhunderts. *ZA* 48 (NF 14), 23-44.
                   1970.   Review of Vollenweider 1967. *AfO* 23, 101-3.

Moortgat-Correns, U. 1964. Beiträge zur mittelassyrischen Glyptik, **in** *Moortgat Festschrift*, 165-177.
                   1969.   Ein mittelelamisches Rollsiegel. *ZA* 59, 295-298.

Negahban, E.O.   1977.   The Seals of Marlik Tepe. *JNES* 36, 81-102.

Nissen, H.J.   1967.   Aus dem Geschäftsleben assyrischer Kaufleute im 14 Jhdt. v. Chr., **in** *Heidelberger Studien zum alten Orient: Adam Falkenstein*, Wiesbaden, Harrassowitz, pp. 111-120.

Oates. D.   1966.   The excavations at Tell al Rimah, 1965. *Iraq* 28, 122-139.

BIBLIOGRAPHY

Oelsner, J.   1980.   Zur Siegelung mittelbabylonischer Rechtsurkunden. *Rocznik Orientalistyczny* 41, 89-95.

Offner, G.   1950.   Note d'archéologie sur deux empreintes inédites de Qatna. *RA* 44, 144-6.

Opificius, R.   1969.   Syrische Glyptik der zweiten Hälfte des zweiten Jahrtausends. *UF* 1, 95-110.

Oppenheim, A.L. 1967.   Letters from Mesopotamia. Chicago, University Press.

von der Osten, H.H. 1934.   Ancient Oriental Seals in the Collection of Mr. Edward T. Newell (*OIP* 22). Chicago, University Press.
          1936.   Ancient Oriental Seals in the Collection of Mrs. Agnes Baldwin Brett (*OIP* 37). Chicago, University Press.

Parker, B.   1949.   Cylinder seals from Palestine. *Iraq* 11, 1-43.
          1955.   Excavations at Nimrud, 1949-1953. Seals and Seal impressions. *Iraq* 17, 93-125.
          1962.   Seals and Seal impressions from the Nimrud Excavations, 1955-1958. *Iraq* 24, 26-40.
          1975.   Cylinder seals from Tell al Rimah. *Iraq* 37, 21-38.
          1977.   Middle Assyrian seal impressions from Tell al Rimah. *Iraq* 39, 257-68.

Peiser, F.E.   1905.   Urkunden aus der Zeit der dritten babylonische Dynastie, in Urschrift, Umschrift und Übersetzung. Berlin, Wolf Peiser.

Petschow, H.P.H. 1974.   Mittelbabylonische Rechts- und Wirtschaftsurkunden der Hilprecht-Sammlung, Jena. *Abhandlungen der Sächsischen Akademie der Wissenschaften zu Leipzig, Philologisch-Historische Klasse* 64/4. Berlin, Akademie Verlag.

Pini, I.   1983.   Mitanni-Rollsiegel des 'Common Style' aus Griechenland. *Praehistorische Zeitschrift* 58,

114-126.

Porada, E.   1947.   Seal impressions of Nuzi. *Annual of the American Schools of Oriental Research* 24 for 1944-5.

1948.   The Collection of the Pierpont Morgan Library. *Corpus of Ancient Near Eastern Seals in North American Collections* I. The Bollingen Series XIV. 2 vols. Washington, The Bollingen Foundation.

1952.   On the problem of Kassite glyptic art, **in** *Archaeologia Orientalia in memoriam Ernst Herzfeld*, Locust Valley, J.J.Augustin, pp. 179-188.

1970.   Tchoga Zanbil IV. La Glyptique. *MDAI* 42.

1971.   Appendix 1: Seals, **in** P. Dikaios, *Enkomi Excavations 1948-1958*, vol. IIIa, Mainz, Philipp von Zabern, pp. 783-810.

1972.   Problems in Iranian iconography, **in** *The memorial volume of the Vth. international congress of Iranian art and archaeology, Tehran - Isfahan - Shiraz, 11th. - 18th, April 1968* I, Tehran, Ministry of Culture and Arts, pp. 163-182.

1981/2.   The cylinder seals found at Thebes in Boeotia. *AfO* 28, 1-70.

1986.   Le cylindre élamite du *British Museum* no. 134766, **in** L. de Meyer, H. Gasche, F. Vallat (eds) *Fragmenta Historiae Elamicae, mélanges offerts à M.J. Steve*, Paris, Editions Recherche sur les Civilisations, pp. 181-185.

Radau, H.   1908.   Letters to Cassite kings from the temple archives of Nippur. *The Babylonian Expedition of the University of Pennsylvania, series A: Cuneiform Texts* XVII part 1. Philadelphia, Department of Archaeology, University of Pennsylvania.

Ravn, O.E.   1960.   A catalogue of the oriental cylinder seals and seal impressions in the Danish National Museum. *Nationalmuseets Skrifter, Arkaeologisk-Historisk Raekke* VIII.

Copenhagen, Nationalmuseet.

Reiner, E. 1970. Légendes des cylindres, **in** Porada 1970, 133-137.

Röllig, W. 1980. Notizen zur Praxis der Siegelung in mittelassyrischer Zeit. *WO* 11, 111-116.

Saporetti, C. 1979. Gli eponimi medio-assiri. *Bibliotheca Mesopotamica* 9. Malibu, Undena.

Schaeffer-Forrer, C.F.A. 1983. Corpus I des cylindres-sceaux de Ras Shamra - Ugarit et d'Enkomi - Alasia. Paris, Editions Recherche sur les civilisations.

Seidl, U. 1968. Die babylonischen Kudurru-Reliefs. *BaM* 4, 1-220; now (1989) republished as *Orbis Biblicus et Orientalis* 87, Freiburg Schweiz, Universitätsverlag, und Göttingen, Vandenhoeck & Rupprecht.
1985. Review of Schaeffer-Forrer 1983. *ZA* 75, 310-313.

Smith, W.S. 1965. Interconnections in the Ancient Near East. New Haven and London, Yale University Press.

Speleers, L. 1917. Catalogue des intailles et empreintes orientales des musées royaux du Cinquantenaire. Bruxelles, Vromant.
1943. Catalogue des intailles et empreintes orientales des musées royaux d'art et d'histoire, supplément. Bruxelles, Vromant.

Stein, D.L. 1987. Seal impressions on texts from Arrapḫa and Nuzi in the Yale Babylonian Collection, **in** D.I. Owen and M.A. Morrison (eds) *Studies on the civilisation and culture of Nuzi and the Hurrians 2: General Studies and Excavations at Nuzi 9/1*, Winona Lake, Indiana, Eisenbrauns, pp. 225-320.
1989. A reappraisal of the "Sauštatar Letter" from Nuzi. *ZA* 79, 36-60.

Teissier, B.   1984.   Ancient Near Eastern cylinders from the
                            Marcopoli Collection. Los Angeles, University
                            of California Press.

Tomabechi, Y.   1983.   Wall paintings from Dur Kurigalzu. *JNES* 42,
                            123-131.

Trokay, M.   1981.   Glyptique cassite tardive ou postcassite?
                            Akkadica 21, 14-47.

Tunca, Ö.   1979.   Catalogue des sceaux-cylindres du Musée
                            Régional d'Adana. *Syro-Mesopotamian Studies*
                            3/1.

Van Buren, E.D. 1954a.   The esoteric significance of Kassite glyptic art.
                            Orientalia NS 23, 1-39.
                    1954b. Seals of the second half of the Layard
                            Collection. *Orientalia* NS 23, 97-113.

Vollenweider, M.-L. 1967. Musée d'Art et d'Histoire de Genève,
                            Catalogue raisonné des sceaux-cylindres et
                            intailles. 2 vols. Genève, Musée d'Art et
                            d'Histoire.

Ward, W.H.   1910.   The seal cylinders of Western Asia. Washington,
                            Carnegie Institution.

Weber, O.   1920.   Altorientalische Siegelbilder. *Der Alte Orient*
                            17/18. Leipzig, J.C.Hinrichs.

Williams-Forte, E.W. 1981. Cylinder seals, in O.W. Muscarella, *Surkh
                            Dum at the Metropolitan Museum of Art: a
                            mini-report*, Journal of Field Archaeology 8,
                            327-359.

Woolley, C.L.   1939.   The ziggurrat and its surroundings. *Ur
                            Excavations* V.

Yadin, Y. et al. 1961.   Hazor III/IV, Plates. Jerusalem, Hebrew
                            University.

1. Seal of Ili-rabi or Ekur-[ ]

2.

3. Nippur I pl. 121:3

4.

5. Nippur I pl. 120:18

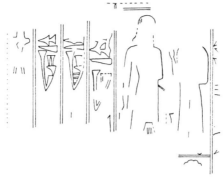

6.

7. Nippur I pl. 120:15

8.

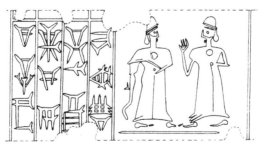

9. PBS XIV 566 (jasper) **not from Nippur**

10. OIC 23 fig. 92:2

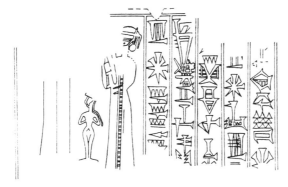

11. PBS XIV 542

12. PBS XIV 543

13. Seal of Taribatum

14.

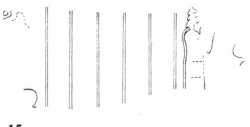

15.

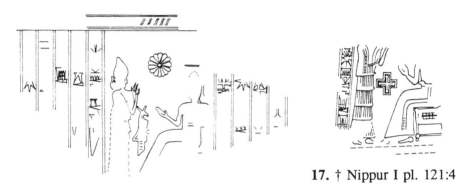

16. PBS XIV 552

17. † Nippur I pl. 121:4

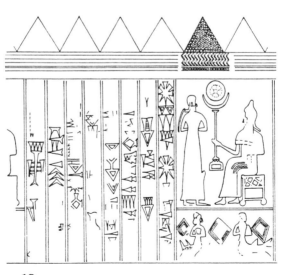

18.

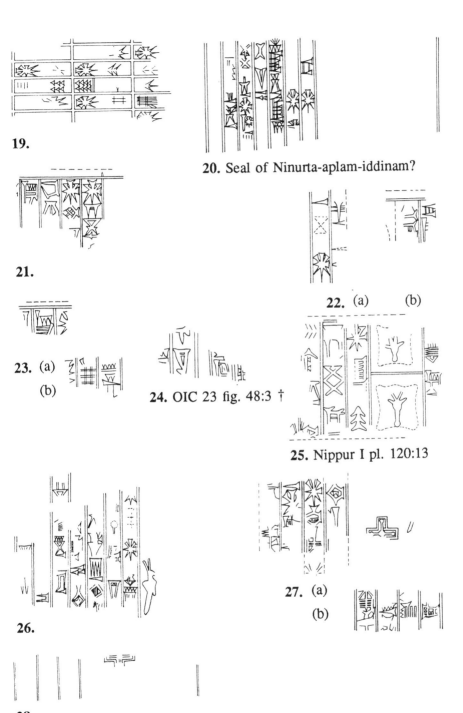

19.

20. Seal of Ninurta-aplam-iddinam?

21.

22. (a)   (b)

23. (a)
(b)

24. OIC 23 fig. 48:3 †

25. Nippur I pl. 120:13

26.

27. (a)
(b)

28.

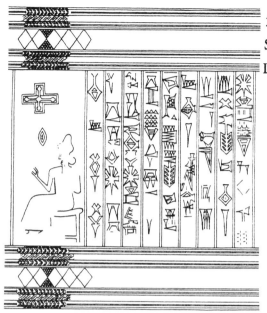

29. PBS XIV 541, 564, 565

Seal of

Luṣa-ana-nur-Ninkarrak(?)

30.

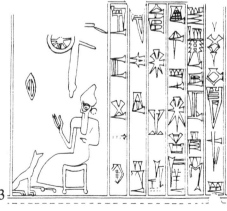

31. PBS XIV 540, 563

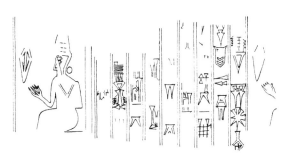

32.

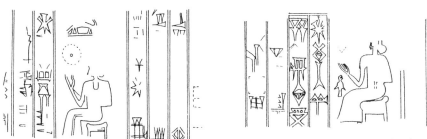

33.

34. Seal of Anu/Ilu-mushtal

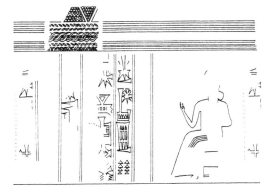

35. Seal of Enlil-shemi?

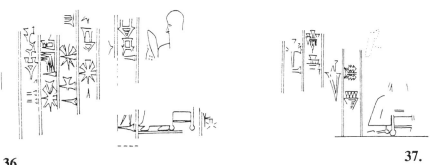

36.

37.

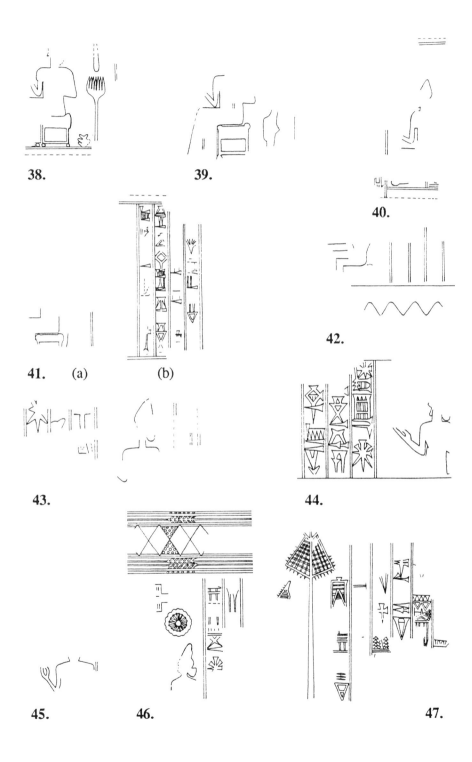

38.

39.

40.

41. (a) (b)

42.

43.

44.

45. **46.** **47.**

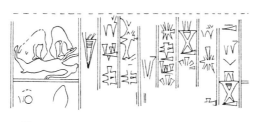

48.

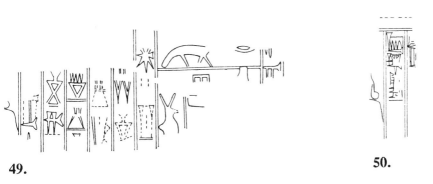

49.

50.

51.

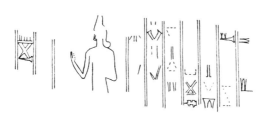

52.

53.

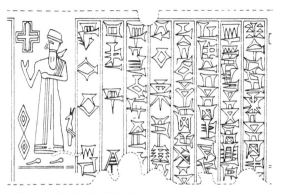

54. PBS XIV 531 (agate)

Seal of Pir'i-Amurru **not from Nippur**

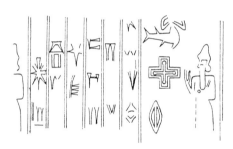

55.

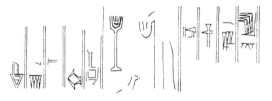

56.

57.

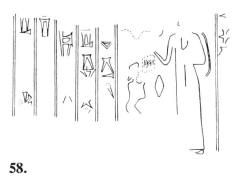

58.

59.

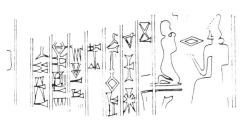

60.

61. Seal of Belanum(?)

63. PBS XIV 554

62.

65. PBS XIV 557

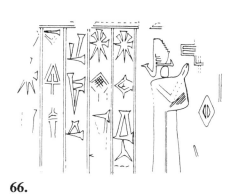

66.

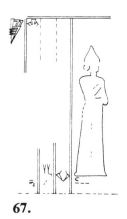

67.

68.

69. PBS XIV 546 (jasper)

provenance uncertain

70. PBS XIV 547 (agate)

not from Nippur

71. OIC 23 fig. 92:1

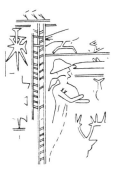

72. PBS XIV 551

73. PBS XIV 266

72 and **73**, combined drawing

74 PBS XIV 553

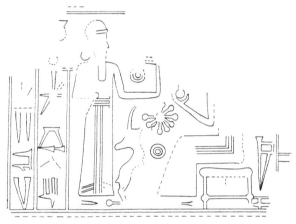

75. PBS XIV 556

76. Nippur I pl. 119:16, 18; pl. 121:10

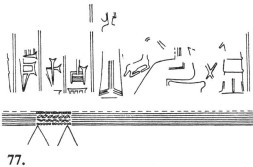

77.

78.

79.

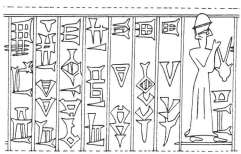

80. (composition) **no provenance**

81. (glass) **no provenance**

82. PBS XIV 555

83.

84

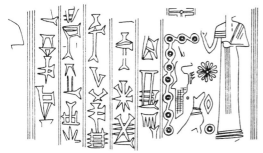

85.

86.

87. no provenance

88. PBS XIV 562

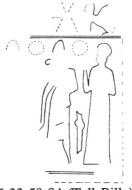

UM 33-58-84 (Tell Billa)

89. PBS XIV 561

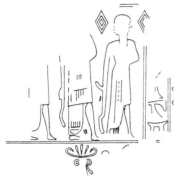

90.

91.

92. OIC 23 fig. 48:4 †

93.

94. (glass)

95. PBS XIV 548

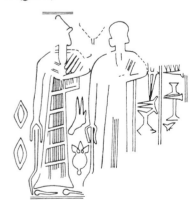

96. PBS XIV 549

97. no provenance

98. PBS XIV 467 (glass)

99.

100.

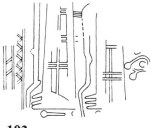

102.

103. † OIC 23 fig. 48:8

105.

104. † Nippur I pl. 121:2

106.

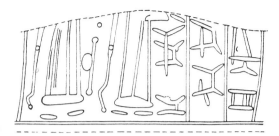

107. PBS XIV 567 (glass)

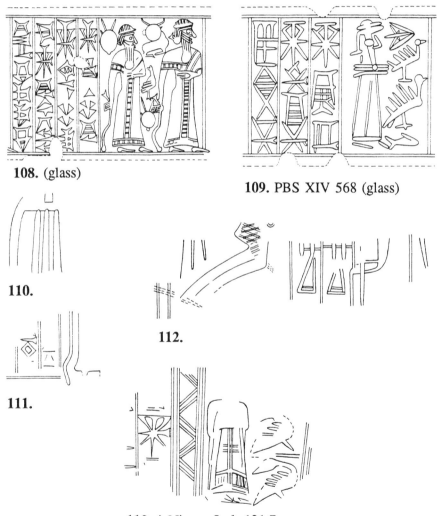

108. (glass)

109. PBS XIV 568 (glass)

110.

111.

112.

113. † Nippur I pl. 121:7

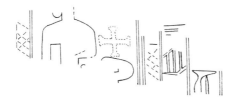

114.

115.

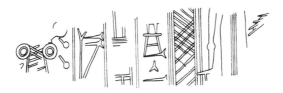

116.

117.

118.

119.

120.

121. PBS XIV 550

122. PBS XIV 570

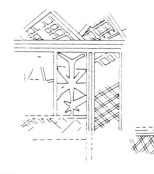

123.

124. PBS XIV 558

125. Nippur I pl. 120:2

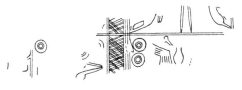

126.

127.

128. Nippur I pl. 119:2

129.

OIC 23 fig. 48:5b

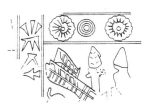

130. PBS XIV 560

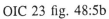

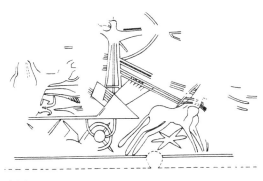

131.

132. Seal of Sin-damaqu

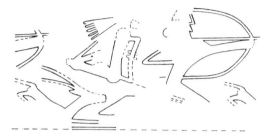

133.

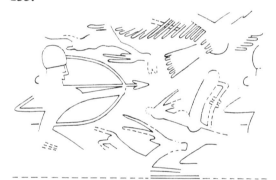

132 and **133**, combined drawing

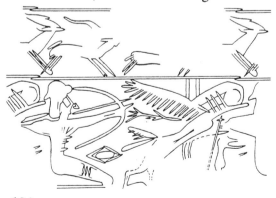

134.

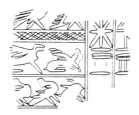

135. Nippur I pl. 121:5

136.

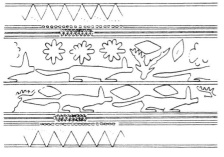

137. OIC 23 fig. 21:2

138. PBS XIV 559

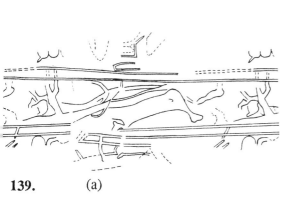

139.   (a)   (b)

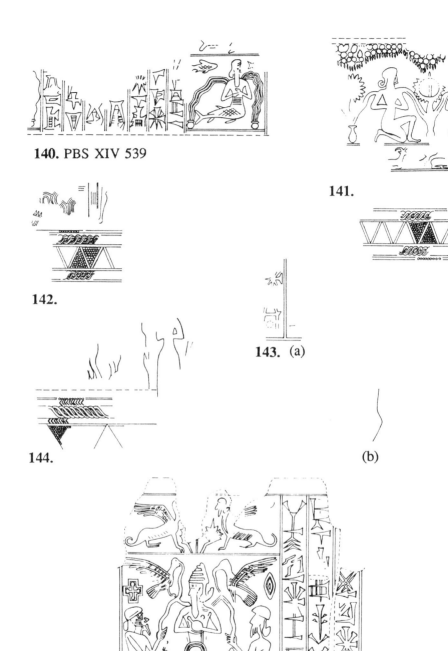

140. PBS XIV 539

141.

142.

143. (a)

144.

(b)

145. (faience)

146 (CBS 7380 only)

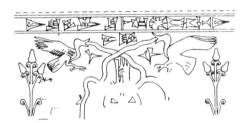

146 (composite with Jena photographs) †

147. Seal of Esagil-lidiš

148. Porada 1952, no. 2; Seal of Rimutu

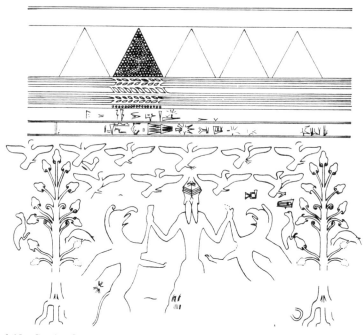

149. Seal of Amil-Marduk

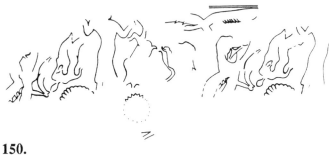

150.

151. †

152. (jasper) not from Nippur

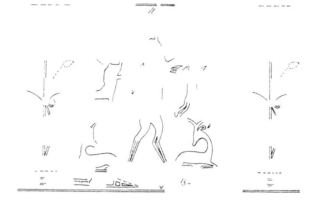

153.

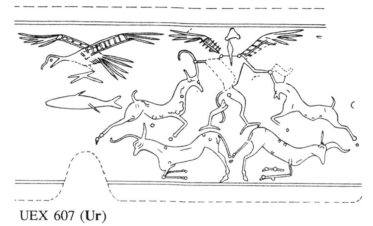

UEX 607 (**Ur**)

154.

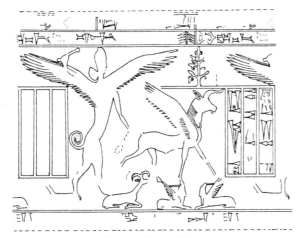

155. Seal of Ninurta-ken-pišu

156.

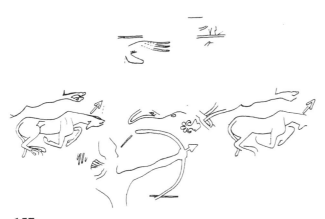

157.

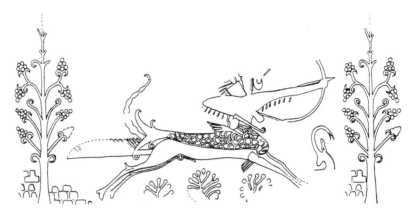

158. Porada 1952, no. 2 (not to scale)

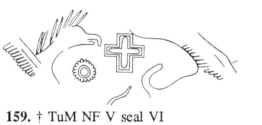

159. † TuM NF V seal VI

160.

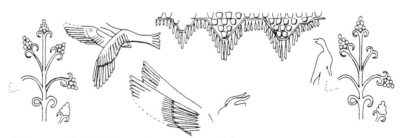

161. Porada 1952, no. 3 (not to scale)

162.

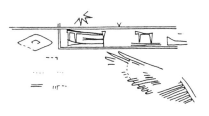

163.

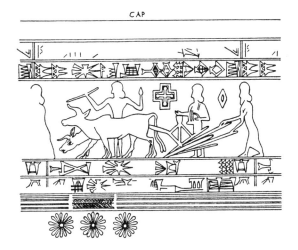

164. PBS XIV 569; TuM NF V seals VII, IX

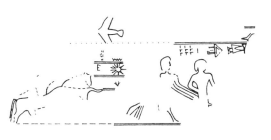

165.

166. † TuM NF V seal IIIb

167.

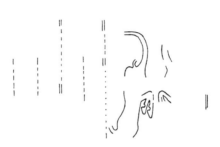

168.

169.

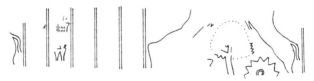

170.

171. † Gibson 1983 fig. 20

172. † Gibson 1983, fig. 21

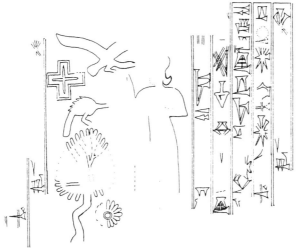

173. Seal of Shigu-Gula

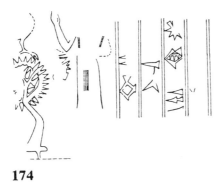

174

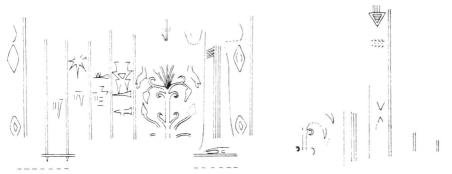

175. Seal of Luṣa-ana-nur Enlil

176.

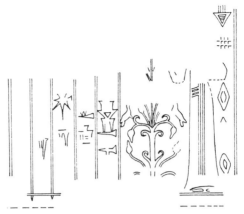

175 and **176**, combined drawing

177.

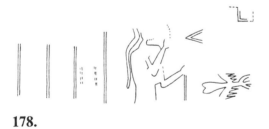

178.

179.

180. (cap only)

181. (cap only)

182.

185. PBS XIV 744

186.

187. Petschow 1974 no. 25

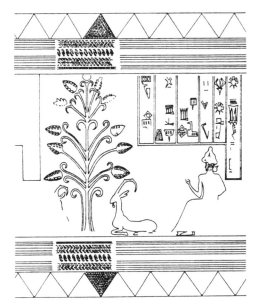

188. Seal of Shamash(?)-[   ]

189. TuM NF V, seals I-IV;

Seal of Enlil-alša, used by Ninurta-nadin-ahhe

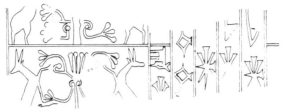

190.

191.

192. † OIC 23 fig. 19:4   **193.** † OIC 23 fig. 21:3

194.

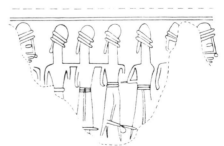

195. PBS XIV 634 (faience)

196. PBS XIV 633 (faience)

197. Nippur I pl. 120:6

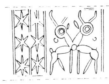

198. † Gibson 1983 fig. 14 (faience)

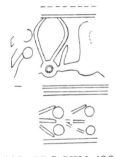

199. PBS XIV 498

200. † Nippur I pl. 113:3 (composition)

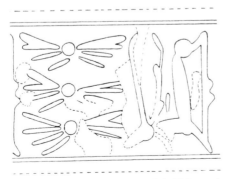

201. Gibson 1978 fig. 24 (faience)

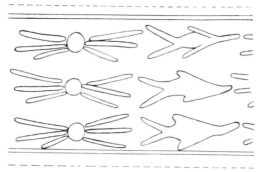

202. PBS XIV 636 (faience)

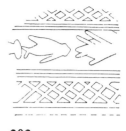

203.

204. PBS XIV 632 (faience)

205. Nippur I pl. 120:17

206. PBS XIV 631 (faience)

207.

208. † TuM NF V, seal IIIa

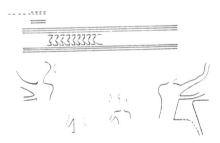

209.

210.

ORBIS BIBLICUS ET ORIENTALIS

Bd. 19   MASSÉO CALOZ: *Etude sur la LXX origénienne du Psautier.* Les relations entre les leçons des Psaumes du Manuscrit Coislin 44, les Fragments des Hexaples et le texte du Psautier Gallican. 480 pages. 1978.

Bd. 20   RAPHAEL GIVEON: *The Impact of Egypt on Canaan.* Iconographical and Related Studies. 156 Seiten, 73 Abbildungen. 1978.

Bd. 21   DOMINIQUE BARTHÉLEMY: *Etudes d'histoire du texte de l'Ancien Testament.* XXV–419 pages. 1978. Epuisé.

Bd. 22/1 CESLAS SPICQ: *Notes de Lexicographie néo-testamentaire.* Tome I: p. 1–524. 1978. Epuisé.

Bd. 22/2 CESLAS SPICQ: *Notes de Lexicographie néo-testamentaire.* Tome II: p. 525–980. 1978. Epuisé.

Bd. 22/3 CESLAS SPICQ: *Notes de Lexicographie néo-testamentaire.* Supplément. 698 pages. 1982.

Bd. 23   BRIAN M. NOLAN: *The Royal Son of God.* The Christology of Matthew 1–2 in the Setting of the Gospel. 282 Seiten. 1979. Out of print.

Bd. 24   KLAUS KIESOW: *Exodustexte im Jesajabuch.* Literarkritische und motivgeschichtliche Analysen. 221 Seiten. 1979. Vergriffen.

Bd. 25/1 MICHAEL LATTKE: *Die Oden Salomos in ihrer Bedeutung für Neues Testament und Gnosis.* Band I. Ausführliche Handschriftenbeschreibung. Edition mit deutscher Parallel-Übersetzung. Hermeneutischer Anhang zur gnostischen Interpretation der Oden Salomos in der Pistis Sophia. XI–237 Seiten. 1979.

Bd. 25/1a MICHAEL LATTKE: *Die Oden Salomos in ihrer Bedeutung für Neues Testament und Gnosis.* Band Ia. Der syrische Text der Edition in Estrangela Faksimile des griechischen Papyrus Bodmer XI. 68 Seiten. 1980.

Bd. 25/2 MICHAEL LATTKE: *Die Oden Salomos in ihrer Bedeutung für Neues Testament und Gnosis.* Band II. Vollständige Wortkonkordanz zur handschriftlichen, griechischen, koptischen, lateinischen und syrischen Überlieferung der Oden Salomos. Mit einem Faksimile des Kodex N. XVI–201 Seiten. 1979.

Bd. 25/3 MICHAEL LATTKE: *Die Oden Salomos in ihrer Bedeutung für Neues Testament und Gnosis.* Band III. XXXIV–478 Seiten. 1986.

Bd. 26   MAX KÜCHLER: *Frühjüdische Weisheitstraditionen.* Zum Fortgang weisheitlichen Denkens im Bereich des frühjüdischen Jahweglaubens. 703 Seiten. 1979. Vergriffen.

Bd. 27   JOSEF M. OESCH: *Petucha und Setuma.* Untersuchungen zu einer überlieferten Gliederung im hebräischen Text des Alten Testaments. XX–392–37* Seiten. 1979.

Bd. 28   ERIK HORNUNG / OTHMAR KEEL (Herausgeber): *Studien zu altägyptischen Lebenslehren.* 394 Seiten. 1979.

Bd. 29   HERMANN ALEXANDER SCHLÖGL: *Der Gott Tatenen.* Nach Texten und Bildern des Neuen Reiches. 216 Seiten, 14 Abbildungen. 1980.

Bd. 30   JOHANN JAKOB STAMM: *Beiträge zur Hebräischen und Altorientalischen Namenkunde.* XVI–264 Seiten. 1980.

Bd. 31   HELMUT UTZSCHNEIDER: *Hosea - Prophet vor dem Ende.* Zum Verhältnis von Geschichte und Institution in der alttestamentlichen Prophetie. 260 Seiten. 1980.

Bd. 32   PETER WEIMAR: *Die Berufung des Mose.* Literaturwissenschaftliche Analyse von Exodus 2, 23–5, 5. 402 Seiten. 1980.

Bd. 33   OTHMAR KEEL: *Das Böcklein in der Milch seiner Mutter und Verwandtes*. Im Lichte eines altorientalischen Bildmotivs. 163 Seiten, 141 Abbildungen. 1980.

Bd. 34   PIERRE AUFFRET: *Hymnes d'Egypte et d'Israël*. Etudes de structures littéraires. 316 pages, 1 illustration. 1981.

Bd. 35   ARIE VAN DER KOOIJ: *Die alten Textzeugen des Jesajabuches*. Ein Beitrag zur Textgeschichte des Alten Testaments. 388 Seiten. 1981.

Bd. 36   CARMEL McCARTHY: *The Tiqqune Sopherim and Other Theological Corrections in the Masoretic Text of the Old Testament*. 280 Seiten. 1981.

Bd. 37   BARBARA L. BEGELSBACHER-FISCHER: *Untersuchungen zur Götterwelt des Alten Reiches im Spiegel der Privatgräber der IV. und V. Dynastie*. 336 Seiten. 1981.

Bd. 38   MÉLANGES DOMINIQUE BARTHÉLEMY. *Etudes bibliques offertes à l'occasion de son 60ᵉ anniversaire*. Edités par Pierre Casetti, Othmar Keel et Adrian Schenker. 724 pages, 31 illustrations. 1981.

Bd. 39   ANDRÉ LEMAIRE: *Les écoles et la formation de la Bible dans l'ancien Israël*. 142 pages, 14 illustrations. 1981.

Bd. 40   JOSEPH HENNINGER: *Arabica Sacra*. Aufsätze zur Religionsgeschichte Arabiens und seiner Randgebiete. Contributions à l'histoire religieuse de l'Arabie et de ses régions limitrophes. 347 Seiten. 1981.

Bd. 41   DANIEL VON ALLMEN: *La famille de Dieu*. La symbolique familiale dans le paulinisme. LXVII–330 pages, 27 planches. 1981.

Bd. 42   ADRIAN SCHENKER: *Der Mächtige im Schmelzofen des Mitleids*. Eine Interpretation von 2 Sam 24. 92 Seiten. 1982.

Bd. 43   PAUL DESELAERS: *Das Buch Tobit*. Studien zu seiner Entstehung, Komposition und Theologie. 532 Seiten + Übersetzung 16 Seiten. 1982.

Bd. 44   PIERRE CASETTI: *Gibt es ein Leben vor dem Tod?* Eine Auslegung von Psalm 49. 315 Seiten. 1982.

Bd. 45   FRANK-LOTHAR HOSSFELD: *Der Dekalog*. Seine späten Fassungen, die originale Komposition und seine Vorstufen. 308 Seiten. 1982. Vergriffen.

Bd. 46   ERIK HORNUNG: *Der ägyptische Mythos von der Himmelskuh*. Eine Ätiologie des Unvollkommenen. Unter Mitarbeit von Andreas Brodbeck, Hermann Schlögl und Elisabeth Staehelin und mit einem Beitrag von Gerhard Fecht. XII–129 Seiten, 10 Abbildungen. 1991. 2. ergänzte Auflage.

Bd. 47   PIERRE CHERIX: *Le Concept de Notre Grande Puissance (CG VI, 4)*. Texte, remarques philologiques, traduction et notes. XIV–95 pages. 1982.

Bd. 48   JAN ASSMANN/WALTER BURKERT/FRITZ STOLZ: *Funktionen und Leistungen des Mythos*. Drei altorientalische Beispiele. 118 Seiten, 17 Abbildungen. 1982. Vergriffen.

Bd. 49   PIERRE AUFFRET: *La sagesse a bâti sa maison*. Etudes de structures littéraires dans l'Ancien Testament et spécialement dans les psaumes. 580 pages. 1982.

Bd. 50/1   DOMINIQUE BARTHÉLEMY: *Critique textuelle de l'Ancien Testament*. 1. Josué, Juges, Ruth, Samuel, Rois, Chroniques, Esdras, Néhémie, Esther. Rapport final du Comité pour l'analyse textuelle de l'Ancien Testament hébreu institué par l'Alliance Biblique Universelle, établi en coopération avec Alexander R. Hulst †, Norbert Lohfink, William D. McHardy, H. Peter Rüger, coéditeur, James A. Sanders, coéditeur. 812 pages. 1982.

Bd. 67   OTHMAR KEEL / SILVIA SCHROER: *Studien zu den Stempelsiegeln aus Palästina/Israel.* Band I. 115 Seiten, 103 Abbildungen. 1985.

Bd. 68   WALTER BEYERLIN: *Weisheitliche Vergewisserung mit Bezug auf den Zionskult.* Studien zum 125. Psalm. 96 Seiten. 1985.

Bd. 69   RAPHAEL VENTURA: *Living in a City of the Dead.* A Selection of Topographical and Administrative Terms in the Documents of the Theban Necropolis. XII–232 Seiten. 1986.

Bd. 70   CLEMENS LOCHER: *Die Ehre einer Frau in Israel.* Exegetische und rechtsvergleichende Studien zu Dtn 22, 13–21. XVIII–464 Seiten. 1986.

Bd. 71   HANS-PETER MATHYS: *Liebe deinen Nächsten wie dich selbst.* Untersuchungen zum alttestamentlichen Gebot der Nächstenliebe (Lev 19,18). XIV–196 Seiten. 1986. Vergriffen. Neuauflage in Vorbereitung.

Bd. 72   FRIEDRICH ABITZ: *Ramses III. in den Gräbern seiner Söhne.* 156 Seiten, 31 Abbildungen. 1986.

Bd. 73   DOMINIQUE BARTHÉLEMY/DAVID W. GOODING/JOHAN LUST/EMANUEL TOV: *The Story of David and Goliath.* 160 Seiten. 1986.

Bd. 74   SILVIA SCHROER: *In Israel gab es Bilder.* Nachrichten von darstellender Kunst im Alten Testament. XVI–553 Seiten, 146 Abbildungen. 1987.

Bd. 75   ALAN R. SCHULMAN: *Ceremonial Execution and Public Rewards.* Some Historical Scenes on New Kingdom Private Stelae. 296 Seiten, 41 Abbildungen. 1987.

Bd. 76   JOŽE KRAŠOVEC: *La justice (Ṣdq) de Dieu dans la Bible hébraïque et l'interprétation juive et chrétienne.* 456 pages. 1988.

Bd. 77   HELMUT UTZSCHNEIDER: *Das Heiligtum und das Gesetz.* Studien zur Bedeutung der sinaitischen Heiligtumstexte (Ez 25–40; Lev 8–9). XIV–326 Seiten. 1988.

Bd. 78   BERNARD GOSSE: *Isaie 13,1–14,23.* Dans la tradition littéraire du livre d'Isaïe et dans la tradition des oracles contre les nations. 308 pages. 1988.

Bd. 79   INKE W. SCHUMACHER: *Der Gott Sopdu - Der Herr der Fremdländer.* XVI–364 Seiten, 6 Abbildungen. 1988.

Bd. 80   HELLMUT BRUNNER: *Das hörende Herz.* Kleine Schriften zur Religions- und Geistesgeschichte Ägyptens. Herausgegeben von Wolfgang Röllig. 449 Seiten, 55 Abbildungen. 1988.

Bd. 81   WALTER BEYERLIN: *Bleilot, Brecheisen oder was sonst?* Revision einer Amos-Vision. 68 Seiten. 1988.

Bd. 82   MANFRED HUTTER: *Behexung, Entsühnung und Heilung.* Das Ritual der Tunnawiya für ein Königspaar aus mittelhethitischer Zeit (KBo XXI 1 – KUB IX 34 – KBo XXI 6). 186 Seiten. 1988.

Bd. 83   RAPHAEL GIVEON: *Scarabs from Recent Excavations in Israel.* 114 Seiten, 9 Tafeln. 1988.

Bd. 84   MIRIAM LICHTHEIM: *Ancient Egyptian Autobiographies chiefly of the Middle Kingdom.* A Study and an Anthology. 200 Seiten, 10 Seiten Abbildungen. 1988.

Bd. 85   ECKART OTTO: *Rechtsgeschichte der Redaktionen im Kodex Ešnunna und im «Bundesbuch».* Eine redaktionsgeschichtliche und rechtsvergleichende Studie zu altbabylonischen und altisraelitischen Rechtsüberlieferungen. 220 Seiten. 1989.

Bd. 86   ANDRZEJ NIWIŃSKI: *Studies on the Illustrated Theban Funerary Papyri of the 11th and 10th Centuries B.C.* 488 Seiten, 80 Seiten Tafeln. 1989.

Bd. 87   URSULA SEIDL: *Die babylonischen Kudurru-Reliefs.* Symbole mesopotamischer Gottheiten. 236 Seiten, 33 Tafeln und 2 Tabellen. 1989.

Bd. 112 EDMUND HERMSEN: *Die zwei Wege des Jenseits*. Das altägyptische Zweiwegebuch und seine Topographie. XII–282 Seiten, 1 mehrfarbige und 19 schwarzweiss-Abbildungen. 1992.

Bd. 113 CHARLES MAYSTRE: *Les grands prêtres de Ptah de Memphis*. XIV–474 pages, 2 planches. 1992.

Bd. 114 SCHNEIDER THOMAS: *Asiatische Personennamen in Ägyptischen Quellen des Neuen Reiches*. 208 Seiten. 1992.

Bd. 115 VON NORDHEIM ECKHARD: *Die Selbstbehauptung Israels in der Welt des Alten Orients*. Religionsgeschichtlicher Vergleich anhand von Gen 15/22/28, dem Aufenthalt Israels in Ägypten, 2 Sam 7, 1 Kön 19 und Psalm 104. 240 Seiten. 1992.

Bd. 116 DONALD M. MATTHEWS: *The Kassite Glyptic of Nippur*. 208 Seiten. 210 Abbildungen. 1992.

ÉDITIONS UNIVERSITAIRES FRIBOURG SUISSE

Summary

This catalogue of cylinder seals from Nippur, the religious centre, presents the first substantial body of dated material from the Kassite period, a time of radical change in Babylonian art. The 210 designs, mainly of First Kassite, Pseudo-Kassite, Second Kassite and Common Mitannian style, are illustrated with line drawings, most of which were reconstructed from ancient impressions in the University Museum, Philadelphia. The chronology is placed on a new foundation, and the relationships, development and usage of the styles are discussed. This book, containing a third of all the known Kassite seal desings, and a much higher proportion of those with some context in space or time, will be indispensible to all those interested in the art of the Late Bronze Age in Mesopotamia.